Herbert Hoover

ENGINEER, HUMANITARIAN, STATESMAN

BOOKS BY

Dorothy
Horton
McGee

SALLY TOWNSEND, PATRIOT

THE BOARDING SCHOOL MYSTERY

FAMOUS SIGNERS OF THE DECLARATION

HERBERT HOOVER: ENGINEER, HUMANITARIAN, STATESMAN

Herbert Hoover

ENGINEER, HUMANITARIAN, STATESMAN

By Dorothy Horton McGee

ILLUSTRATED WITH PHOTOGRAPHS

Dodd, Mead
& Company

NEW YORK 1965

The extracts from *Herbert Hoover, A Reminiscent Biography* by Will
Irwin published by The Century Company are copyrighted 1928 by Will
Irwin. The extracts from *Hoover Off The Record* by Theodore Joslin, copy-
right 1934 by Doubleday & Company, Inc., are reprinted by permission of
the publisher. The extracts from *Our Unknown Ex-President* by Eugene
Lyons, copyright 1948 by Eugene Lyons, copyright 1947 by The Reader's
Digest Association, Inc. are reprinted by permission of Doubleday & Com-
pany, Inc.

Extracts from the following are reprinted with permission: from The
Macmillan Company, *The Memoirs of Herbert Hoover* by Herbert Hoover,
copyright 1951–1952; Doubleday & Company, Inc., *The Life and Letters
of Walter Hines Page,* edited by Burton J. Hendrick; Funk and Wagnalls
Company, *27 Masters of Politics* by Raymond Moley; *Nevada County
Nugget and Nevada City-Grass Valley Nugget,* June 19, 1958, article by
Gerald Wallace; *New York Herald Tribune,* August 1949; *Scribner's Maga-
zine,* September, 1930, article by Frank Kent; Charles Scribner's Sons,
The Economic Consequences of the Peace by John Maynard Keynes, *The
Hoover Administration* by W. S. Myers and W. H. Newton, *The Hoover
Policies* by Ray Lyman Wilbur and Arthur M. Hyde; from The Macmillan
Company, *The Economics of Recovery* by Leonard P. Ayres; from *An Amer-
ican Epic, Volumes I–IV,* by Herbert Hoover; from speeches, statements and
writings by Herbert Hoover.

LIBRARY OF CONGRESS CATALOG CARD NUMBER: 65-26316

PRINTED IN THE UNITED STATES OF AMERICA

BY VAIL-BALLOU PRESS, INC., BINGHAMTON, N. Y.

To my mother

AND THE MEMORY OF

my father

Acknowledgments

APPRECIATION is extended to the Honorable Herbert C. Hoover for his kind permission to use material from the three volumes of his *The Memoirs of Herbert Hoover;* also to the following officers of Dodd, Mead & Company: Dorothy M. Bryan, Vice-President, for editing the manuscript; S. Phelps Platt, Jr., Vice-President, for processing the manufacture; D. Fred Slota, Secretary-Treasurer, for the book idea; and to the following for valuable assistance in the preparation of the manuscript—Bernice Miller, Secretary to Mr. Hoover; Walter B. French, Senior Deputy Manager, The American Bankers Association; William A. Irwin, former Professor of Economics, Washburn College and former Economist, The American Bankers Association; Acosta Nichols, Groton School; Winifred A. Teague, Administrative Assistant and Thomas T. Thalken, Archivist, Herbert Hoover Archives, both of The Hoover Institution on War, Revolution and Peace, Stanford University; Ruth Scibird, Curator, Stanford Collection, The Stanford University Libraries; Perrin C. Galpin, President, Belgian American Educational Foundation, Inc.; Major General George L. Van Deusen; the Honorable Steven B. Derounian, Member of Congress, Second District, New York; and to staff members of the Reference Collection and Photographic Service, The New York Public Library, Fifth Avenue and Forty-second Street, New York.

DOROTHY HORTON MCGEE
July, 1959

APPRECIATION is extended to Colonel Frank E. Mason for assistance in the preparation of the revised edition; and to the following for research information—Dr. Rita R. Campbell, Archivist and Research Associate, Herbert Hoover Archives, The Hoover Institution on War, Revolution, and Peace, Stanford University; Ralph W. Hansen, Curator, Stanford Collection, The Stanford University Libraries; Franz G. Lassner, Director, Dwight M. Miller, Archivist, Herbert Hoover Presidential Library, James B. Rhoads, Office of Presidential Libraries, National Archives and Records Service, General Services Administration; Ernest Kirkendall, Secretary and General Manager, United Engineering Trustees, Inc.; Mrs. Sylvia K. Cornman, Boys' Clubs of America; Robert A. Harper, Director, Office of School Relations, School of Engineering and Applied Science, Columbia University.

D. H. M.

July, 1965

Contents

1. NEW HORIZONS, 1

2. A DIPLOMA EARNED, 18

3. THE ENGINEER TAKES A PARTNER, 29

4. CHINA STORY, 45

5. WORLD-WIDE ENGINEERING, 73

6. "PLUMS IN A PUDDING," 88

7. STRANDED AMERICANS, 99

8. FEEDING A NATION, 113

9. "FOOD WILL WIN THE WAR," 134

10. "FOOD REGULATOR OF THE WORLD," 150

11. "GAUNT REALITIES," 173

12. SECRETARY OF COMMERCE, 184

13. ORPHAN TO PRESIDENT, 212

14. BATTLE ON A THOUSAND FRONTS, 224

15. AGAINST ALL ODDS, 248

16. NEVER BROOK DEFEAT, 266

17. KEEPING HIS WORD, 277

18. ALL ALONG THE WAY, 300

BIBLIOGRAPHY, 318

INDEX, 321

Illustrations

Following page 150

Herbert Hoover at the age of five with his brother, Theodore

Hoover's birthplace at West Branch, Iowa

Hoover's geology class at Stanford University

Stanford football team, 1894, showing Hoover as financial manager

Herbert Hoover in Western Australia

Sons of Gwalia Mine at Mount Leonora, Western Australia, showing the plant installed by Hoover in 1898

Mrs. Hoover in the White House

Herbert Hoover delivering his Inaugural Address

Former President Hoover with his two sons, Herbert, Jr., and Allan

Herbert Hoover with Polish children in Warsaw, in 1946

Admiring members of Boys' Clubs of America surround former President Hoover, Chairman of the Board since 1936

President Eisenhower shakes hands with former President Hoover on White House portico, July 21, 1953, after luncheon meeting on plans for bipartisan commission to study government operation

Former President Hoover is met by Prince Albert on arrival in Belgium, July 3, 1958, to represent President Eisenhower at Brussels World Fair

New
Horizons

CHAPTER 1

The birthplace of Herbert Hoover, the first President of the United States to be born west of the Mississippi River, is in West Branch, Iowa. Now a national shrine, it is a very humble dwelling, as was the log cabin where Abraham Lincoln was born. Herbert's birth, on August 10, 1874, was announced by his father, Jesse Hoover, the village blacksmith, as the arrival of another General Grant—the President at that time. This was more the customary confident aspirations of many an American father than a prophecy. The fact that the baby boy did achieve his country's highest honor and become the thirty-first president of the United States is only part of the amazing story of Herbert Hoover. His is a fabulous, inspiring tale of success through hard work and dedication in the best American traditions, and it is an outstanding tribute to the boundless opportunities given to all in the United States—in his case to a poor orphan boy.

With only the slenderest financial resources in reserve, his chosen career in engineering seemed out of reach for young

Hoover. He had been obliged to leave school and go to work for his living as an office boy in the employ of the Oregon Land Company when he was about fifteen. His early ambition to drive a railway locomotive shifted to bookkeeping as he learned to keep the firm's accounts.

Then one day an engineer from the East came into the Land Company Office, in Salem, Oregon. This proved a fateful visit for Herbert. Making the acquaintance of the office boy, the newcomer talked to him about the advantages of college training for any profession. He spoke very persuasively about engineering, too. For a year, Herbert mulled over this as a possible career for himself. He haunted the little foundry, the sawmill and repair shops in Salem, asking questions. He collected catalogues and pertinent information on universities in general and engineering in particular. Finally he made up his mind. He determined to become an engineer. At first he leaned to the mechanical side, but on a visit to a mining prospect in the Cascades with a mining engineer he was persuaded that this branch of the profession offered more choice. The older man's study of the mine's geology and his deductions that the prospect was no good excited the boy's imagination. But how could the poor orphan with a "thimbleful" of preparatory education achieve this goal? The only possibility he had of achieving a degree was through a scholarship at a college which did not give engineering courses.

Could anyone who looked into the unpretentious office of the Oregon Land Company in Salem, on a day in 1891, and saw the tall, lean office boy, sitting at a little corner table with shoulders hunched over a copy of the *Oregon Statesman* in between his duties, have dreamed what his future would be? When the office boy suddenly sat up straight and reread a certain notice, could anyone have grasped the significance of the incident to the United States—and indeed to the world?

Public examinations, Herbert read, would be held for entrance to the new university which had been founded by Senator Leland Stanford at Palo Alto, California. The institution was to be opened shortly—and it was to be free!

Probably the earliest description we have of Herbert Hoover comes from an aunt who visited his mother, Huldah Minthorn Hoover, and the new baby son when he was not yet one day old. He was round and plump, she recalled, and looked about "very cordial." The Hoover family had come to West Branch, Iowa, by prairie schooner from Ohio twenty-one years before Herbert's birth. The Minthorns had come by wagon from Canada about seven years after the Hoovers. They were originally from New England. Herbert's family on both sides were members of the Society of Friends, also known as Quakers.

Herbert Hoover remembered little of his father, who died when he was only six years old. According to report, Jesse Hoover was a man of gregarious charm who possessed a mechanical talent. In addition to this mechanical bent, his second son inherited his humor.

Of one incident in his father's blacksmith shop Herbert had retained a vivid recollection. Once, while playing around the shop barefoot, the boy stepped on a chip of hot iron, and he carried this brand of his Iowa childhood on his foot all his life.

The farm implement business which Jesse Hoover established some time before his death provided the occasion for Herbert's first scientific experiment. In the implement shop there was a machine for putting barbs on wire. "After the barbs were fixed," as the grown-up scientist told the story, "the bundles of wire were dipped in hot tar to prevent rust. While no one was looking, I undertook an experiment in combustion by putting a lighted stick in the caldron. It produced a smoke that brought the town running and me speeding the other way in complete terror." Even a picture of a volcanic eruption reminded the scientist of that terror to the end! Another experiment in wood carving nearly cost Herbert a forefinger.

Herbert remembered his mother as a sweet-faced woman who

took in sewing to maintain her little family after her husband died. She carefully saved his insurance money so that it would help in her children's education. She had been trained to be a schoolteacher and had received more schooling than most girls of that time. A devout Friend, she was in demand as a speaker at Quaker Meetings.

To aid her in the struggle to bring up her family, an uncle, Major Laban Miles, took Herbert, then almost seven, for a long visit with his family in Oklahoma. Major Miles was the United States Indian Agent to the Osage Nation and lived at the agency in Pawhuska. Herbert and his cousins attended the agency school with the Indian children. He learned much aboriginal lore of the woods and streams from the young Indians. They also taught him the art of making bows and arrows and their use.

At home, Herbert and his older brother Theodore, known as Tad, aided their mother not only by chopping and carrying in wood but by washing the dishes and sweeping, too. An aunt affirmed that Bertie was always very helpful.

Herbert's Quaker family was unwilling in those days to have the children exposed to books other than the Bible, the encyclopedia, school books or those great novels in which the hero overcomes the "demon rum," so some of the boys' early reading was surreptitious of necessity.

Tad borrowed *Robinson Crusoe* and later the *Leatherstocking Tales,* which he and a cousin, George Hoover, used to read secretly, lying on the floor of an upper bedroom in Huldah Hoover's house. They took turns reading, with Bertie, as the lookout, stationed on the stairs, with orders to whistle if anyone approached. He had his Defoe at second hand! Sometimes he would forget his job, creep into the room and ask in an excited whisper, "What are they doing now?" The boy who didn't have the book would drag him back to his post. Afterward, the trio acted out the stories. To Bertie fell the role of the colonial army, commanded by his brother, and also that of the maiden bound to the stake who was rescued by the Deerslayer, played by Tad.

After George Hoover saw a circus in Iowa City, the three boys dressed up an old white mare belonging to George's father as a circus horse. Bertie acted as the post in the center of a ring, holding the end of the halter line while the horse docilely circled around him. But neither of the two older boys could remain standing on the mare's back at a gallop, so they decided to have a menagerie instead.

A faithful big yellow hound dog became a Numidian lion; a fierce tomcat shut in an empty apple crate a Bengal tiger; and squirrels and chipmunks were trapped to portray panthers and leopards. A bull calf played the elephant.

Admission was paid in pins, and the audience was just assembling when the lion broke his leash and knocked over the apple crate to battle the Bengal tiger. In the fray, the boys upset the other cages and panthers, leopards and even the elephant escaped to the "jungle"!

The following winter brought great sorrow to Bertie, Tad and their younger sister May when their mother died in February. To his mother Herbert owed his idealism and integrity, and he reflected her spiritual quality.

After her death, the Minthorns and the Hoover relatives met to decide who should have the "joy," rather than the duty, of adding the three young orphans to their "own broods." Theodore went to live with a Hoover uncle, May was taken in by her Grandmother Minthorn, and Herbert by his uncle Allan Hoover, who lived on a farm just outside of West Branch.

Eight-year-old Herbert took his loss very hard. He went off to his new home with his lips pressed tightly together and his grief showing in his eyes. But after he recovered, he was very happy with his Uncle Allan and Aunt Millie and their children. He found a great friend in his cousin Walter. The two boys walked side by side to school or, in winter, rode, mounted double, on a farm horse. They did farm chores and played together.

Hoover had a vivid memory of his Iowa boyhood. There was Cook's Hill where, on cold winter nights, he and his companions slid down the long, steep incline at a terrific pace with their "tummies" pressed tight to homemade sleds. And there was the swimming hole under the willows, down by the railroad bridge.

There were pigeons at times in the forest and prairie chickens in the hedges to be hunted. A young Indian from a neighboring Indian school showed the boys how to use bows and arrows. Herbert, of course, had already received training in this art while living with Major Miles in Indian territory. Shooting arrows by volleys, in "battalion" formation, the young hunters sometimes brought down a pigeon or a chicken. The fanciest hotel, Herbert declared, never provided game of such wondrous flavor as one of these birds, plucked and half-cooked over the small boys' campfire.

There were sunfish and catfish to be caught. The boys did not have modern equipment in the form of artificial lures and tackle assembled from Damascus steel, bamboos of Siam, Bangkok tin, Chinese lacquer or Colorado silver. They were still in the days of the willow poles with a butcher-string line and hooks ten for a dime. And that dime was hard to earn! Their lure was a segment of an angleworm and their incantation was to spit on the bait. They lived in a time when a fish used to bite instead of strike. They knew a fish was biting when a cork on the line bobbed. And moreover, they ate the fish immediately afterward!

Young Herbert acquired a pair of second-hand skates by trade and barter. He learned to use them by skimming over the frozen swimming hole on winter days. He played one-old-cat, absorbing the rudiments of baseball, with a hickory stick and a ball made by winding yarn around and around a piece of rubber.

The railroad track was an inspiring place to Herbert. The ties were ballasted with glacial gravels in which, by hard search, he found gems of agate and fossil coral. These, he discovered, could be polished on the grindstone at the cost of infinite backaches. Their fine points came out wonderfully when the specimens were wet. The young geologist licked each precious piece when preparing an exhibit! The West Branch village dentist recalled in later years that Herbert often pored over the collection of geological specimens in his office, yearning to find out all about them, while the other children were out playing. The dentist was doubtless influenced by later knowledge in his recollections, but Herbert's early interest in geology is evident!

His boyhood was not all adventure and outdoor life, however. There were the school days in the West Branch Free School. His first teacher remembered him as a sweet little boy with rosy cheeks who learned his lessons readily and never made any trouble. He seemed more interested, though, in getting outdoors to play than in his studies. And there were the chores outside of school hours—planting corn, hoeing gardens, learning to milk, sawing wood, currying horses, and the other tasks then shared by Iowan children which helped to build strong, healthy bodies, along with a sense of values.

The pioneer farms of those days were almost entirely self-sufficient. On Allan Hoover's farm, they ground their own wheat and corn for a toll at the mill, slaughtered their hogs for meat, repaired their own machinery, put up their own buildings, made their own soap, preserved their own fruit and grew their vegetables. They wove most of their own clothing. Herbert's clothes, partly homespun and dyed with butternuts, showed no influence of Paris or London!

When fuel was cut and hauled from the woods, ten miles away on the river, walnuts and hickory nuts were incidentally gathered for the winter. These and popcorn balls cemented with sorghum molasses were the Hoovers' main Christmas confections.

Herbert and Walter became fascinated by a new mowing machine which Allan Hoover bought for the farm. When Herbert discovered a crosscut saw with many teeth missing in the abandoned farm trash, he decided that he and his cousin would make a mowing machine of their own. It did not take them long. Available for motive power was a young heifer of whom the boys had made a special pet. They rigged a harness for her out of old rope ends and disintegrating straps and gave her a few preliminary lessons in driving. Then they hitched her up to the contrived machine. When the clatter sounded behind her, she uttered a frightened bleat and bolted, dragging behind her the machine and Herbert, too, at the end of the lines. After cutting a swath through the vegetable garden, she smashed the machine against a tree trunk. It was a total wreck!

A worn-out clothes wringer attracted the boys next. They converted this find into a sorghum mill and hitched the heifer to the long pole for propulsion power. One boy pulled her and the other pushed and braked from behind and she worked out quite well. They actually managed to grind out a few spoonfuls of "somewhat tinged" molasses which tasted sweeter to them by far than any Aunt Millie served at the table. This despite the fact that Herbert often extolled the cooking of his aunt.

At a very early age, Herbert learned the value of money and the importance of thrift and frugality. One summer, he earned over five dollars picking strawberries—a handsome sum for which he could easily forget the backaches and sunburn involved.

The prevailing rate for picking potato bugs was one cent a hundred—but if you wanted firecrackers on the Fourth of July, you accepted it! A few more pennies could be earned for the firecracker fund by selling old iron to the only Democrat in West Branch.

An integral part of Herbert's boyhood was his religious training. Among the Friends, this began almost from birth. The babies were present at the invariable family prayers and Bible readings every morning. They were even taken to Meeting every Sunday, as there was no other place to leave them.

Their cries and the resultant hushings were often the only break in the long silences.

The religious characteristics of the faith are a literal belief in the Bible, great tolerance of beliefs, practices or habits differing from their own and a conviction that spiritual inspiration springs from the "inward light" in each person. The Friends have always held strongly to education, thrift and individual enterprise. Due to plain living and hard work, extreme poverty has never been their lot. The Friends of Cedar County, Iowa, many of whom were Herbert's relatives, held to the "plain language" of *thee* and *thou* and the "plain clothes." Even then, he noted that the pride of his "aunts" in their Quaker bonnets and flowing gray skirts contained grains of relieving worldliness in the formalism of their worship. To the principles behind it they held fast.

Herbert received a thorough grounding in the meaning and significance of his faith. But, like many small Quaker boys, he found it difficult to keep from wriggling during the solemn hours of meeting and observance of the Friends' silent worship custom. For him, it was strong training in patience!

Individual Bible reading was an important part of Quaker education. Although Herbert was only ten when he left Iowa, he had already read the Bible in daily stints, cover to cover.

His earliest recollection of sensing national events was through the torchlight parade in West Branch during the Garfield Presidential Campaign—and later the stir caused by the news of Garfield's assassination and death. The flag over the main village store was flown at half-mast, and this brought to Herbert the realization that the loss to the nation of the man at the helm of his country was a great one.

In 1884, ten-year-old Herbert was sent to Newberg, Oregon, to live with his uncle, Dr. Henry John Minthorn, the doctor's wife and three daughters, in place of the only son who had recently died. To most people, it would seem that the childhood of the poor orphan, passed from relative to relative, must have been unhappy. Herbert, however, always found a warm welcome and generous, kind treatment. Also, he was grateful for the opportunities and free education offered everywhere. "It is the entry to life that I could wish for every American boy and girl," he later stated.

The trip from Iowa to Oregon took Herbert seven days, traveling in an emigrant train. Dr. Minthorn met him at Portland and took him to his home at Newberg, a Quaker settlement in the Willamette River Valley. When the boy arrived at the Minthorns, his aunt and three girl cousins were making the winter supply of pear butter in a wash boiler over a fire in their yard. Herbert was asked to stir the butter and invited to eat as much of the ripe fruit as he wanted. He had never tasted pears before and found them delicious. However, after his enthusiasm had led to a two-day diet of almost nothing but pears he had had enough. He did not indulge in them again for years! On two counts Dr. Minthorn was a romantic figure to his nephew. As a boy in Iowa, he had driven wagon teams for the Underground Railroad, that remarkable system of co-operation among certain antislavery people in the United States whereby fugitive slaves were secretly helped to reach the North or Canada. Later, the doctor had run away from home to join the Union Army. Herbert listened eagerly to his tales of the Battle of Shiloh, in which he had taken part, during the War between the States.

In addition to his medical practice, Dr. Minthorn helped conduct the Newberg Academy (Pacific College) and taught history and literature there. The academy was run by Quakers, who, although a small sect, played such an important role in pioneer education in America.

Herbert was put in school and given special chores to do, which included feeding the doctor's team of ponies twice a day and hitching them up when required. This routine, plus his attendance at religious meetings, kept Herbert pretty busy, but he soon managed to find time for baseball, jigsaws, building dams, swimming, fishing and exploring the woods with other village boys.

Later on, he was asked to help his uncle clear a piece of fir forest. One summer, he took a job weeding onions in the great bottom lands north of Newberg for fifty cents a day. He returned with about thirty dollars. This was a princely sum to Herbert and he treasured part of it for a long time.

At the age of twelve, he graduated from the grammar course at the Newberg Academy, taking an active part in the commencement exercises. Early in the program, Bertie Hoover gave a declamation entitled, "Keeping His Word." Whether this was his own choice or an assigned subject, there could not have been a more suitable theme for the tall, earnest boy dressed in homespun!

Bertie continued his studies at the academy until his uncle moved to Salem, where he established a Quaker land-settlement business with several partners while keeping on with his medical practice. This was the time, recounted earlier, when Herbert had to go to work when he was about fifteen and was given the job of office boy in Dr. Minthorn's new venture. He then had little or no hope of any educational future. But he did his work with alacrity and was later described as a walking encyclopedia of knowledge on all the company business and records. He studied school books at every opportunity and made the most of what came his way, including night sessions at a newly opened, small business college. The teacher was very proficient in mathematics and knew some Latin. On discovering Herbert's predilection for mathematics, he taught him algebra, geometry and higher arithmetic thoroughly, but with Latin he was not as successful.

Herbert developed a firm, clear handwriting in helping the bookkeeper with the books, and the stenographer taught him how to type. A kind lady who was interested in furthering the education of boys working in stores or offices took Herbert to the library and borrowed *Ivanhoe* for him. Introduced to this great imaginative world, he promptly read much of Scott and Dickens, often at the loss of sleep.

His first business venture in repairing and reselling old sewing machines failed. The machines worked but the prospective buyers could not be induced to believe that such low-priced wares would be reliable.

At this time, Herbert managed to buy a second-hand high bicycle, which he mastered with many bumps. Soon, the new safety bicycles arrived on the market and one of these, with cushion tires, absorbed several months of his salary.

Bertie went on hunts for grouse in the Oregon forests and on expeditions for trout in the mountain streams when he could. The fishing in the upper Santiam River was very productive and the evening climb out of its one-thousand-foot canyon no effort at all in those days!

As time passed and Herbert's heart became set on an engineering career, any hope of achieving this ambition must have been very dim. Then came that momentous day when he read the notice about the opening of the Leland Stanford Junior University!

Because of his incomplete schooling, the office boy hardly dared to dream of entering the new university. A family barrier arose, too. His Quaker relatives viewed the new institution suspiciously, as they feared it to be godless.

Imagine Herbert's relief when it was announced that entrance examinations would be conducted in Portland by Joseph Swain, Professor of Mathematics at Leland Stanford—and a well-known Quaker. His association with the new university allayed the fears of the Minthorn family about its religious nature.

Herbert arrived in Portland to take the examinations at the Esmond Hotel with little hope, yet anxious determination. He did his best with the subjects given him. Mathematics came easily, due to the night-school courses and his aptitude. Fortunately, this was the professor's own field and Herbert's skill did not go unnoticed. But, although he had once studied them at the Newberg Academy, the boy was sadly deficient in the other studies needed, which included English composition, geography, history, Latin and physics.

Professor Swain recognized great promise in the young man and he must have been touched by his pupil's earnest efforts. He called Hoover into his room at the hotel. Overcoming the boy's diffidence, he talked to him about the new university and discussed his neglected schooling, due to his having to pay his own way with his uncle at the early age of fifteen. Professor Swain inquired into Herbert's financial resources, which only amounted to a third share of the small legacy left by his parents and managed by his legal guardian, Laurie Tatum.

As the professor went on talking, the boy probably felt increasingly that there was no solution to his educational problem. Any chance of entering the university seemed doomed to failure, in spite of his mentor's kindly interest.

Suddenly, Herbert heard the examiner suggest, "Why don't you come down to the university two months early, engage a tutor and take some of the subjects over again?"

Hoover felt a wave of hope. But how could he afford college when some of his precious reserve would have to be spent on advance board and tutoring?

"I think," asserted Professor Swain, sensing his companion's inner conflict, "that you can earn your way through college."

Heartened by the professor's support, Hoover quickly made plans to try.

"I resigned my great office," he later described this turning point of his life, "and gathered up all my possessions—being $160 of savings, two suits of clothes and a bicycle (and one-third of the Tatum reserve). The Minthorn family added $50 and put me on the train with blessings, affections—and food."

Young Herbert traveled to California with a Salem boy, Fred Williams, the son of a local banker. The boys alighted from the train at Menlo Park, California, as there was then no station at Palo Alto. With his bicycle and satchel, Herbert followed Professor Swain's directions and reported at Adelante Villa, where a Miss Fletcher was to provide both board and tutoring.

With charm and patience, Miss Fletcher worked hard to fill in the gaps in her tall, shy pupil's education. Herbert worked hard, too—desperately hard—to meet the entrance requirements. His whole future was at stake. One factor, however, was in his favor. The university authorities did not know how many students would enroll for the first year. Their anxiety to have enough entrants, Herbert felt, helped carry him along when the crucial day came for retaking his examinations in the subjects in which he had failed.

He passed the tests, answerable to some conditions—only to find a new obstacle in his path. He was one subject short, and there now was no time to make up the deficiency!

Not willing to admit that this might be the end of his college hopes, Herbert earnestly looked over the various elective alternatives for a spot where he might attack the final citadel. The long dissertations of his uncle, Dr. Minthorn, while on horse-and-buggy trips to visit the doctor's patients came to mind. He decided to risk his entrance on physiology. By polishing a sound memory and boning all night on two textbooks, he passed triumphantly—and entered the university!

Professor Swain's judgment and faith in Herbert were vindicated. On his return to Stanford after interviewing prospective students, he had described Hoover to Dr. Jordan as "a young Quaker employed as a clerk in some store in a back room of which he slept and studied up for college . . . none too well prepared but showing remarkable keenness."

Encina Hall, the men's dormitory, was not yet open but Herbert moved in just the same, along with Fred Williams. The two Freshmen were proud to be the first inhabitants. Due to the wide selection of food at Encina Hall, Herbert was able to declare his complete independence from the mush and milk which, under family direction for health and economy, had been his major breakfast course ever since he could remember.

Now Herbert's immediate need was to find a way to earn his living. He had the $210—less the bill for Miss Fletcher's services and his board—and the backlog of his father's insurance, which had been safeguarded and increased by Laurie Tatum to $600. Professor Swain, true to his word, secured a job for the promising young student in the university office at five dollars a week.

The mathematics teacher also guided Herbert in his choice of subjects to study. The head of the Department of Geology and Mining, Dr. John Branner, had not yet arrived, so Professor Swain arranged for Herbert to take those freshman studies best suited to prepare him for later work in Dr. Branner's department.

The formal opening of the Leland Stanford Junior University (Stanford University) was scheduled for October 1, 1891. It was a great day for the institution—and for California. Senator and Mrs. Stanford were present, of course, to dedicate their long-planned project, built on their country estate in memory of their only son, Leland, Junior, who had died in Italy of malaria at sixteen years of age.

More than 400 students gathered in the open court of the inner quadrangle of the Spanish mission-type buildings. A stand for the speakers and distinguished guests had been built in front of the arch at one end of the quadrangle. The decorations for this rostrum included flags, bunting, pampas plumes, palms, eucalyptus and grapevines hung with clusters of fruits. Brilliant sunshine flooded the scene. Throngs of people from near and far crowded the court in front of the speakers.

In tribute to the Founders, the students, assembled for the first time, uttered the college yell. "Wah-HOO! Wah-HOO! L-S-J-U! STAN-ford!" they shouted and thus marked the entrance of the new university into the world.

Senator Stanford, Judge Shafter for the Trustees, President Kellogg of the University of California and President Jordan of Stanford all spoke in the dedication of the university to the service of humanity.

"All that we can do for you," advised the donor, "is to place the opportunities within your reach. Remember that life is, above all, practical; that you are here to fit yourselves for a useful career; also, that learning should not only make you wise in the arts and sciences, but should fully develop your moral and religious natures."

The aim of Stanford, as Senator Stanford had previously outlined it to the Trustees, was not alone to give the student a technical education to fit him for success in a profession but, also, to instill in him an appreciation of the blessings of the government of the United States, a reverence for its institutions and a love for God and humanity.

Herbert listened to each speaker's words intently, completely entranced. To the tall youngster from the farms and small towns of the pioneer West, Stanford was opening new horizons of intellectual experience—and a degree of fellowship and friendship previously unknown to him.

On the arrival of Dr. Branner to head the Department of Geology and Mining, young Hoover indeed found a lode star to follow and a sure focus for his college study. He started work in geology right away under Dr. Branner, but mining engineering was not given until the second year. In his own words, "I came under the spell of a great scientist and a great teacher, whose friendship lasted over his lifetime."

In that first geology class, there were very few students, so Herbert had full opportunity to receive personal attention from the professor. On his part, Dr. Branner immediately recognized in the eager, quiet Freshman an ability to concentrate, quick comprehension—and a special talent for geology.

Knowing of his pupil's need for financial support, Dr. Branner gave Herbert a job in his department because of his ability to typewrite. Hoover also had established a laundry agency and a newspaper route on the campus, with two partners. These enterprises were sublet, so brought in only a very small, though regular, income. With his financial pressure lessened, Herbert was free to concentrate on his studies. He could even take part in college activities during his spare time.

When summer came, Dr. Branner obtained a job for his gifted student on the Arkansas Geological Survey, as an assistant. To Herbert, the sixty dollars a month salary, plus expenses, for three months seemed a fortune. Dr. Branner's obvious special interest in Herbert, however, had brought his star pupil the envy of several fellow students. Aware of this, the professor explained firmly that it was not pull or luck that helped Hoover—but character.

"So many fumble assignments," Dr. Branner said, "but I can tell Hoover to do a thing and never think of it again. If I told him to start to Kamchatka tomorrow to bring me back a walrus tooth, I'd never hear of it again until he came back with the tooth. And then I'd ask him how he'd done it."

And so Dr. Branner sent Herbert off to work on the Arkansas Geological Survey with confidence that his favored pupil would do him credit.

A
Diploma
Earned

CHAPTER 2

On reaching Arkansas early in his Freshman summer, Herbert tackled the geological survey work with his customary determination. The job consisted of mapping the geologic outcrops, or layers of rock at the surface, on the north side of the Ozarks. He worked mostly alone, on foot, and stopped for the nights at any nearby cabin that offered a welcome. The mountain people were naturally hospitable, but they were suspicious of all government agents. Moonshiners felt the "gawky boy" might even be a spy. When Herbert tried to explain his presence in terms of rocks, suspicion only increased. Talk of making a survey or tracing zinc- or coal-bearing formations was worse. The local inhabitants wanted no check-up on their landholdings or invasion by mining concerns. Finally, Herbert gave up trying to explain—but, due to his disarming, friendly personality, he never failed to find someone who would take him in for the night. His hosts often refused any payment for his lodging.

The substandard diet and crowded living conditions of many of these people appalled Herbert. But neither he nor his hosts could ever have imagined that, years later, the "gawky boy" would be able to reward that most helpful hospitality a hundred fold! As relief director in the aftermath of a great Mississippi flood, he arranged for the providing of proper food and improved living conditions for other people similarly situated who lived in the flooded Southern counties.

Herbert returned to Stanford University for his Sophomore year "lean as a greyhound, as hard as nails, and as brown as a berry." In addition, he had cleared almost $200 for his college expenses.

At Stanford, the Greek-letter fraternities had begun organizing chapters among the students. The members of these chapters combined for the purpose of securing all the student offices and elective honors. Herbert and three steadfast friends—Lester Hinsdale, Herbert Hicks and a Freshman, Ray Lyman Wilbur—resented the snobbery that accompanied the fraternity system, as did many other students. They suspected favoritism by the "frats" in handling student enterprises and were critical of the accounting of funds. They helped to organize a party of "barbarians" and declared war for reform. A slate of "barbs" was put up to oppose the frats in the student elections. Vigorous campaigning rocked the campus. Hoover was assigned to deliver the vote of the poorest students who lived in a row of shacks, known as the "Camp," which had been used by the workmen building the university. The barb ticket won on a close vote.

His fellow barb, Lester Hinsdale, recounted that his early impression of Herbert was of an earnest student, "very immature in appearance, probably the youngest looking of us all. He seemed shy to the point of timidity—rarely spoke unless spoken to. It wasn't until later, when we got into (campus) politics on the same side and I began to see under his surface, that I realized how much it was possible to like him." Lester became a lifelong friend, as have many of Herbert's early associates in college and engineering, and his later colleagues in relief work and government.

During his Sophomore and Junior vacations, Herbert was given the wonderful opportunity of working under Dr. Waldemar Lindgren on the United States Geological Survey in the high Sierra Nevadas, the Nevada deserts and among mining camps in the region. One summer, probably after his Sophomore year, there was for a time uncertainty about Herbert's getting the Survey job. As he needed funds badly, he joined some other students in canvassing San Francisco business firms for contracts to put up or paint advertising signs along the roads. Due to the very modest rates offered, the boys succeeded in getting a few hundred dollars' worth of sign contracts. They bought a team, wagon and camping outfit and started off toward Yosemite Valley, putting up "eyesores" along the way, with permission from the landowners, which advertised coffee, tea and newspapers.

A few days after the group reached the Valley, Herbert received a telegram announcing that he could join the Survey party. There was not enough money left among Herbert's sign-painting partners to pay his stage fare to the railroad. He did not give up, however. This was an opportunity he could not afford to miss. He arrived at the appointed place on time—by walking eighty miles in three days!

This job, as cub assistant to Dr. Lindgren, was a far happier assignment for Herbert than the Ozarks Survey. In the high mountains, the party camped out with teamsters, horses and pack mules and, of matching importance—a good camp cook! Most of the work was done on horseback and the cub assistant considered that, during those two summers, he put in enough mileage by that mode of transportation to take care of his normal lifetime share. On the long mountain rides over rough trails and through the hampering brush, he concluded finally that a horse was one of the original mistakes of creation for use in that type of country. The horse, he felt, was too high off the ground for convenience and safety on mountain trails and could have negotiated them better if he had been given "a dozen legs so that he had the smooth and sure pace of a centipede. Furthermore he should have had scales as protection against flies, and a larger water-tank like a camel."

The Survey party was once visited by a foreign geologist, who, it developed, had never seen a rattlesnake. One hot day, as Herbert rode along a trail, a rattlesnake alarm went off and his horse shied violently, giving the rider double notice. Resolving to take the snake's corpse to the visitor, who was not present, Herbert dismounted and carefully hit the poisonous snake on the head with a stout stick. He then wrapped him in a bandanna handkerchief which he hung on the pommel of his saddle.

A few minutes afterward, while the horse and his rider were toiling along to camp, drowsy in the sun, the rattler woke up and indignantly sounded another alarm. This proved too much for the horse, who quickly shed his rider. When Herbert extricated himself from the brush, he had to walk five miles back to camp. It added to his prejudices against horses in general!

As the youngest member of the Survey, the cub assistant was made disbursing officer. Before long, Herbert came to realize that this appointment was not a distinction but a liability. It was his job to purchase supplies and keep the records in conformity with the elaborate book of regulations, which provided excellent safeguards for the public funds.

One morning, when the party was encamped high in the Sierras, a pack mule was found dead. The regulations stated that the disbursing officer and two witnesses must prepare and sign an affidavit explaining the circumstances of such a catastrophe; otherwise the disbursing officer was held personally responsible for the animal's value. Herbert was therefore involved to the amount of sixty dollars—a large sum in view of the fact that he was earning his way through college.

An autopsy disclosed that the mule had died from a broken neck. In scratching his head with his hind foot, the halter rope had become wedged in the caulk of his shoe. The mule had jerked back and broken his neck. Herbert filed an elaborate affidavit to this effect with the government authorities in Washington. Two months later, he was advised that sixty dollars had been deducted from his pay. The story was too highly improbable! Knowing what this sum represented to his assistant, Dr. Lindgren kindly paid Herbert the deducted amount, planning to recover it from the government bureau when he returned to Washington the following winter.

A great engineer and scientist, Dr. Lindgren was, in addition, a great teacher. Herbert listened intently to the conversations around the mines and absorbed a large amount of engineering lore and practice. The geological party spent the evenings of the two long summers around campfires in the high mountains, at foothill hotels or at the homes of mine managers, when in the mining districts.

In the wintertime, Dr. Lindgren and other leading members of the party lived in Washington, D.C., so their illuminating conversations around the fire embraced a vast amount of objective observation on government outside of the scientific bureaus, all of which was eagerly absorbed by the cub assistant.

The summers of hard physical exertion in the mines and the mountains blessed Herbert Hoover with a physique equal to any subsequent strain, as well as increasing his knowledge of geology and mining immeasurably.

He also earned his first recognition toward his chosen profession. On the published Survey maps, alongside the name of Dr. Lindgren, appeared that of a coming young geologist and engineer—Herbert Hoover. Before he could achieve success as a mining engineer, he first had to become expert in geology.

On the Stanford University campus in those years there was a particularly close association between the professors and their pupils, due in part to their mutual stake in the new institution. This greatly benefited the students in absorbing education. Physics, chemistry, geology, mathematics, mechanics and engineering all came easily to young Hoover. He was able, therefore, to take an unusual amount of instruction in history, economics and English and French literature for an engineering student. Although he did not achieve *A* grades in his courses, he failed in only one, German. As far as boning for marks was concerned, he had too many interests and occupations in noncurricular activities for that.

Among these was managing the baseball team. Herbert had made the Freshman baseball team but in one game had stopped a ball too short, spraining a finger so badly that he had to drop out of playing. In time, too, his teammates decided he would make a better manager than shortstop!

It was Herbert's job as manager to raise money for equipment and uniforms, arrange games for the new, untried team and collect the gate receipts. Through the latter activity, the manager had his first encounter with a great public figure. Former President Benjamin Harrison was giving a course of lectures on government at Stanford, and he came to a baseball game one afternoon. The playing field was not enclosed and the twenty-five cent admission charge was collected by student outposts. Benjamin Harrison was apparently unaware that he should pay admission and the outpost was too overcome with shyness to insist, so it became the stern duty of the manager to collect! This Herbert did, selling the former President an admission for that afternoon and an advance ticket for the next week's game. Later on, feeling that "justice must occasionally be done, even to ex-Presidents," the one-time manager disclosed in his *Memoirs* that Harrison then took two more tickets!

In Herbert's Junior year, the barbs had another campaign to wage. During vacation, he had evolved a plan for organizing all campus activities which he drew up in written form. This constitution was voted into effect and, under the plan, Herbert was elected treasurer or financial manager. This gave him the responsibility for the receipts from all the athletic games and other collegiate activities. It was a paid job, but Herbert refused the salary, in spite of his need for it. Benefiting from the training he had received from the Land Company bookkeeper, he set up full accounts of all the student enterprises and published them in the campus newspaper. College football was then becoming big business, and Herbert handled many tens of thousands of dollars in game receipts and athletic and other disbursements. With the student body finances thus organized, it became possible to help deserving undergraduates in distress. But all this extra work reduced Hoover's studying time and cut down his earnings.

As financial manager, Herbert had a busy time at a football game played in San Francisco with the University of California on an early Stanford Thanksgiving Day. Tickets were printed for ten thousand spectators and when almost twice that number came, an alley of college boys was set up to collect.

The receipts, in gold and silver, piled up in the box offices. The two financial managers had to rent a wash boiler and a dishpan from nearby residents—for the price of a free ticket— to hold the overflow. In the midst of this rush, the two football captains demanded a football, to begin the play. This detail had been overlooked—and the start of the game was delayed half an hour while the managers sent downtown for two pigskins!

Herbert had no chance to see the game, which Stanford won. He and the California manager took the money, now transferred to grain bags, to a hotel and sat up most of the night counting the receipts. The cash added up to over thirty thousand dollars—an amount that Herbert had never seen before. The team was well financed for the next season.

Another non-curricular activity was a concert and lecture forum bequeathed to Herbert by its originator when he left college. On one occasion, as impresario, Hoover presented as a speaker a young congressman, who, being virtually unknown, failed to draw a crowd. Two years later, the same man would have filled a large auditorium. His name—William Jennings Bryan.

Another crisis arose for the young impresario and his partner when a scheduled concert by Ignace Paderewski failed to draw an attendance large enough to cover the famous pianist's fee, owing to a vacation conflict. The two college boys were $400 short and Hoover offered his note for the debt, based on good faith. Declining to accept the note, Paderewski graciously canceled the obligation.

After World War I, at a large public reception for Herbert Hoover at Lodz, in Poland, Paderewski, now Prime Minister of his country, thanked Hoover for saving tens of thousands of Polish lives through famine relief. In turn, Hoover recalled the long-ago concert and his host's generous action. Thunderous applause demonstrated the feeling of everyone that the concert debt had been repaid more than a thousandfold!

His lifelong friend and admiring biographer, Will Irwin, has given a description of Hoover in his last year at Stanford. Entering that year as a Freshman, Irwin's first impression of Herbert resembled that of some great impersonal force. The football captain and other campus celebrities were cheered or joked with from the bleachers. "But Hoover," Will stated, "while he walked humanly among us, was a kind of legend too; a supernally able personage." Standing, rather than popularity, seemed a better word to express his influence on his fellow students.

The first distinct memory Irwin had of the eminent Senior was when the former broke his ankle playing football and Herbert came to see him in the dormitory room and arrange for the necessary medical supplies. Standing in the doorway, he was tall, just under six feet, broad shouldered and had a lean build. Irwin noticed a slight stoop, suggesting excess muscular development rather than midnight oil. The visitor's hair was mouse colored, straight as an Indian's, and his hazel eyes were so contemplative as to appear dreamy. There was not a single straight line in his round, strong face. As he discussed Irwin's needs with the team's rubber, who was acting as nurse, he stood with one foot forward, jingling the keys in his trousers' pocket.

When arrangements were completed, Irwin made a little joke to keep up his courage in his suffering. Hoover chuckled —a deep, rich chuckle that originated far down inside and seemed to lose much of its force in inner mirth before reaching the surface. As he was leaving, the sensitive Senior turned to the patient and said, with obvious sincerity, "I'm sorry." To Irwin, this brief word of sympathy was equal to another man's tears.

"Then and there, I suppose, I put myself under his leadership," Will Irwin recalls. "That kind of thing was always happening at Stanford. Even men who opposed him in the 'great frat-barb war,' coming afterward into association with him, began to lean on his sane and unruffled judgment. The whimsies of life have permitted some of us to follow him since in affairs and struggles whose actors were kings, principalities and powers, dynasties and armies, violences of which the nineteenth century never dreamed, incredible human sacrifices, Godlike benevolences. But the game was the same. . . ."

Another Freshman who was conscious of Herbert by reputation was a girl from Monterey, California, named Lou Henry. She planned to major in geology and later teach the subject. One afternoon, Miss Henry was in Dr. Branner's laboratory and the professor was showing her some new specimens which Hoover had brought in from the field. She did not appear to notice the sunburned, immature-looking boy who stood nearby, gazing at her fascinated. Such attention was no novelty to this tall, handsome girl.

Dr. Branner declared his view that the geological specimens were pre-carboniferous. "What is your opinion, Hoover?" He asked his assistant's judgment.

But Herbert, blushing, was tongue-tied.

As handy boy in the geology and mining department, it became his pleasure and duty to aid the young lady in her studies, both in the laboratory and the field. He was greatly attracted by her whimsical mind, her blue eyes and a "broad, grinnish smile," inherited from an Irish ancestor. He soon learned that Lou Henry had been born in Iowa the same year as he. Her father, a Monterey banker who liked hunting and fishing, had brought her up in the out-of-door life of a boy, as he had no sons. According to contemporary sources, Lou Henry was the only co-ed to receive attention from the busy Senior.

With his studies, the time spent in earning his way and all his varied interests—including his affection for the tall girl from Monterey—Herbert had never worked off the conditions on entrance credits under which he had been admitted to the university as a Freshman. Suddenly, he discovered that he would not receive his diploma with his own class at graduation! It took the active intervention of his friends, Dr. Branner and Professor J. Perrin Smith, to make his degree possible. They insisted, among other things, that he was proficient in English composition!

The diploma was duly granted to him—Bachelor of Arts in Geology—"with all the Rights, Privileges and Honors here or elsewhere thereunto appertaining." He was now a full-fledged graduate in geology and mining engineering—ready to take up his long-dreamed-of career as an engineer wherever opportunity offered.

Since then, Mr. Hoover was tendered and given many honorary degrees—totaling ninety-three—often, he commented wryly, in exchange for commencement addresses. But not one of these ever had the stature or, in his opinion, the importance of the first one.

However, as he marched up to receive that diploma, the thrill of the occasion was somewhat marred by the sinking realization of his shortage of working capital and the necessity of finding an immediate job. He had exactly forty dollars in reserve.

The poor orphan boy, having worked his way through college and obtained an education through his own strenuous effort and initiative, now faced the task of making a living and being able to plan with confidence for the time when he could provide for a wife and family—with a stake of forty dollars. Herbert had an understanding with Miss Henry that, when his career permitted, they would marry.

The
Engineer
Takes a
Partner

CHAPTER 3

Ａfter his graduation, Herbert needed at once to find "some person with a profit motive" who could use the services of the fledgling mining engineer to help him earn money. This free-enterprise test for a job, as Hoover whimsically put it when speaking to the graduating class at Stanford University in 1935, has some advantages. It does not require qualifications as to ancestry, religion, good looks or ability to get votes.

To begin his search, Herbert went to the gold-mining districts of Nevada City and Grass Valley, in the Sierra Nevada foothills, where he had had some engineering experience with Dr. Lindgren the previous summer. To make his job hunting more difficult, the depression of 1893 was then being felt in California. But Herbert had lived all his life in hard times and the situation did not affect him. He knew how to surmount it and went determinedly ahead to find employment.

He did not succeed right away in impressing the profit-and-loss takers with the high potentialities of his diploma or experience. The mines were mostly managed by Cornishmen who had worked their way up from foremen. They held a certain rooted scepticism toward "them college-educated fellers." Herbert was not trying for a top job. He would have been glad to get a start anywhere near the bottom of any mine staff.

He had no luck, however, in finding a position, no matter how lowly, on the technical staff of a mining corporation. Soon the white collar possibilities—and the forty dollars—were exhausted, as well as some credit from a kind hotel keeper. Herbert finally got a job pushing a car in the lower levels of the Reward Mine, at Nevada City, for two dollars a day, on a ten-hour night shift and a seven-day week. He started literally at the bottom—far underground. He shoveled the wet mixture of dirt and rocks, working as a mucker. His first serious entrance into the economic world was by manual labor, but he did not feel like a "down-trodden wage slave." The young engineering graduate was confident that, when he had saved up forty or fifty dollars from his laborer's wages, he would have enough security ahead to exercise the option of leaving his job to look for a better opening.

At first, the Cornish miners on his shift were offish toward the young college boy but, won over by his genuine friendliness, they soon started teaching him the tricks of the trade. Among other pointers, he learned how to keep warm in a wet underground level of the mine while the smoke of blasting cleared. To do this, he curled up in a steel wheelbarrow which was heated by several candles burning underneath. Herbert also picked up some Cornish dialect.

In two or three months, the young engineer was appointed helper on a drill by the foreman. He was then acknowledged as a real miner. The Cornishmen on his level of the mine celebrated his promotion by bringing extra Cornish pasties for their midnight lunch. Over thirty years later, the survivors of this group celebrated Herbert Hoover's nomination for president by organizing a special campaign committee for his election. They won the vote of every Cornish family in the region. After some brushing up on the Cornish dialect, their fellow miner was able to thank them in their own tongue some years later, at a Fourth of July speech.

Herbert lost his job as a miner after a while, however. The Reward Mine slackened down and he was let go. He then learned what the "bottom levels of real human despair are paved with. That is the ceaseless tramping and ceaseless refusal at the employment office day by day."

Finally, he found steady employment at the Mayflower Mine, near Grass Valley, at full miner's wages. Hiking up the side of Banner Mountain, he reported to the shift boss, Thomas Ninnis.

"So you want to learn mining. There's only one way," he was advised by the veteran worker. "Get in there and dig. It can't be learned by sticking your nose in a book. You need a nose for gold. You'll develop it by working where the gold is."

Herbert started right in. He pounded a drill, shoved handcars and performed his other duties with alacrity. The shift boss did not think much of the young "whippersnappers" who came to the mines. He felt that the old hard-rock miners had to tell them what to do too often, but he grew to have a high regard for Herbert, whom he called "the Professor." He conducted him through the different mine levels, drifts and stopes. They took samples, checked veins and discussed mining problems. Herbert absorbed a great store of practical mining and promptly linked this knowledge and experience with his theoretical study of geology.

He overlooked no opportunity to increase his fund of information. Old-timers in Nevada City, the "Gold Capital," described his making the rounds from the Plaza to Ott's assay office, the National Hotel and the Wells Fargo Express Office. "Always he talked and asked questions about gold mines and mining," they remembered.

After some time at the Mayflower Mine, Herbert took stock of his situation. He had saved up $100. There had been a change in his family picture. His Grandmother Minthorn had died, leaving his sister May without support. His older brother Theodore had been compelled to interrupt his studies at Penn College to take care of her. They were living in a house in Oakland, California, where Theodore was working as a linotype operator. It was nearing Christmas in 1895—and Oakland was not far from Palo Alto, where a special young lady was attending Stanford University.

Herbert joined his brother and sister. His cousin, Harriet Miles, whose father young Herbert had visited in Indian Territory in Arkansas, also became a member of the household. For the first time since their mother's death, the three young Hoovers were reunited.

Dr. Lindgren had once casually introduced his cub assistant to the outstanding mining engineer on the Pacific Coast—Louis Janin of San Francisco. Herbert called at his office and succeeded in seeing Mr. Janin. He explained the details of his meager experience and told him that he wanted a tryout in his office in any capacity.

"Why don't you come to lunch with me at my club and we can talk then?" the kindly, convivial engineer suggested. Herbert promptly accepted and observed that his host spent more on their lunch than the young engineer needed for a week's support!

Mr. Janin explained gently to Hoover that he had no places open.

"I have already more assistants than I know how to keep busy," he said. "As far as I know, none of the mines with which I am connected need staff."

Then, to emphasize the fact that there were no openings for engineers, he concluded, "The only job vacancy I know of is that of copyist in my office."

Visions of his diminishing $100 raced through Herbert's mind. Also, the thought that something might turn up if he kept near the throne. He disclosed at once that he could type and would like the job in question.

"But—er—" Mr. Janin was startled. Then he laughed. "All right, my boy. You are hired."

The episode made a favorable impression on the older man. A few days later, Mr. Janin sent for his new copyist. "I have a few months' work to be done on an extensive engineering project in northern Colorado," he said. "Would you go as an assistant for $150 a month and expenses?"

Hoover accepted with dispatch. From that day on, he had never again asked for or looked for engineering jobs of any kind. Since then, offers had come to him "of their own accord." By starting from the bottom, literally far underground, and doing each successive job thoroughly and wholeheartedly, he made a permanent name for himself—the hard way.

When the Colorado assignment was finished, Mr. Janin sent Herbert as assistant manager to a mine at Steeple Rock, New Mexico, which employed Mexican miners. It was a tough locality. There was lots of gambling, and often serious trouble arose, especially after paydays. The mine manager was also a deputy sheriff. When murder was committed, or near-murder, he took direct action. Unarmed, he captured the culprit. As there was no jail, he secured prisoners by lowering them down a disused mine shaft and throwing the rope down, too. There they remained snugly until the sheriff arrived.

On this assignment, Herbert's chief work consisted of helping the manager in the mine engineering. He assisted in superintending the co-ordination and efficiency of the staff and the miners, and the purchase and consumption of supplies.

When Herbert had been at the New Mexico mine for some

time, Mr. Janin asked him to join the staff of his office in San
Francisco, where an opening had occurred due to the promotion of a young staff engineer to a mine superintendency. The
offer was accepted at once!

At that time, Mr. Janin was serving as the technical expert
in a great mining litigation in Grass Valley. Herbert had studied the geology of the mines involved, under Dr. Lindgren, and
he was assigned to work up the details for his employer's technical report. This providential assignment brought him two
blessings—a special fee and the acquaintance of Judge Curtis
Lindley, who later became a great friend.

On one occasion, when Herbert was working at the North
Pole Mine, he prepared a report on the mine for Mr. Janin.
The completeness of the account surprised his employer. Matter of factly, the young engineer explained his familiarity with
the situation. "I worked underground in that mine, pushing a
car."

Often Herbert Hoover's success has been due to having been
in the right places at the right times—but, most importantly,
he had always made full use of any opportunities that were offered.

When Herbert returned to the San Francisco office from
New Mexico, he again lived with his brother and sister, who
had meanwhile moved to a house in Berkeley. He had regis-
tered there as a Republican for his first vote but did not have
the opportunity to exercise his rights, owing to absence. He
closely followed the 1896 presidential campaign between William McKinley and William Jennings Bryan through the newspapers. Certain features of the campaign provided his first
shock over the realization that intellectual dishonesty could be
used as a basis for national economics.

Ever since leaving his job as a laborer in the Mayflower
Mine, Hoover's work schedule had given him some spare time
in the afternoons and evenings. In college, due to his intensive
program of preparing for his profession, earning his living and

dabbling in extra-curricular activities, he had had less general education than he felt was imperative for a well-rounded existence. Now that he had some free time, he began insatiable reading in the field of economics. New continents of thought opened up to the young engineer through diligent study.

One significant day in October, 1897, Mr. Janin called Herbert into his office. He showed him a cable he had received from an important British mining firm—Bewick, Moreing and Company—asking him to recommend to them an engineer skilled in American gold-mining practice for work in Australia. There was a gold rush booming in the colony of Western Australia and, since American machinery and technical practices in gold mining were far ahead of those of the Australians and British at the time, they felt the need of assistance from the United States.

"I do not like losing your services," Mr. Janin admitted, "but this means $600 a month for you, instead of $200. I would like to have you take it." He reported later that his assistant had stood for a moment so dazzled that he could not speak when he offered him the post.

After Herbert had caught his breath, he responded that the British firm might be disappointed in his age—he was then only twenty-three—and his lack of experience.

"Don't worry about your age," Mr. Janin encouraged him, "or the amount of time you've been working, for that matter. I'll guarantee to fix all that. I am going to write a very good letter of recommendation for you."

This exciting opportunity gave Herbert the chance to contribute enough to the support of his brother and sister so that Theodore could leave his job and finish his college education. Theodore later graduated from Stanford and, after a successful business career as a mining engineer, returned to his Alma Mater as Dean of the Engineering School.

For the first time in his life, Hoover was able to buy some extra clothes. With the advice of his friend, Lester Hinsdale, and another Stanford man, he ordered three new suits and then was persuaded by Lester into adding a sporting Scotch tweed. About a year later, Hinsdale received a package from Australia containing the Scotch-tweed suit and a note from Hoover saying, "Since you like this, take it. I haven't worn it yet."

Herbert said good-by to his family and friends—and to Miss Lou Henry. He had had few chances to be with her since leaving college. Sometimes he had gone to Stanford on a week end to see her, staying with his friend Will Irwin. Herbert Hoover and Lou Henry had corresponded busily, however, so, when they parted, there was still an understanding between them that, as soon as his career permitted, they would marry.

With considerable trepidation, Herbert left for London, where the head office of his new firm was located. Crossing the Mississippi River and the eastern half of the United States for the first time, he boarded a White Star liner of seven thousand tons for the ocean trip. Unhappily for him, this ship proved unable to overcome the waves to his satisfaction!

Arriving in London, Hoover promptly presented himself at the office of Bewick, Moreing and Company. At first he was startled by the pomp and circumstance of British business. When the uniformed doormen "ultimately deigned" to pass him in to the head of the firm, Mr. Charles Algernon Moreing proved much less formidable. Another experience awaited the young American at Mr. Moreing's country place, to which he had been invited for a week end. It was shock enough for him to find that the footman, Buttons, insisted upon helping him prepare for dinner but, in addition, the visitor sensed deeply the scantiness of his wardrobe as Buttons dissected it, piece by piece. At Mr. Janin's suggestion, Herbert had brought dinner clothes. Otherwise, Buttons' sniffs would have frightened him to flight!

Bewick, Moreing and Company had acquired a number of gold mines in the newly discovered fields in the central part of Western Australia. The American engineer's employment was for general engineering work among a group of some ten mines and a number of prospecting ventures. He was to be subordinate to a resident member of the firm.

The journey to Western Australia brought Herbert glimpses of France, Italy, Egypt and India. History became a reality—and America a contrast.

Herbert Hoover spent his first two weeks in Australia in a quarantine station at Albany, then the chief seaport of Western Australia. Smallpox had broken out on his ship before it docked. When released, he traveled about 500 miles on a newly constructed narrow-gauge railway to the desert mining town of Coolgardie. At the height of a mining boom, the town, as he came to know it, had all the characteristics of a western American mining camp, with some special Australian attachments. Violence was absent, because of a rigid form of self-government in the colony, but "petty crime, immorality and good cheer" were as abundant generally as they were in California during the heyday of the forty-niners.

The nth degree of optimism pervaded all. Everyone lived in a tinted atmosphere of fortunes already estimated or being calculated. In time, however, the gorgeous surface showings of the Coolgardie mines faded out. When the mines were worked downward, the poor results quickly dissolved many astronomic hopes. Later on, the gold fields at Kalgoorlie, in a nearby district, took over the center of the stage.

The young engineer was immediately absorbed in technical work with his firm's mine managers at Coolgardie and Kalgoorlie. He planned and superintended plant layouts and development projects, the ordering of American equipment and the examination of new mining prospects. The amazement which the managers, staff and miners must have felt on meeting such a youthful gold-mining expert soon faded out and in its place an appreciation of his abilities mushroomed. Later this most efficient engineer became known to those who worked with him as "the Chief." Down through the years, to those closely associated with him in all the different enterprises which he has managed and in which he has taken an active part Herbert Hoover continued to be—the Chief.

The Bewick, Moreing mines at Kalgoorlie were unbelievably rich. They were of the impregnation or replacement type, with gold ore deposits distributed "like plums in a pudding." However, these mines presented difficult metallurgical problems which were intensified by the lack of water. Fuel was provided by the scraggly bush of the desert, while the limited water available came from shallow wells in salty depressions and had to be distilled for domestic purposes.

These conditions required extensive alterations in the mining practices previously known. Herbert was faced with the problem of recovering all the water he could from the metallurgical processes, in order to re-use the commodity, which was rarer even than the sought-for gold. He solved this problem by introducing for the first time a filter press, copied from one used in sugar refining. This press has since been largely adopted by the mining industry.

Coolgardie and Kalgoorlie were described by Herbert as being among the hottest, driest and dustiest places on earth. The temperature was over 100 degrees at midnight for days at a time. The country was flat and uninteresting. It was covered by the Australian bush, dwarf or stunted half-starved trees and shrubs, eight or ten feet high, consisting mostly of eucalyptus and acacias. The annual rainfall of a little more than one inch usually came all at one time. This did have a doubly redeeming feature. After the rain, the whole desert was transformed into a lovely Persian carpet of many-colored immortelles.

With water at 2½ cents a gallon, the inhabitants, including Herbert, were restricted to shower baths—most of which came from a suspended bucket with a few nail holes in the bottom. Whenever rain fell, every person in town dropped his current occupation to collect free water from the heavens. Flat roofs, blankets, buckets and tubs were all pressed into service.

Herbert tried to improve the diet at the corrugated-iron staff residence, named the Iron House, by starting a vegetable garden. Soon a variety of "creeping things" entered into enthusiastic competition with each other over the growing plants. Only two cabbages were pulled through the garden experiment. The neighbors would gather on the fence in the evenings for the novelty of watching green plants grow, but it proved to be an expensive show. The bookkeeper informed Herbert that $250 worth of water had been expended for each cabbage!

The American was delegated to sit on an advisory board of mine operators, concentrating on the scant water supply. Relief was finally obtained by building a 400-mile pipeline from the coast. The water consumption estimate was based on the statistics for an average civilized city. The figures proved 75 per cent too high when water finally came, for the people had been so trained to economy in using the rarity that it went against their natures to be at all lavish with the liquid, even when it arrived in quantity.

At one time, Herbert took over the mine manager's job at Hannan's Brownhill Mine, near Kalgoorlie, so the manager might have a vacation. While he was in charge, the Governor of Australia paid a visit to the district. As Brownhill was a show mine, the local reception committee asked to have their honored guest taken below. Herbert directed the foreman to have the mine all spic and span for the state visit.

When the Governor and his party came, Herbert met them at the mine shaft, dressed in his usual work togs. He himself conducted the visiting dignitary on the mine tour, doing his best to make it interesting. As he progressed, he realized that, unknown to him, the foreman had plastered the walls with bright, powdered iron pyrites, or fool's gold, sprayed through a cement gun, as part of the spic-and-span program. He could not bear to call the foreman down for his well-meant deceit— or reveal the true situation. He did not explain that all was not gold that glittered so brilliantly under the strings of electric lights! When the party came to the surface, the Governor thanked Herbert kindly—and gave him a five shilling tip!

Some of the Bewick, Moreing and Company mines were situated far in the interior of the colony and the only practical transportation to reach them was by means of Afghan camels. After riding these glamorous "ships of the desert" on inspection trips, Herbert was completely disillusioned. A camel, he could state authoritatively, did not fulfill all the anticipations of romantic literature. In fact, the animal was an even less successful creation than the horse, in his estimation, and needed water oftener than the school books indicated. Its motion caused aches in muscles previously unknown to Herbert, and no amount of petting could inspire the beast with affection. His mount's long neck permitted the perverse creature to bite Herbert's leg, which it was prone to do unless constantly watched!

On camel back, the inspection party traveled twenty to thirty miles a day and usually slept on the ground at night, under the "cold" stars. The mining men cooked their own food, and Herbert soon reduced his culinary operations to a menu of toast, cocoa and sardines or baked beans heated in the can. The sun and stars dominated the atmosphere above, but the chief undertones were generally flies, sand and dirt.

Later on, when more salt wells were dug in the desert and a crude distilling apparatus was available, the camels were replaced by horses, usually harnessed in tandem to two-wheeled carts.

On one of his early inspection tours, 150 miles in the interior, Herbert camped overnight near a mine prospect named the Sons of Gwalia. This was being worked by Welshmen for the owners in Wales. In the evening, the American engineer called at the mine and was conducted over their "show" and their small mill. He was most impressed by what he saw.

As soon as Herbert reached a telegraph office the next day, he cabled Mr. Moreing that he thought the prospect well worth further examination, if the senior partner could get an option from the Welsh financial backers. This prospect gave evidence of great riches, and Hoover's "nose for gold," developed by working where gold actually was, following the instructions of his shift boss at the Mayflower Mine, told him that the Sons of Gwalia was a real find.

The option was secured, and a few weeks later Herbert completed his examination. He recommended that the firm buy a two-thirds interest for $250,000 and provide a working capital of $250,000. This was his first assumption of responsibility for what seemed to him a huge sum of money.

The mine more than justified his recommendations. Over the succeeding fifty years of continuous operation, the Sons of Gwalia produced $55,000,000 worth of gold and paid $10,-000,000 in dividends!

The partners of Bewick, Moreing and Company gave Herbert a small percentage of the mine ownership, and he was appointed the mine's first manager, at $10,000 a year salary, plus expenses. The firm was naturally pleased with this venture!

The new manager built a corrugated-iron residence at the site, under the shadow of a high peak, Mount Leonora, and at once undertook a vigorous development of the mine and the installation of a large metallurgical plant.

Life at far-off Gwalia may have seemed desperate at times to some of the personnel, but the American engineer-manager said in retrospect that no one need sympathize with men engaged in constructive work at the outposts of civilization. Except for an occasional toot by the foreman, Herbert and his staff enjoyed every minute of it.

"To feel great works grow under one's feet and to have more men constantly getting good jobs," he later wrote, " is to be the master of contentment."

Herbert Hoover's reputation began to spread in Australia and his name began to appear in Australian and London mining journals and financial journals. To some he was known as

"Boy Hoover." Another appellation was "Hail, Columbia" Hoover.

Hoover found time for reading for his own pleasure—chiefly on the history and government of Australasia. And there were light moments, too, at the Sons of Gwalia, such as the time the Austrian cook served American canned corn as a tempting dessert—direct from the tin. Also, there was the burro who made the error of eating wax matches and had to have his internal fire put out by pouring a bucket of water in through a funnel.

Herbert was, of course, always "panning" for good men to work under him. One day there appeared at the mine a lanky young fellow seeking employment. After telling Hoover of his qualifications—a degree and summer work at the mines in New Zealand—he asked for any kind of job to get started. Remembering his own experience at Nevada City, Herbert gave him work as an underground miner. Promotion was rapid and the young man, whose name was John A. Agnew, was associated with Herbert until the latter's retirement in 1914.

The young manager worked hard in the evenings—planning, figuring, conjecturing—in his corrugated-iron office, under the summit of serene Mount Leonora and over the hurly-burly of the camp life. He read hard, too. Not only must he lose no time in the struggle to earn a place in his profession—but he must also cover up his loneliness for the girl who waited in Monterey—a continent and an ocean away.

In the summer of 1898, Mr. Moreing was in Peking, China, in connection with a bond issue which had been floated in England, Belgium, France and Germany, to provide development capital for the Chinese Engineering and Mining Company. This was a large coal-mining and cement-manufacturing concern, of which the majority interest was Chinese owned. The business management was Chinese, but the operations were under a European technical staff. The purpose of the capital was to open further mines and to build an ice-free, coal-loading port and connecting railway at Chinwangtao, on the Gulf of Chihli.

The director-general of the company, Chang Yen-mao, had recently been appointed head of the Bureau of Mines, a newly created department of the Chinese government, arising from the "reform and progress" movement of the Young Emperor, Kwang Hsu. Chang consulted Mr. Moreing about the technical staff for the Bureau, as he was being buffeted by the various European governments who wished appointments for their nationals, in order to control the technical staff.

Mr. Moreing suggested that the director-general by-pass these political pressures by selecting an American as chief engineer. He explained that he had in his employ an American who could qualify for the position, and, at the same time, look after the interests of the bondholders in the new development projects planned by the Chinese Engineering and Mining Company.

With Chang's authorization, Mr. Moreing cabled to the young American in far-off Western Australia.

The cable, offering Herbert the dual job, with an aggregate annual salary of about $20,000, plus expenses, reached him as he was working late at night, far above the camp hubbub. Never was a message more enthusiastically received! To the young man, sweltering in the high temperatures, even at night, the prospect of a new and romantic world was enthralling.

And, what was even more important, he cabled Miss Lou Henry at Monterey. Would she agree that the time had come for them to be married—and go to China?

The answer came back with record speed. She would. The uncertain and turbulent life of an engineer offered no obstacles to her.

En route to California, Herbert stopped in London, in January, 1899, to receive a briefing on his new assignment.

Meanwhile, Lou Henry was busy at home with the wedding preparations. Having determined to adopt the religious faith of her future husband, she wanted a Quaker ceremony. However, there was no Friends' Meeting in that part of California, so this was not possible, as the meeting is an essential part of the marriage ceremony.

Herbert reached Monterey on February 10, 1899. The ceremony took place in the living room of the Henry house on the same day, in the presence of relatives. Since no Protestant minister was in the town at the moment, a Catholic priest, who was an old friend of Miss Henry's family, secured a special dispensation to marry the couple. The bride was given in marriage by her father.

The next morning, Mr. and Mrs. Herbert Hoover caught the steamer for China. Among their household goods were all the books on China and Chinese life and customs that could be corralled. The newlyweds little suspected that an adventure awaited them in China that was stranger than any related in those history books and along a route unmarked on any of the suggested guidebook tours!

China
Story

On reaching China, in March, 1899, the Hoovers went at once to Peking, to see Chang Yen-mao, the Imperial Commissioner of Mines, who also held the quasi-political post of director-general of the Chinese Engineering and Mining Company. After lengthy sessions with Chang and his many advisers, it was arranged that Hoover would assemble the necessary engineering staff for both the Bureau of Mines and the coal and cement company, and that he and Mrs. Hoover would live at Tientsin, where the main offices of the company were located.

The Hoovers rented a house on the edge of the foreign settlement at Tientsin. Mrs. Hoover was kept busy with the exciting job of furnishing their first home from the Chinese merchants' wares and planning for the "necessary" number of Chinese servants. From the start, she developed a unique talent for making a charming home in each of the many different places all over the world where she and her husband lived.

Herbert sent to Australia for John Agnew, Wilfred New-

berry and Daniel Francis of the Sons of Gwalia staff, and to the
United States for geologists George Wilson and John Means,
both Stanford men. From England he engaged a harbor engineer named John Hughes.

When Hoover was able to get the actual work started on the
proposed harbor project at Chinwangtao, the temperature was
ten degrees below zero—but the building of the new port was
begun without further delay. Herbert could grapple easily with
the problem of constructing the new ice-free, coal-loading port
and the necessary railway connections. Planning to open an
additional coal mine with more modern equipment was also—
to him—part of the day's work. These were concrete projects
upon which he could get a sure hold.

His major job, however, that of chief engineer to the Department of Mines, was not only intangible, but derived from
an authority which no longer existed. The "reform and progress" movement, advocated by the Young Emperor, Kwang
Hsu, which had promoted Western methods and education,
had been swept away. The Empress Dowager had dethroned
and imprisoned Kwang Hsu in September, 1898, and banished
his ideas and reforms. A drastic reaction to Western ideas was
rising—accompanied by a resurgence of anti-foreign feeling.

Kwang Hsu's tutor and adviser on reform had fled for his
life. Six of the most prominent "reformers" were executed and
many others arrested. Chang Yen-mao feared for his own future.

The "reform" period had brought to China an increasing
number of foreign concession hunters, demanding large mining areas. Hoover was disturbed by the lack of any Chinese
laws on the development and production of minerals or on the
conditions of employment. He therefore drafted a decree which
was a compound of American and Australian principles of
mining law, in an early attempt to safeguard China from foreign exploitation.

Chang Yen-mao said the decree was good but the political

climate was unfavorable for promoting it, as they both knew. Moreover, Chang was busy molding himself into the new political form as fast as he could—and, incidentally, helping a few concession hunters!

Chang was not wholly in sympathy with "reform." As Hoover was later told, he was a palace creation, who had risen from the status of groom by "well-applied corruption." As an agent of a highly placed Manchu, Prince Kung, he had worked his way into profitable places. Another patron of his was Li Hung-chang, Viceroy of Chihli and Superintendent of Trade. By intrigue and the support of his patrons, Chang had managed to have himself appointed director-general of the coal and cement company which had a semi-official standing.

Among Chang's advisers was a German, Gustav Detring, a retired commissioner of the Maritime Customs of China and shareholder in the coal and cement company. With Mr. Moreing, Herr Detring had negotiated the foreign loans for the Chinese Engineering and Mining Company—the bond issue which had been the cause of Hoover's going to China.

During the political uncertainty, Chang determined that it would be very helpful if he and Hoover could discover some fabulous gold mine and show an example of profit for his ministry. His chief engineer argued that China's primary need was industrial metals. Chang, however, had heard of some rich gold mines in Jehol, and he asked Hoover to go up and look at them, with a view to using American machinery to take out large amounts of the valuable ore.

Mrs. Hoover could not accompany her husband to Jehol or, in fact, on most of his journeys into the interior, as the trips were made under circumstances which precluded even the minimum of comfort or privacy for a woman. To fill in the time during her husband's absences, Mrs. Hoover took up the study of the Chinese language. She engaged a Chinese teacher and never failed to have her daily lesson when she was at home. Aided by a natural gift for languages, she made great progress in this difficult tongue. Hoover never managed to absorb more than a hundred words, but he did not forget these. Even after they left China, Mrs. Hoover made it a point to keep those hundred words in use by speaking to her husband in Chinese from time to time, if she needed to say something to him privately when there were others present.

The Jehol gold mines were about 150 miles from the Shanhaikwan Railway. Hoover planned that George Wilson, an interpreter and himself, mounted on saddle ponies, plus a Chinese "Boy" and a cook with two or three pack mules, would constitute the personnel and equipment needed for the expedition. However, the Chinese official assigned as guardian for the trip protested violently. He had already started to organize the expedition and his ideas were on a grand scale. He knew what the dignity of Hoover's position as chief engineer and representative of the Imperial Bureau of Mines required—and how to attain such Oriental splendor! After many arguments, Hoover gave up and told the official to let him know when he would be ready to start from the railway station nearest the mines.

On learning of the appointed day, Hoover and Wilson, with their servants, took the train at Tientsin. The private car of Tong Shao-yi, director-general of the Northern Railways of China, was attached to their train. Tong, an alumnus of Columbia University, was aboard. He invited Hoover and his associate to ride with him. The American engineer found Tong to be a man of great ability, fine integrity and high ideals for the future of China. Tong was later appointed twice to serve his country as prime minister.

During the conversation in his private car, Tong Shao-yi exploded in his antagonism to Chang Yen-mao and revealed the man's background. He informed the two Americans that the Chinese Engineering and Mining Company had been the creation of his uncle, the late Tong King-sing, and that the stock of the concern was largely owned by the Tong family. Grabbing the post of director-general through intrigue after Tong

King-sing's death, Chang was currently, according to their host, "looting the company."

A firm friendship developed between Tong Shao-yi and Hoover as a result of that meeting—a friendship which was to have curious ramifications in later years.

Hoover and Wilson themselves were carrying meager luggage for their journey, but when it was added to the great quantity of baggage brought by their own servants, a sizable heap resulted. This proved to be but a molehill, however, in comparison with the mountain of baggage and equipment they found awaiting them at the station where they disembarked from the Shanhaikwan Railway train.

Gathered in the compound of an inn nearby, the two Americans found 100 mules, 10 riding ponies and half a dozen carts. A company of 100 Chinese cavalrymen and 20 officers were milling around among mounds of bags, boxes, packages and rolls of rice matting.

It took the expedition a couple of days to get underway. Finally, the caravan of about 200 animals started off, amid great tumult and clamor, with advance heralds and rear guards— and banners flying!

At the head was the cavalry general, with two staff officers, his mounted orderlies and grooms. Next came Hoover's official guardian, with his staff and grooms; then the two American engineers with mounted servants and grooms, followed by their Chinese interpreter and his staff. After these trailed the heavily laden carts. Dozens of miscellaneous mounted men brought up the rear, each in his place, according to rank.

The cavalcade lumbered along, barely making twenty miles a day. The trip lasted a full week. Hoover found many opportunities to read, and he thereupon began his education in French literature by studying the cheap paperbacked translations of Balzac, Dumas, Zola, Victor Hugo, Rousseau and Montaigne, which he had brought with him.

The interpreter assigned to Hoover was most proficient—

except for an inadequate knowledge of American terms of dismay. When things went wrong, he reported with great solemnity that matters were "really damn." Hoover and Wilson promptly nicknamed him Really Damn.

Each night, the expedition took over an inn. Cleaning operations were immediately started, but no amount of sweeping or using fresh mats deterred the bugs already in residence. The two engineers experimented and arrived at a partial solution by putting the legs of their cots in pans of water. Periodic invasions continued, nevertheless, and Hoover began to suspect that the spiders collaborated with the bugs by building bridges for them!

Dinner each night was an elaborate five-course meal. The cook had once worked in the French Legation and felt it was necessary to maintain suitable style, even en route. When the "foreign" supplies gave out and he was limited to native chicken and eggs, that born chef still managed five courses—chicken soup, Welsh rarebit, hot roast chicken, cold chicken salad and sweet omelet—all cooked over charcoal-fired pots in the courtyard of the current inn. Any less pretentious dinner would have meant a loss of face and dignity for the Americans. Fortunately for them, the "henhouse" dishes were all very good to eat!

On reaching the mines, the cavalcade was met by an immense crowd of Chinese. Hoover asked Really Damn if this mob planned violence.

"No," answered the interpreter, "but word was sent ahead that a great foreign mandarin was coming who could see through the ground and find gold."

To add to the excitement, Hoover's Chinese Boy assured everyone within earshot that this special talent on the part of the engineers was due to their green eyes. Many of the Chinese were anxious to verify this mystic color. The intimacy of their investigations proved rather embarrassing to the pair.

The two Americans began their task by surveying the mining scene from the top of a low knoll with their allegedly valuable special-eye equipment. Hundreds of mat-shaded stone mills dotted the valley below, every one turned by a circling pony or mule. They were the same type of mill that was used in ancient Egypt for grinding grain. Each of these mills ground a few score pounds of hard quartz a day and the free gold was washed out over a blanket. The tailings, or residue materials left over after the ore extraction, were jealously saved for reworking, for the Chinese believed that gold grew in them—as indeed it did, due to oxidation.

The richly clad, elderly official in charge of the mines came up to the visitors. Apparently, he was trying to speak but no sound could be heard. The interpreter stood by attentively. Finally, words came from the mine official's lips.

"Hello, boss," he greeted Hoover with extreme dignity.

This was the English that he remembered from the days when he had been a shift boss at a well-known mine in far-off California!

The next day, with proper ceremony, the two engineers inspected the mine. Steam clouds issuing from below through three or four shafts proved to be due to the leaky steam pumps which the former shift boss had installed on opening up the mine that had been flooded for some centuries. Underground, Hoover found a small, fairly rich vein of gold-bearing quartz. With labor at only six cents a day, the mine seemed to pay, despite the number of workers and the increasing amount of water at the current working depth. The Chinese official demanded that Hoover look hard and tell him where there were more profitable veins of less depth.

Hoover did look hard—but informed the official that he could report his observations only to his superior in Peking. This enabled the engineers to get away without being mobbed or losing face over the fact that they had not found rich deposits in spite of their "green eyes."

The Chinese had prospected the surrounding land, inch by inch, without any significant results. Later, Hoover reported to Chang that, without a doubt, the Jehol gold mine possessed no likely possibilities of significant profit.

After lingering for a few days, in order to give a convincing show of an exhaustive examination, Hoover asked his official guardian if it were possible to return to the railway more quickly by running the rapids of the Lanchow River. This could be done in small boats, the official replied, but he made it clear that such a method of travel would not be proper. Only two persons and a boatman could go in one boat—and the engineers would thus lose face. Hoover and Wilson insisted, nevertheless, and reached the railway in two days instead of seven.

At Chang's request, Hoover went on more gold-hunting journeys, to track down rumors of gold mines in the Gobi Desert, Manchuria and the provinces of Shantung, Shansi and Shensi. Each time it was a question of rainbow chasing—the pots of gold never materialized. However, the American had opportunities to make side excursions, in the hope of finding evidence of the presence of such industrial metals as iron, copper and lead.

Some of the trips lasted as long as two months. On one horseback trip Hoover reached Urga, the Mongol holy city, to the north of the Gobi Desert. The Mongol camps and the ceremonies of hospitality, he felt, had been accurately described by Marco Polo and showed no foreign influence for good since that time. This trip was enlivened by a visit to the Hutuktu Lama, or Living Buddha, at the Kuren or Lamasery in Urga. The Lama entertained the American by playing Russian records provided by the Russian consul. A bicycle had also been supplied by the same source.

Returning from a trip to Shensi during the winter, Hoover pushed the caravan for days in the hope of reaching Tientsin in time to spend Christmas with Mrs. Hoover. This proved impossible. Two days before Christmas, the travelers came into Kalgan, a gate to the Great Wall of China, in a driving snowstorm and temperatures below zero. The caravan retinue badly needed rest, so they stayed over for a while.

Hoover called on the Tao Tai, or local governor, to thank him for a cavalry escort he had provided. The Tao Tai told the visitor about the large American mission in Kalgan and of the good the missionaries did in their educational and medical work among the people.

A visit to the mission brought Hoover an invitation for Christmas dinner the next day. This was a lively, happy occasion. Among the presents sent from the United States for the mission children were four secondhand footballs. The head missionary's daughter did not know how to make use of them. Hoover was experienced in that line. With the daughter's help, he divided the three hundred Chinese children, wearing their native dress and loose Chinese sandals, into two equal squads. He then organized a football game in which all four pigskins were put in play simultaneously. Three hundred pairs of loose sandals immediately came flying off in the snow. But playing in their stocking feet on the snowy field did not lessen the interest nor the agility of the children.

During the Boxer Rebellion, the next summer, these same missionaries were driven out on the Gobi Desert. With protection provided by the Tao Tai, they managed to cross the desert to the Russian frontier under great hardship. When the rebellion was over, they returned to their mission work. Many of the foreign missionaries in China were ruthlessly killed in the uprising.

Hoover protested many times to Chang about the time and money wasted on mining expeditions. He felt that there were far more important duties to be performed for the Chinese people. The engineer became convinced, however, that Chang was hoping to discover a gold mine for himself and his colleagues at government expense, and, at the same time, he expected to achieve a certain standing by his display of ministerial vigor. At long last, the American persuaded Chang to agree

to a survey of the anthracite coal fields which extended inland
west of Peking, and Hoover assigned Agnew, Means and Newberry to do the job.

One expedition was of a different nature. Hoover was asked
by Li Hung-chang to inspect the flood-control works of the
great Hwang-ho or Yellow River and advise him about their
efficiency, as the river's threatening behavior was giving him
much anxiety. Hoover protested that flood control was not his
engineering field but Li would not accept a refusal.

Even one break in the river, known as the "Sorrow of
China," would result in a fearful loss of life—a change in the
river mouth meant the drowning of millions. For a thousand
years, the Chinese had built dikes and more dikes. Along the
river banks in some places, willow forests had been planted.
These extended many miles both in length and width. The
Chinese believed that, when the stream broke out of its channel and the river mouth changed, it was an infallible omen
of the fall of the ruling dynasty, in spite of the fact that, at the
time of the last disastrous change of outlet in 1855, the dynasty
had not fallen.

An important official was appointed to guide the inspection
trip. Mrs. Hoover was able to go, this time, as they traveled
by boat through the waterways. On examining the flood-control
situation, Hoover found that the Chinese engineers had been
capable enough but the works were in poor condition. The
vital need was to keep the complicated system in repair. He also
reported that the river and the whole setup of official conservation which related to it required an exhaustive engineering
study of a year's duration. He further concluded privately that
the superstition regarding the floods and the fall of the ruling
dynasty had a sound foundation. As a dynasty became old
and corrupt, the appropriations for the flood-control works
were used up in graft and the willows were cut for fuel. There
was much evidence of long-standing graft and negligence in

what Hoover saw. The dynasty fell in 1912—"according to portent."

Hoover's travels in China gave him much opportunity to observe the life and customs of the Chinese people and to continue his reading. The latter included such diverse subjects as Chinese history, Confucius, Mencius, economics, sociology, fiction, Plato, Shakespeare, Schiller and Goethe.

Abruptly, Hoover's journeys were ended by the Boxer Rebellion. A violent reaction to the encroachment of the European powers—Russia, Great Britain, Germany and France— and to that of Japan, swept over North China. During the winter and spring of 1900, the foreign colony had begun to hear of a new secret society named the I Ho Tuan, or the Mailed Fist. Its avowed purpose was to expel all foreigners from China and to root out all Western ideas and influences—houses, railways, telegraphs, mines, books. Included among those who were the objects of the society's wrath were Christian Chinese and all those Chinese who had had anything to do with Westerners and Western things. Known to foreigners as the Boxers, the members of this fanatical association believed themselves possessed of great powers, among which was supernatural protection from foreign bullets. The extent to which some of the officials around the Empress originally encouraged the Boxer movement is not entirely clear, but it is certain that the Imperial group joined it later.

The danger to foreigners had become so great by May 1 that Hoover recalled his geological expeditions from the interior, even though their findings had outlined a field of coal larger than all other known anthracite fields in the world combined.

Anxious about the internal situation, Hoover went to Peking in June to see Chang, taking Mrs. Hoover with him. Chang was at his country place outside the city. The American found him greatly agitated over events in general. He was particularly upset by the palace intrigues, through which the Empress was currently encouraging the Boxers. A force of these fanatics was at the moment drilling in a neighboring village. Peking was in a turmoil. Murder and pillage were daily occurrences in nearby regions.

On his return to the city from the visit to Chang in the country nearby, Hoover found his wife quite ill. He had her carried to the station and they took the first train to Tientsin. Here, their doctor quickly cured her of what proved to be sinus trouble.

The atmosphere in Tientsin was just as alarming as it had been in Peking. Rumors of attacks on missionaries and massacres of native converts frightened the members of the foreign colony. Foreign-drilled Chinese troops were brought up to protect the settlement. These numbered 25,000 and they were equipped with modern artillery. The alien residents breathed easier with this protection. Two missionaries had recently been murdered near Peking.

On the tenth of June, a Sunday morning, the Hoovers and the rest of the colony were rudely awakened by shells bursting overhead—shells from modern artillery. Everyone was upset, naturally, but all thought it must be due to misdirected fire from the Chinese troops, trying to hit groups of Boxers on the other side of the settlement, so would only be temporary.

But soon some of the foreign officers in charge of drilling the Chinese army came into the settlement—running for their lives. They gasped out that the troops had turned on the European officers and had killed some of their comrades.

In the midst of the horror and fear that swept the foreign colony, the alarm bell on the town hall was rung. Everyone expected the worst. The settlement had no defense works of any consequence. The only hope—and this was a fleeting one— was the presence of about 1,100 sailors and marines of various nationalities who had recently been sent to Peking from warships in the Port of Taku. They had been ordered there to protect the foreign legations in the capital. To oppose the modern artillery of the Chinese army, this limited force had only two small cannon and a dozen machine guns.

The day dragged by—with no direct assault. The Chinese army could easily have overrun the settlement then. Later it was learned that the foreign-drilled troops had "no stomach" for the attack which was urged by the Boxers and that, in the absence of the European officers, they were wrangling over the choice of leaders to command the army.

Desperate, the foreigners pulled themselves together. All the troops there, Japanese, German, Russian, French, American and Italian, accepted the command of Colonel Wogack, a Russian, who outranked the other officers. There was one exception—the British contingent was under the command of a "naval bully."

Learning of the presence of Hoover and his engineering staff, Colonel Wogack promptly directed the American to organize the Christian Chinese, who had fled into the settlement to save their lives, to build barricades.

The foreign settlement, protected by the Hun Ho River on one side, was about a mile long and a quarter of a mile wide. Frantic for material to construct the barricades, the engineers went to the great godowns, or warehouses, filled with sacked sugar, peanuts, rice and other grain. Before long, Hoover, his staff and the other foreigners he had enlisted had organized the transportation of the bags of grain and sugar by a thousand terrified Chinese. The sacks were piled up to make a series of walls along the exposed sides of the town and at the cross streets.

On the second day, the big attack was launched. But the small force of sailors and marines repulsed the assault from behind the sacks.

The Hoovers' house, on the edge of the settlement, was exposed to constant rifle and artillery fire. With other American families, they moved into the home of Edward Drew, the Commissioner of Customs. His residence, near the center of the

settlement, was considered safer, since it was partially surrounded by godowns. However, it proved to be in danger,
owing to the poor aim of artillerymen trying to set the warehouses on fire. Fortunately, the Hoovers could call on two of
their servants to run the Drew kitchen. They had remained
loyal, although most of the other servants in the settlement
had run away.

The day of the shelling brought Hoover an additional anxiety
and responsibility. As the Boxer warfare was also directed at
those Chinese who had had anything to do with foreigners,
Tong Shao-yi and Chang Yen-mao took refuge in the settlement with their families. About five or six hundred minor
Chinese officials and foreign-educated Chinese rushed in also—
to save their lives. Housing was found for all these refugees in
a compound belonging to the Chinese Engineering and Mining
Company, across the street from the Hoovers' house.

To supply their need for sustenance, Hoover, with the aid
of some of the Chinese men, transported provisions of water,
rice and any other food he could get from the godowns to the
refugee compound each morning.

Mainly, however, he and his staff were absorbed in the desperate work of strengthening the barricades and safeguarding
the water supply. The waterworks were outside these barricades. Under the guard of British Tommies, water was boiled
at night in the boilers of the municipal waterworks. In the
morning, the precious liquid was brought into the settlement
in the municipal street-sprinkling carts.

The most acute danger came first from the possibility of
mass attack and secondly from the incessant and furious artillery fire. The early assaults were mostly sporadic but some on-
slaughts were concentrated against the place where the foreign
settlement adjoined the Chinese city of Tientsin. There the
Boxers and the Chinese troops were able to approach with
protection from the houses. In the face of this warfare, the besieged foreigners and Chinese were shocked by the knowledge

that they could not hold out at all should the attackers simultaneously bring pressure upon the other sides of the settlement. At times, the defending forces could not post a man even every hundred yards upon those barricades. About 60,000 shells were fired into the settlement during the siege. Under the constant rain of rifle bullets and shells, the defenders soon found that the best protection against being hit was to keep in the lee of the walls when moving about—or trying to catch a brief sleep.

In the siege of Tientsin, a group of civilian men, women and children, aided by a small force of a few hundred sailors and marines, were fighting for life itself against a horde of fanatics. The defenders, with only two small cannon for artillery, were trying to stand off tens of thousands of attackers, who were foreign drilled and equipped with modern artillery. There were only two helpful factors on the side of the besieged—inside lines and greater intelligence. The foreigners and the Chinese in the settlement were fully aware of the form of death that awaited them if they should lose. Everyone forbore from mentioning it, except one appalling person who asked Hoover at intervals whether he intended to shoot his wife first if the fanatics closed in on the colony. The others tried to free their minds of such horror with whatever gleam of humor they could muster.

The number of civilian and military wounded increased constantly. The resident physician, one army doctor and one nurse constituted the only medical staff available. Colonel Wogack turned the settlement club into a hospital and soon all the floors were occupied by the wounded. Mrs. Hoover immediately volunteered to help and spent most of her time at the hospital. Years later, she wistfully said, "I didn't see much of Bert in those days."

The colony herd of cattle had been rescued from their pasture about a mile outside the settlement by Wilfred Newberry. Mounted on a pony, he had driven the animals in, under fire all the way. Mrs. Hoover found some Christian Chinese women to milk the cows, and the herd proved invaluable in providing milk and meat for the hospital. On her occasional trips to the Drew house to eat or get some sleep, she became very expert in riding her bicycle close to the walls of buildings, to escape stray bullets and shells. One day, however, one of her bicycle tires was punctured by a bullet.

Stray bullets fired from long distances outside the colony came close to causing a tragedy. Some nearly hysterical foreign civilians jumped to the conclusion that the bullets were being fired by Chinese within the settlement. The 600 Chinese in the company compound, including Tong Shao-yi and Chang Yen-mao, were arrested and taken off for trial. Hoover learned of this one evening, after an exhausting day. He rushed off to the place where the drumhead trial was being conducted by a British bully, under torchlights. Irresponsible wharf rats were testifying to impossible happenings. When Hoover tried to intervene, the "judge" ordered him to leave. Some Chinese, he was told, had already been executed on the river bank. In desperate haste, the American bicycled to the headquarters of Colonel Wogack. The colonel understood the situation instantly and went to the trial with Hoover, accompanied by a platoon of Russian soldiers. He stopped the proceedings on the spot and the Chinese were turned over to Hoover for safe return to their compound.

After a while, the Hoovers and their engineering staff moved back to their own house on the edge of the colony, as it had not been hit. One evening, very late, a shell banged through a back window. It exploded inside, blowing out the front door and shattering the nearby surroundings. Worn out from a long day at the hospital, Mrs. Hoover was playing solitaire in a side room. She did not stop the game.

A few evenings after that, several shells came very close. One exploded in the compound across the street, where the Chinese were staying. Hoover and John Agnew rushed over to find that it had struck Tong Shao-yi's place, killing his wife and baby. One of his other children was injured, too. The distracted father helped the engineers gather up his surviving children. The three men each carried a child and led the others across to the Hoover house, where Mrs. Hoover took charge of the children and Tong was able to apply his Oriental discipline to recover his composure.

Many years later, when Hoover was War Food Administrator in Washington, he and his wife received an invitation to dine with the Chinese Minister and Mrs. Koo at their legation. As Hoover escorted the Minister's wife in to dinner, Mrs. Koo addressed him in perfect English: "I have met you before. I am Tong Shao-yi's daughter whom you carried across the street during the siege of Tientsin!"

About the fifteenth night of the siege, a Chinese messenger reached the settlement with the news that relief armies were on their way from Taku and would be on hand the next day. The defenders were warned not to shoot at the rescue forces in error.

In the morning, the Chinese stopped firing. Someone claimed to hear far-off cannonading. Ears were strained to the aching point. The noise increased—plainer, louder. Climbing to the roof of the highest warehouse, the defenders saw the relief columns coming across the plain. They proved to be American Marines and Welsh Fusiliers. As the Marines entered the settlement, their bugles were playing, "There'll be a Hot Time in the Old Town Tonight." To the defenders—it was the most satisfying musical performance ever heard.

The rescue forces consisted of only a few hundred soldiers all told, but they had some artillery and machine guns. The besieged felt better for a while.

Then the Chinese closed the circle again. The attacks became even more violent and dangerous. Finally, in late July, forces arrived which were strong enough to drive the Chinese back sufficiently for a respite, if not for peace. Most of the wounded, as well as the unharmed women and children and many civilian men were then evacuated down the river under guard. Mrs. Hoover and a few other women refused to go, as there were wounded to care for who could not be moved.

When adequate reinforcements came, it was decided to attack the Chinese army. Colonel Waller of the American Marines requested that Hoover accompany his command as a guide in their part of the attack on the Chinese city. He was familiar with the adjoining topography from carefree horseback rides outside the settlement with Mrs. Hoover in happier days. As the Marines advanced, they were exposed to sharp fire from Chinese posted on the old walls of the city. In the open plains, the Americans had little cover except Chinese graves. Hoover admitted to being scared, especially when some Marines next to him were hit. He was unarmed and he could scarcely propel his feet forward. He asked for a rifle. On being given one which belonged to a wounded Marine, he was suddenly no longer afraid. Although he did not fire a shot, carrying the rifle was a great comfort.

A number of American newspaper correspondents accompanied the final relief forces. The Hoovers opened their house to all who would forage for their own food. Floor space to sleep upon was provided for some, including Joaquin Miller, the California poet. Miller hired a rickshaw to take him on to Peking. His hosts warned him that foreigners were still under siege there, and that there were a few armies in between. These arguments failed to deter Joaquin. Finally, Mrs. Hoover bribed the rickshaw boy to give out and the poet remained safely with his friends in Tientsin.

Although the foreigners in Peking suffered a longer siege and they did not have the advantage of food warehouses, their losses were small compared with those suffered in the Tientsin settlement. Also, there were no foreign-drilled troops or modern artillery opposing them. The South African War was then being fought and the sieges of Kimberley, Mafeking and Lady-smith had just been relieved. The total losses of the defenders in these three cities combined did not equal the foreign losses in Tientsin, to say nothing of the Chinese refugee casualties. But, as Hoover commented, their publicity arrangements were better.

On the relief of Peking, the Empress Dowager and her government fled to the interior. Hoover felt that he had been given a strong hint, "by way of artillery," that his engineering employment by the Chinese Bureau of Mines had terminated. The Hoovers prepared to return to the United States.

In the wake of war, the Chinese Engineering and Mining Company fared badly. The Russian army seized the coal mines and the extensive shops at Tongshan; the German army took over the coalyards at Taku and Tientsin; while the British navy appropriated the harbor works and coal stocks at Chinwangtao. The Japanese army occupied the company's offices in Tientsin and the American army took over the twelve coal steamers. A "grand grab" was underway.

The Hoovers were about ready to sail for home in early August when Chang and Herr Detring sent for Herbert. They had prepared a plan by which the bondholders of the company could intervene to save its assets. They suggested that Mr. Moreing accept a deed for all the property and reorganize the company into a British corporation. They wanted Hoover to sign at once for Mr. Moreing, to make it easier for them to defend the property from the seizures. The engineer telegraphed to Mr. Moreing, who authorized the signing on his behalf, subject to his subsequent approval of the terms. Hoover had had no experience in international high finance at that time, and the terms had been made by Chang and Detring.

The Hoovers left immediately for London, starting off by tugboat to Taku, while his engineering staff stayed behind to await developments. Chang rode down the river with them. A great red moon rose that evening. Chang observed that it was a bad omen for China. His chief engineer felt it was a little late as a portent. From Taku, the Americans continued their journey via the Red Sea—without benefit of air conditioning!

In London, Hoover presented the deed to Mr. Moreing and advocated the possibilities of continuing the work of the company under foreign management. The bondholders and Moreing accepted the terms offered by Chang and Detring, which included raising new capital to pay off the creditors and repair property damage resulting from the Rebellion. Hoover was appointed general manager of the new corporation at an increase of salary, and Mr. Moreing gave him a small share of ownership in the reorganized business. In order to effect the recovery of the property from five different countries and to obtain the approval of the Chinese government for the transfer contract, Chevalier de Wouters, a member of the Belgian Foreign Office who was then in China, was engaged as a special agent, to deal with the negotiation and the diplomatic aspects of the company affairs. In addition to the commercial value involved, the coal mines, the projected harbor works in the ice-free port and the connecting railroad were all of vital strategic importance to the defense of North China.

On their way back to the Orient, the Hoovers spent a few days in California. They arrived in Japan in January, 1901, where Mrs. Hoover remained for the winter. Her husband went on to Shanghai, planning to find some way to reach North China from there. In the interests of the company, he had circled the globe!

Travel arrangements proved very difficult as the Port of Taku was frozen over and there was then no railway connection between Shanghai and the north. Finally, Hoover, with four American and British army officers, chartered a 1,200-ton steamer to take them to Chinwangtao, where they thought the ice would be open enough for passage. The ship ran into a terrible storm. On the second day, the Chinese crew threatened the Norwegian officers and the passengers with mutiny unless they returned to Shanghai. The passengers were too seasick to fight. Fortunately, the sea subsided somewhat, so they continued on their way and, on the third day, arrived off Chinwangtao. The ship entered the harbor, which was full of floating ice. The captain promptly rammed the vessel in near the beach as far as he dared. The passengers disembarked on the ice, to walk ashore. About twenty feet from the shallow beach, the ice had been beaten to slush by the waves. The travelers plunged into ice water up to their hips and struggled to dry land, each burdened by a suitcase. Hoover expected to find his engineering staff, who had been constructing the new harbor works, on hand to welcome him, but they had not returned and their buildings had been burned by the Boxers. It was dark by then, and the five weary men stumbled seven miles to the railway, in sub-zero temperatures. Near the tracks, they lit a bonfire, which, combined with the walk, probably saved them from pneumonia and from freezing. Before daylight, they signaled a troop train and Hoover went aboard with the British officer. The engine broke down at dawn, unable to pull the long string of cars up a steep grade. Hoover persuaded the Russian engineer to detach the locomotive and first car and proceed to Tongshan, about 150 miles away, where another engine could be sent back to pick up the rest of the cars.

When Hoover reached Tientsin, he found a total disruption of all business. There were armies of eleven nationalities occupying various zones in North China. Each was intent on getting a piece of China, with a view to protecting its "national interest."

Chevalier de Wouters had secured nominal repossession of the company's coal mines from the Russian army. These were at Tongshan and Linsi, about thirty miles apart, and were equipped to produce 5,000 tons of coal a day. At Tongshan, there were also large machine shops, a coking plant and cement factories. Surrounded by high walls, these works employed about 25,000 men. Hoover placed Agnew in charge at Tongshan and Newberry at Linsi. The two engineers had been in

Tientsin, awaiting word from the Chief. Operations and reorganization were started at once. The new general manager immediately set to work to survey the "depredations" of the foreign armies on the company's properties, to determine what amount of reparation payment they should demand.

Hoover again made his headquarters in Tientsin. Household and food supplies were almost impossible to obtain. He solved the greater part of this problem by inviting General Humphries, the American quartermaster general, to live with him, so they were able to purchase quartermaster's supplies. Herbert bought a cow and her calf, in order to have fresh milk and butter, and engaged a proper Chinese keeper to look after them.

Late one night, Hoover's startled Number One Boy rushed to him with the news, "The cow he lost!"

Herbert summoned the cow's keeper. With his Boy acting as interpreter, the keeper did not throw much light on the disappearance but he did suggest a constructive move.

"His cow's pup he have stay. Cow he have go. Pup he cry. Maybe pup he walk road he cry. Cow he cry. We find cow."

At that time, Chinese were not allowed on the streets of the settlement at night unless they were accompanied by a foreigner. So the general, Hoover and a guest, the Number One Boy and the cow's keeper started out in the dark in solemn parade, taking two lantern bearers with them. The pup did cry and the "cow he cry" in answer—from inside a German army barracks.

Addressing a sentry in his best German, the guest, J. Bromley Eames, demanded to know if a cow had recently been acquired. The sentry listened to the duet of cow cries and solemnly asked if the calf belonged to the cow. On learning that it did, he announced, "Then I'll take 'he calf.'" He promptly did.

The sentry proved immune to the general's explosive English and Eames' legal arguments in German. He remained unimpressed by the general's rank. The cow hunters finally retreated to reorganize their moral forces. The following morning, General Humphries called on the German general in person. Hoover did not know what transpired, as he was not present —but "he cow" and "he cow's pup" came home.

The daily work of producing and transporting coal soon became involved with all the occupying armies. The officers with whom Hoover dealt seemed determined to regard civilians as a great bother, though any real fighting was long since over. However, the military needed coal and cement, of which Hoover's company was the only producer in the area—and they needed help in reconstructing the railways and ports.

Hoover went frequently to Peking with de Wouters, to see the ministers of the various foreign countries upon matters involved in the company contracts with the occupying troops. He also maintained constant relations with the different military commands, as well as contact with the temporary Chinese government set up under the veteran Li Hung-chang.

The Northern Railways of China had been torn up and wrecked to a large degree by the Boxers in their anti-foreign frenzies. The railways were very much needed by the military authorities, to move troops for police duties, and by the Chinese Engineering and Mining Company for coal transport. A board of officers was set up by the military to take charge of the reconstruction. Hoover's co-operation was requested and he assigned members of his engineering staff, both Chinese and foreign, to aid in the operations.

The Boxers and other Chinese had unbolted the fishplates and pulled out the spikes for long stretches of track. They had taken all the metal, rails and fastenings away off into the interior. The loot was distributed among a thousand villages, and the inhabitants of each were overjoyed at the opportune amount of iron which would supply their blacksmith shops for years to come. The railroad ties had been taken away also, to be used for building material and fuel. A great deal of thought was given to the recovery of this urgently needed maial. Hoover and the board members suggested that the Chinese would soon realize that the rails were made of steel, not of iron, and that it was not even possible to chip pieces of the metal off the long bars. Hoover and his associates felt that, when the villagers discovered this, they would be happy to sell the rails back, if a tempting price was offered, accompanied by a promise of immunity and forceful threats if they did not comply! Per rail, the price offered was $5 Mexican. The Mexican dollar was then the chief silver circulation unit in China and had a value of about fifty cents on the American dollar.

The price offer soon brought results. Before long, the whole countryside for miles along the torn up segments of the railroad was alive with caterpillar-like processions of thirty or forty villagers, bringing back the rails—one rail forming the body of each caterpillar.

Recovering the amounts of reparations demanded from the foreign governments proved to be a long process for the general manager. The British refused to consider the company claims for damages unless they were filed in triplicate on the proper forms. But they eventually paid in full, after the claims had passed through a maze of red tape. The Germans announced that they had occupied the property as an act of war and would accept no claims for coal or anything else they had appropriated. Payment was obtained after a year, through pressure from bondholders of the company in Berlin. The Japanese brushed aside all communications and refused to give up the Tientsin offices.

On receiving a bill for the use and repair of the twelve company coal steamers, the American quartermaster general immediately protested to Hoover. The American Army had saved the company, he maintained, and the government should not have to pay any compensation claim now. Hoover countered that the United States was asking the total cost of the expedition from the Chinese government, and there was no reason why a private company should give the United States this whole sum as profit. In the spirit of democracy, the general and Hoover compromised on the payment in cash of 75 per cent of the claim of $300,000 Mexican.

The Russians were the worst offenders, for they loaded several trains with machinery and supplies from the mines and shipped them off on the railroad into Manchuria. Hoover sent them a claim for $700,000 Mexican. Finally, after some weeks, an agent appeared. His offer to settle included a commission for himself of $150,000 Mexican. Hoover refused this. The same agent returned later with the full amount in silver and a large extra sum. This extra was taken back by the agent. Months later, the commander of the Russian forces in Manchuria made Hoover an offer to sell back all the machinery and stores for around $200,000 Mexican. The general manager bought back the property, but he has always been curious as to the entries for the transaction made in the Imperial ledgers.

In the reorganization of the Chinese Engineering and Mining Company management, Hoover soon ran up against the Chinese "squeeze" in large dimensions, plus the general inability of the Chinese laborers to handle machinery that was at all complicated.

Squeeze in China, Hoover found, did not have exactly the same moral implications that graft does to foreigners. Venerated by agelong custom and subject to certain limitations, it was a kind of appendage to the profit system. According to Chinese concepts, officials were expected to make something beyond their nominal salaries.

With so large a ratio of squeeze, it was hopeless to try to carry on Western industrial operations, so Hoover and his associates steadily slashed this ratio. By cutting the squeeze alone, a losing business was turned into a prospering concern in only ninety days, although, for humane and economic reasons, Hoover had raised the workers' wages about 40 per cent above the rates in nearby towns, so the company's employees would have enough to eat.

But the drastic decrease in squeeze caused wide and long-range aftereffects. Chang Yen-mao was sharply hit. As Chinese director-general, he suddenly found himself with only his nominal salary of $500 Mexican a month. He began to stir up trouble for de Wouters over transfer details of various properties from the Chinese to the British company.

De Wouters effected a settlement with Chang by obtaining a stock interest in the company for him and his advisers in lieu of their squeeze privileges. In addition, a memorandum setting up the reorganized company under British law was signed by the Belgian and Hoover. It agreed to make Chang the head of a local board to represent the Chinese ownership in the business at an increased salary. The memorandum provisions designed to save face for Chang caused trouble for Hoover in his 1928 presidential nomination and election campaigns, due to subsequent litigation, and the settlement proved to be only temporary.

Foreigners found it difficult to understand the Chinese squeeze. The Hoovers experienced an example of the latter in their own household. At the time the Number One Boy had been hired, they had known that he was penniless. Yet he produced evidence of $900 in losses suffered during the siege which the reparations authorities duly honored when Hoover put in the damage claim for him. All this had accumulated from a salary of $15 Mexican per month, through squeeze.

As well as enjoying the fruits of the squeeze system, it was a part of the job to limit others to the minimum of its benefits, which he faithfully carried out. The household bills were high—in fact, Mrs. Hoover discovered that they were about twice as high as those of a neighbor whose establishment was about the same size. She complained to the Boy about this.

"Master have two times pay of Mr. Francis," was his ready explanation. But the Hoovers could and did entrust the family valuables to their ten servants whose nominal salaries combined totaled only $108 Mexican a month.

For a while, all went well for Hoover as general manager. New equipment was brought in, the ice-free port at Chinwang-tao was sufficiently completed to start coal loading in winter and the business was expanding rapidly. Technical methods were revised and a new American staff was imported. There was a constant increase in profits, and the equivalent in new stock of the original Chinese shares gained 500 per cent in market value. The largest Chinese stockholder, Tong Shao-yi, was fully informed on the company's progress by Hoover. Tong was especially pleased as he had long since given up hope of any return on his holdings, due to Chang's control.

In 1901, Hoover was officially notified from London that control of the business had been purchased from other European and Chinese interests by a group of Belgians. Mr. Emile Francqui, a Belgian director, came to China to run the company affairs there. He was followed by a Belgian technical staff which replaced the Americans. Francqui assured Hoover, though, that he would remain as general manager.

The new head soon declared that the memorandum agreement was not binding and ended the co-operation with the Chinese board on the grounds that they were still grafting. This charge was substantiated in part by the fact that Chang had sold in his own name property in Hong Kong which was proved to have belonged to the company long before he had come into the concern. However, Hoover and de Wouters both maintained that the memorandum was legally and morally binding and that it was up to management to check graft.

Hoover found Francqui very able but determined. Their discussion over the repudiation of the agreement was most heated and outspoken. In September, both Hoover and de Wouters resigned. Hoover immediately telegraphed this news to Mr. Moreing, adding that he would return to the United States.

Shortly afterward, a cable came from Moreing, offering the American a junior partnership in Bewick, Moreing and Company. This was accepted and the twenty-seven-year-old engineer was delighted to leave China for a larger engineering world. With de Wouters, the Hoovers took a tramp steamer to Nagasaki and then traveled to London via California.

Herbert Hoover had worked as an engineer in China for about two and one-half years, except for time out for a round-the-world trip. When he left, he held an abiding admiration for the Chinese people as a whole. And he cautioned Western minds that China was not going to be made Occidental.

Tong Shao-yi attributed to Hoover the transformation of the Chinese Engineering and Mining Company, in which he held a large interest, from a financially unsuccessful business to a highly profitable concern. He asserted that the engineer's record in China was "not only clean and honorable, but highly creditable and in many ways remarkable."

But his warmest admiration and respect for Hoover had been won by the engineer's fearless, humane conduct in the Boxer Rebellion, when he had supplied the thousand Chinese refugees in the foreign settlement with provisions. In following Hoover's career in international relief through the years, Tong Shao-yi always felt that the American's first actual relief work began in China during the siege of Tientsin.

World-wide
Engineering

CHAPTER 5

London was the center of the metal-mining world at the time of the Hoovers' arrival there in early November, 1901, so that Herbert could take up his partnership in Bewick, Moreing and Company, a very old and respected mining firm. It had management and engineering contracts with about twenty mines in different parts of the world, as well as with two substantial exploration syndicates whose purpose was to discover and develop new ventures. Herbert's job was to operate all the mines—both as an engineer and an administrator. Unlike the previous partners in the organization, Hoover decided to work in the field.

If he had changed at all in the more than five active, successful years since his Stanford graduation, the change was expressed in a deepening of his powers, even in his sense of humor, according to a college friend. But one entirely new quality had been added—under his modesty and shyness now lay an air of authority. This was not revealed in his speech, but in his attitude and approach to life in general and his work in particular. The exciting times in China had added greatly to his depth of experience and ability to assume responsibility. From then on, he was unmistakably the Herbert Hoover whom most of the world came to know, admire, rely upon and hold in deep affection.

As a partner of Bewick, Moreing and Company, Herbert's first tour of inspection was in Australia, where the largest single area of the company's business was located. When Hoover had first worked for the firm in the continent down under, he had built up its operations with American methods and machinery. After his departure from the Sons of Gwalia to take over his jobs in China, the Bewick, Moreing engineering work in Australia had largely relapsed into British and Colonial methods and practices. It was anxiety over this situation that had brought Hoover back into the concern.

The Hoovers reached Kalgoorlie in December, 1901, and Herbert found that the temperature in those hot precincts had not diminished!

Western Australia's gigantic gold boom had collapsed, and the whole area was suffering the "bitter headache" of the morning after. The causes were unscrupulous stock promotion, poor standards of technical engineering and geological conditions. Many mines, promising at first, had turned out to be only flashes in the pan when worked "in depth."

To insure integrity and reliability in management, and to cut costs by using improved equipment and thereby increasing recoveries of metals, Hoover sent to the United States for university-trained mine managers, metallurgists and mechanical engineers. He also recalled Agnew and Newberry from China.

He then went to work to stiffen the whole operation by setting up stronger centralized ore inspection and consolidating the purchase of supplies. In time, this resulted in greatly reduced costs, although wages were increased. Of the original Australasian mines under Bewick, Moreing management when Hoover became a partner, three in Western Australia, including the Sons of Gwalia, and one in New Zealand, were great mines. Six other previously large producers were petering out in depth and had to be abandoned within a few years. Four mines, formerly profitable, were exhausted and had to be closed. Hoover's realistic cleanup cut seriously into the firm's income by reducing the number of management fees.

However, this gloomy outlook was brightened by a fortunate circumstance. On the voyage from Marseilles to Australia, Hoover had met an English investment banker named Francis Govette, the newly elected chairman of the Lake View and Ivanhoe companies which operated two of the most important mines at Kalgoorlie. These concerns had suffered from stock manipulation and fraud, all of which had finally exploded in the conviction and death of the chief manipulator of the enterprise. The stockholders had chosen Govette, an Englishman of wide outlook and high integrity, to reorganize and salvage the business, although he had had no previous experience with mines. After a few days in Kalgoorlie, Govette went to Hoover, admitted that he was in a complete fog over the mine operations and requested that Hoover's firm take entire charge of the reorganization. This was the start of a most important expansion of Bewick, Moreing's connections, entirely due to Hoover, for Govette, working in co-operation with the firm over a period of years, directed his own and his friends' interests more and more into the industrial mining field. In addition to the close business association of the two men, Govette and his wife became great personal friends of Herbert and Lou Hoover.

The shining example of systematic improvement in the Lake View and Ivanhoe mines brought other management business to Hoover from the wreckage of the Australian boom. Many producing mines were added to his engineering group. However, two subsequent additions caused him great trouble. Finding that his reports, which were adverse, were being withheld from the stockholders, Hoover resigned from the management of these two mines.

An important part of his firm's business was second-stage development of prospectors' strikes, and Hoover directed a thorough combing of prospectors' finds for possible new mines. He soon found that the government terms on which prospectors were allowed title to their discoveries were too strict and often starved them out. He interested his friend Walter James, the Premier of Western Australia, in the situation, and the Premier secured changes in the mining law more favorable to the prospectors.

Large capital was required for equipment to develop each prospect. Many so-called finds were tried out and discarded by Hoover. Some which the firm did equip, failed in depth. Their fanciful names, such as Lancefield and Nundydroog, ever rose up to remind him that, even under the most careful technical controls, gold mining is a hazardous business. They were among Hoover's painful memories.

The greatest disaster that Hoover was to meet while he was a partner in Bewick, Moreing and Company confronted him just a year after he joined the firm and only two months following his return to the London office from work in the field. One morning he reached his desk to find a confession from an associate in the firm, revealing that he had been speculating in American railroad stock and had suffered huge losses, in spite of the fact that all speculation was prohibited in the partnership agreement. To recoup, he had embezzled money from the firm and, in addition, by forgery, from other companies they managed and certain trust funds. The total loss proved to be about a million dollars when the final accounting was rendered!

Hoover immediately called in Wellstead, another junior partner. Mr. Moreing, head of the firm, was in Manchuria, hunting tigers, and could not be reached by cable for a week. Mr. Bewick, a retired partner, who could be counted on for advice, was hunting moose in Canada. In all, Hoover had had less than three months of actual business experience in the

London office and did not even know all the firm's London and New York business associates. Though only twenty-eight years old, he was temporarily the senior partner on the job and so had the major responsibility. Hoover and Wellstead, who was thirty-two, decided to call upon their elders for advice. They telephoned a few important men located in London who were business allies of the firm and asked them to come over quickly, saying the partnership was in trouble. None of these men, who included Francis Govette and Sir Frederick Hamilton, had suffered from the embezzlement.

When the serious group assembled an hour later, Hoover admitted his ignorance of English business customs and asked the firm's lawyer to read the confession aloud. When the lawyer finished, the almost unanimous reaction was one of stunned disbelief. Some were all the more surprised because they had known and trusted the man in question for years.

The lawyer, who was also Moreing's best friend, pointed out that the firm had no legal liability for the forgeries.

After some discussion, Govette turned to Hoover, saying, "Young man, you are new in this firm and you are new in English business. We all wish to help you. We first want to know if you have any ideas as to what you would like to do."

"What I would *like* to do," Hoover declared, "is to pay back every dime over the counter, whether we are liable or not— and have no public noise about it. But I do not have any such resources—and neither does Wellstead," he added. "Moreing and Bewick are, of course, rich men. They can pay and not feel it."

"You should say 'tuppence' instead of dime," Govette remarked, relieving the tension by giving the English version of the expression.

They all agreed that Moreing should feel even more strongly about making the losses good. He had chosen the man and his own, as well as his firm's, reputation was at stake. The standing of the mining industry was involved, too, as Bewick, Moreing was one of few firms which had emerged from the Australian boom with "clean hands."

Taking the chance of Moreing's disapproval, Hoover sent a statement to the press, disclosing the embezzlement and adding that the firm would make good all losses, although not legally obligated to do so.

On his return to London, Moreing backed up his junior partner's decision and the entire loss was repaid in three years, even though the new partners were still repaying the good-will value of the firm to the previous members. The culprit was sentenced to a ten-year prison term. Mrs. Hoover gave his wife an allowance to maintain their four children until he was released.

After joining Bewick, Moreing, Hoover circled the globe five times. During his term as a partner, he visited an average of six countries a year. Mrs. Hoover went on most of the journeys. The two had many interesting experiences, traveling on passenger liners, tramp steamers and tugs, by railway, automobiles, buggies, horses and camels. There were diverting and educational contacts with leaders of men, heads of governments and public officials; with snobs and crooks; with plain, good people and intellectually inspiring people; and with human "boll weevils."

But work continued to be Hoover's main occupation, even en route. On most of his voyages, he took along a secretary or an engineering assistant and his cabin became a floating office between ports. At each stop, he received a bagful of reports and at each wirehead, or telegraph station, a sheaf of cables. While the vessel coaled, he hurried to prepare answers for these communications. There was ample opportunity for reading, too. At times he had thought he might exhaust all the books on earth—but the supply held out!

Housekeeping is always difficult for globe trotters, yet the Hoovers preferred to live in houses instead of hotels, whenever possible, while they were in foreign lands. In addition, they felt they should have a "mooring" in the United States and joined with Mrs. Hoover's father in building a cottage in Monterey, in 1902. Five years later, their geographical anchor was moved to a six-room cottage at Stanford University.

During their first year in England, Mrs. Hoover thought they were going to settle down for the summer, so she rented a small country house at Walton-on-Thames. Her husband was promptly called away to the United States—but this time she stuck to the house. In the fall, it seemed necessary to have a European headquarters, even if they were seldom there, so Mrs. Hoover took a flat at Hyde Park Gate, in London, and furnished it to her heart's desire.

Their first child, Herbert, Jr., was born there on August 4, 1903. When he was only five weeks old, his parents took him to Australia—in a basket—accompanied by a nurse.

Hoover had been requested to take over the management of an ill-fated enterprise in the Australian state of Victoria earlier that year. Whitaker Wright and his fellow operators had secured title to twenty miles of buried rivers with gold-bearing bedrock gravels in the Lodden River System. The placer miners of the 1850 gold boom had worked the rich gravel beds until the water at the lowered mining depths proved too much for the pumps of that time. Wright had spent a great deal on shafts and pumps but the project did not work out well financially.

Hoover engaged Dr. Lindgren to examine the area, as he had made a long study of similar rivers in California. When the engineer met his former employer at the steamer in Melbourne, Lindgren's first words were, "Do you know that bureaucrat never would pay me that sixty dollars? And do you know I have since seen a hundred mules scratch their heads with their hind feet?"

But in spite of Hoover's determined insistence, the geologist would not accept the sixty dollars dunned originally from his cub assistant's pay for the dead California pack mule.

Lindgren thought there was a chance of solving the water problem. Hoover warned the stockholders that any success was highly speculative. However, they put up more money and Hoover started the greatest pumping operation in mining history. But the water again proved too much and the project was abandoned. Hoover was also asked to try to salvage certain supposedly large copper mines in British Columbia and California which had been Wright ventures, too. He personally inspected the properties but was compelled to decline as the mines had little future value. Always, Herbert Hoover lived up to the fine tradition of engineers for integrity, no matter if giving the true facts might cut off a profitable association.

Recognizing that an automobile would be ideal for transportation in desert mining work—even though it did not go all the time and required a highly professional nurse—Hoover took a car to Australia. It was one of the first introduced in the mining fields. The very high monthly cost of maintaining horse-and-buggy relays for mine inspection trips did not improve Hoover's views on horses. He had great hopes for the car.

The automobile worked, he discovered, only with much coaxing, but it did make an unheard of 125 miles over bush tracks in a single day. A surprising obstacle to the progress of automobiles in the desert proved to be the long camel trains which followed the bush tracks, too. The Afghan drivers disliked halting their beasts of burden and moving them off their well-worn path. However, after the custom of giving three large bottles of beer for this service was established, at the sound of a long-distance honk, the road would promptly be cleared—with cheers from the Afghans.

In view of his mechanical training, Hoover thought that a little gas engine on wheels would present no problem. He was used to building and running powerful steam engines and electric generators, with vast and complicated machinery tied to them; yet the early automobile had him down in the Australian dirt almost every hour of the day. Cars there often caught a disease called sand-in-the-carburetor. The tires had to be bandaged in split steam hose, in spite of which they could only be used for a little while. Nevertheless, four automobiles ultimately displaced the horses.

During July and August, 1904, Hoover was in the Transvaal, in South Africa, in connection with a coal company and some gold mines managed by his firm. The coal beds proved to be over gold-bearing ore. After a consolidation of the different interests involved—the coal mines became extremely successful gold mines! In the Transvaal, Hoover was entertained by an old friend and Stanford classmate, Herbert Stark, manager of the Crown mines.

Soon after joining Bewick, Moreing as a partner, Hoover had determined that the firm should devote more attention to the base metals—lead, zinc, copper and tin. These industries were less romantic—but also less speculative—than gold. Mining development was undertaken in Australia. Although the usual routine number of prospects did not mature, a successful copper mine was established in Queensland. Intent on his policy of developing base metals, Hoover visited the great Australian silver-lead district at Broken Hill in the summer of 1905. He found that the out-of-date mining operations there were recovering the lead which contained most of the silver but not the zinc—a large element in the ore. Mountains of tailings, or ore residues, had piled up with the zinc still in them. New processes had recently been discovered that could solve the recovery of this metal, and Hoover had already instituted systematic research on the subject in the firm's testing laboratories.

For Bewick, Moreing, Hoover formed an association with W. L. Ballieu and W. S. Robinson of Melbourne, and Govette in London. With Ballieu, he bought control of 5,000,000 tons of tailings. Contracts were obtained for future outputs and dominant interests were acquired in some low-grade mines and prospective ore-bearing land nearby. The organizers encountered all the difficulties that go with pioneering new processes but a feasible method of recovery was finally achieved.

Four highly successful concerns emerged from this operation, two managed by Bewick, Moreing and two by the Ballieu firm. Due to this enterprise, planned by Hoover and carried out by him and his associates, employment in the district was greatly expanded. In addition, living conditions and the stability of the area were much improved. Although there was considerable labor trouble elsewhere in the Broken Hill area, no strikes occurred in the mines managed by Hoover.

Broken Hill lay in the middle of the desert. It was unbelievably hot in summer. All water had to be hauled in or distilled. Vegetation was almost nonexistent—while the tailings blew into every crack, corner, dish and bed on every "wisp of wind."

In January, 1905, Chang Yen-mao brought suit in the English courts against the Chinese Engineering and Mining Company, to establish his rights and those of the China board under the organization memorandum of February 19, 1901, signed by Hoover and de Wouters. Both Hoover and Bewick, Moreing and Company were brought into the action as defendants. The memorandum was found binding as a result of Hoover's and de Wouters' testimony in its favor. The trial excited great interest and Chang, in full Mandarin dress, was a picturesque plaintiff.

Hoover was again to experience the clash between Oriental and Occidental civilizations, with engineering as a catalyst. In late 1904, when returning by steamer from a tin-mine inspection trip in Penang, Hoover heard of some enormous, abandoned mine workings near the Lashio railway terminal, in North Burma, from the contractor, A. C. Martin, who had been building the line. Martin had taken a lease on his find, said to be a lead and copper mine, and had enlisted the support of a small London promoter. He wanted Bewick, Moreing to join in the project, too. On reaching London, Hoover found that the promoter had already sent some machinery out to Burma—all of the wrong kind. He had some reports on hand —made by unreliable men—and he lacked the financial strength to carry out the undertaking as well. With some of the firm's clients, Bewick, Moreing took an option on a controlling interest in the venture.

A young engineer who was sent to Burma to inspect the mine cabled back ecstatic descriptions of the inaccessible mine and reported 500,000 tons of lead piled up on the surface in slags. Skeptical that any such amount of loose lead could exist in the world, Hoover dispatched C. D. Clark, an American engineer who had had a great deal of experience with lead. His report was even more impressive. Hoover went out to take a look himself.

From Mandalay, Hoover and Clark rode up on the railway to Hsipaw, the Shan State, where the mine was located. They were met at the capital, also named Hsipaw, with great enthusiasm by the Sawbwa, or native prince, who ruled the state. The Prince invited the engineers to his palace, speaking with a perfect Oxford accent. At dinner, he spoke of his situation and problems. Educated in England, he had then come back to rule a primitive kingdom of about 200,000 Shans with insufficient funds. A quarter of the net revenues went to the British Superintendent of the Shan States and, from the remainder, the Prince had to pay the expenses of the state, including the costs of schools, police and road maintenance. His family had ruled for a thousand years and the traditional hospitality offered his numerous relatives was expensive. Besides, to comply with the spiritual and ceremonial needs of the people and the state, he had to buy a new white elephant, as the former one had died—and these rare creatures were costly. The Prince spoke vigorously, with humor and some despair.

In Hoover and the proposed establishment of a large industrial mining concern, he saw great possibilities for increasing commerce and employment, with a resulting improvement in the standard of living for his principality, through royalties and taxes. He saw hope for more schools and progress in civilization, as well as sufficient income for him to maintain his regal dignity and to attend the Imperial and Indian Courts with the pomp and elegance befitting his rank. He questioned Hoover eagerly about the mine prospects and what the engineer planned to do.

Hoover and Clark traveled to the mine area through the dripping jungle, mostly on horseback. Located in a mountainous region, the workings were surrounded by grassy hills. One open pit was nearly 1,000 feet long and 300 feet deep. Hundreds of dumps and tunnels extended over almost three miles. For four and a half centuries, up to 1850, the Chinese had mined the workings, taking out great amounts of silver. But the mines had apparently been so inaccessible that the ancient Chinese had not been able to transport the greater quantities of less valuable lead to market, so they had thrown the lead residues on the dumps.

The miners of old had only worked the ore near the surface. Operations at lower depths had been blocked by metallurgical and water-flooding obstacles. Hoover and Clark determined to enter the old workings, to study the deposits. The tunnels were fairly well preserved because they had been made through hard rock, and the two engineers started to investigate. They crawled into one after another of them, only to be stopped each time by an old roof cave-in.

Undaunted, Hoover chose still another tunnel and crawled in, carrying a candle in one hand. Clark followed in similar fashion. Hoover happened to see, just ahead in the dim light, the fresh tracks of a Bengal tiger! Hoover pointed out the prints to Clark. The tiger had been going in. There was no appeal whatever to either engineer in fighting a Bengal tiger with miners' candlesticks! The pair made for the tunnel entrance with no delay and steadily increasing panic. The tiger, fortunately, was not of an inquiring mind and did not put in an appearance. But Hoover and Clark ventured into no more tunnels. Further underground exploration was not resumed for some years.

Hoover decided there was sufficient lead in the surface tailings to justify building a railway to the main line and putting up a smelter at Mandalay. This report cheered the Sawbwa. He promised to recruit laborers from the hill tribes to construct the railroad in Asiatic fashion. With the co-operation of the British Superintendent, wage scales were arranged with the Sawbwa and the adjoining state. These were higher than any previously known in the jungle. Thousands working for the first time had never had money before.

On his return to London, where his wife and baby were awaiting him at Hyde Park Gate, Hoover arranged for the necessary financing of the project. He departed from his usual rule of not investing very much of his own savings in any mine and took the largest chance of his career in the Burma lead mines.

Among the interests of Bewick, Moreing during Hoover's partnership was a turquoise mine at Mount Sinai. Before he became a member, the Egyptian government had asked the firm to reopen some ancient workings on the Sinai Peninsula, in an area where copper had once been mined. A Cornish foreman and a prospecting party were sent into the territory to explore. They discovered a large dump and a partly buried tunnel portal made of large stones covered with ancient Egyptian inscriptions. The portal being too small to suit the investigators, they enlarged the entrance with dynamite—to Hoover's later grief. The mine, surprisingly, turned out to be turquoise, fashionable with Egyptian women three or four thousand years before.

When Hoover took charge for his firm, the Cornishmen informed him that they had found a large underground storehouse full of "gravestones," in addition to other such markers on the nearby hills. Warning the miners not to touch them, the engineer sent for Dr. Flinders Petrie, a noted Egyptologist. From the inscriptions on the stones, the expert was able to revise and enlarge the chronology and dynastic succession of ancient Egypt. In a subsequent book, however, Dr. Petrie criticized the Cornishmen for blasting the ancient portal and also accused them of other destruction which they had not done. Egyptian gossip unjustly laid the blame for this at Hoover's door.

And no jeweler could be found, anywhere, to buy the bucketfuls of greenish turquoise stones from the mines so sought after in antiquity.

One side activity of Bewick, Moreing was a survey of the mineral resources of Abyssinia, made at the request of the King of Kings. Hoover did not go in person, but the report of the geologists and engineers who were sent revealed that the probability of substantial mineral development was very remote, and extended irrigation was recommended by the firm instead. Forty years later, Herbert Hoover, Jr., was asked to advise on the same subject and came to the same conclusions that his father had reached.

Bewick, Moreing was also requested by the authorities of northern Italy to report on the abandoned mines in the Alps from which the Romans had produced iron to arm their legions. Mr. and Mrs. Hoover made this inspection themselves, combining business with a two-week holiday. On a modern scale, the mines proved disappointing in size. The Empire had not needed much iron for munitions—a little of the ore made a lot of short swords!

In 1907, Mr. and Mrs. Hoover rented an old house with a garden in Campden Hill, London, as they needed more room. It was called the Red House. The original lease of ancient date required the tenants to keep their cows from wandering in High Street and to refrain from hanging their laundry in sight of the neighbors. The Hoovers' second son, Allan Henry, was born at Hyde Park Gate, July 17, 1907, while they were still furnishing Red House. Like his brother, he went off on a long trip at the age of five weeks. This time it was from England to Burma. Traveling with babies, his father commented, is easier than with most grownups. Both parents contracted malaria on this Burma visit from which it took them months to recover completely.

Early the next year, Herbert Hoover determined to retire from Bewick, Moreing and go into business on his own. He and Mrs. Hoover wanted to spend more time in the United States, and the boys would soon need systematic American schooling. Hoover wished to manage fewer projects at a time and have less routine business to handle. He had saved and invested enough to assure a modest income and had high hopes for his Burma mine holdings. He also hoped to serve in American public life, due to his Quaker feeling for helping others and his sense of gratitude to his country for the opportunities he had received.

His firm's business had tripled during his membership and his share of the profits, as a partner, was netting one of the largest amounts earned in engineering at that time. Although pressed to stay, he did not renew his partnership contract when it expired in July.

Herbert Hoover had a most important asset for starting his own business—his enviable reputation for successful work in the clannish mining industry.

He had first won recognition in the mining world as an alert and expert technician. As the years passed, the true scope of his powers was revealed—as co-ordinator, administrator of industrial enterprises, eliminator of waste and folly—and as a wise, understanding and sympathetic judge of men.

"Plums
in a
Pudding"

CHAPTER 6

Hoover asked a number of young engineers to join his new organization, guaranteeing that they would earn a minimum annual amount in fees. He had no partners in a legal sense and no formal company. The top-ranking mining engineer opened offices in New York, London, San Francisco and subsequently in Petrograd and Paris. The entrance doors to his modest business suites were marked simply—*Herbert C. Hoover*.

The following six years proved to be a period of even larger engineering undertakings all over the globe—from the Equator to the Arctic regions—for Herbert Hoover. He became pivot man and leader of a group of engineers, mostly American, who used American mining methods and machinery. So he continually spread our culture.

Hoover and his associates operated on the theory that, besides new prospects, there were many sound engineering projects in the world which returned little or no profit, due to incompetence or outworn methods. If they could reorganize such concerns, bring the work up to date and provide efficient management, they deserved a fair share of the increased profits.

One of his oldest and closest associates has declared very aptly that Hoover became, at the height of his engineering career, a great doctor of sick companies. When a concern which, according to its owners, ought to produce and pay, did not, and it was given up as hopeless by everyone else, Hoover was called in. He diagnosed the trouble and, if he found the outlook promising, he cured the industrial patient almost every time. From among all opportunities which came to him, he was able to create many mining "plums" that were as valuable and as irregularly distributed about the surface of our planet as the rich gold deposits in the Kalgoorlie mines which followed a pattern of recurrence known in the profession as "plums in a pudding."

Among Hoover's associates were Agnew, Gilman Brown, Dean Mitchell, Louis Chevrillon, Amor Kuehn, T. L. Jones and his own brother, Theodore. Theirs was a "happy shop." They had, in Hoover's words, the sheer joy of creating productive enterprises, of giving jobs to men and women, of fighting against the whims of nature and of correcting the perversities and the incompetence of men.

Naturally, many of the investigations that Hoover made of ailing companies and prospects for new ones came to nothing. In 1910, a group of Japanese bankers asked Hoover to participate in an allegedly large, rich group of copper and gold mines in Korea. He made a long and tedious round trip over the Trans-Siberian Railway to inspect the properties, but his only profit from the inquiry was the view of the magnificent Yalu River scenery from a junk and the ornamental Korean chests purchased and shipped home.

Hoover became managing director of Burma Mines, in the

Shan State of Hsipaw in North Burma, which, as a Bewick, Moreing partner, he had developed from infancy. Later, he was elected chairman of the board as well. The railway connection to the main line was now in operation and lead was being produced at the smelter in Mandalay, but Hoover and his associates had not been able to get under the old workings into the mines to start underground production. They had waged a losing struggle against caving ground, tropical conditions, untrained labor and huge amounts of water. Diamond drilling did not work, as the ground was too soft and shattered, so they drove a tunnel, but this struck the old workings above the possible ore. However, they sank a shaft from there and had a glimpse of the rich ore bodies before being drowned out.

The next attempt was a deep tunnel, almost two miles long, named the "Tiger," for the undesired companion Hoover had almost met on his first exploration at the site. Through this, the mines were opened 700 feet below the old workings. Heavy slides delayed the completion of the underground passageway. Great lengths of it had to be supported by arched masonry. But the reward finally came in the discovery of one of the largest and richest lead-zinc-silver ore bodies ever known.

Headed by Hoover, the management built hydroelectric plants and large mills for ore concentration, developed coal mines and constructed houses, hospitals, schools, recreation grounds—in fact, whole towns.

Large production was underway in 1916. The enterprise provided a living, directly and indirectly, for over 100,000 Chinese, Shans and Indians—with a higher standard of living than they had ever known, plus some special features of mechanized civilization.

The Sawbwa became rich. He was able to support his king-sized role under both the Oriental and Western civilizations!

In 1918, Hoover received an offer for the American interests in Burma Mines, which he reluctantly sold. These mines were taken over by the Japanese in 1942. Later they were seized by Communist forces in Burma and closed, leaving 100,000 people destitute. These have since been reopened with the government as co-owner.

Great mining opportunities in Russia were offered Hoover, and he spent much time in that country. In 1910, he was asked to provide financial and engineering help to complete the modernization of the industry on the Kyshtim estate, in the Ural Mountains, near Ekaterinburg, which belonged to a distant branch of the ruling Romanoff family. The property comprised 1,500,000 acres and had a population of about 100,000. The major industry was copper mining and smelting and the marketing of related chemical by-products.

Until he was able to visit Kyshtim in person, Hoover sent an engineer to inspect the property. Meanwhile, he arranged for the reorganization of the company's finances. Gilman Brown took charge of the technical direction of the copper production and experienced mining men were brought from Butte, Montana, where similar ore is treated. As soon as the new furnaces were fired, the company made money and everybody benefited—the whole community, as well as the creditors and engineers.

Hoover found Kyshtim the most interesting of his Russian ventures—to him the estate was Imperial Russia in miniature. The agricultural land was poor, so the current owner, Baron Mellor Zakomelsky, had built up the forests with careful cultivation and replanting as a supplementary living for the peasants. A small cottage industry produced sheet iron which was unusually rust resistant, owing to a secret process. Many of the American stovepipes were made of this product. Iron ornamental forms were cast and sold in Asia and also in the United States. In the latter country, they took the form of ramping cows, horses and warriors. The market for these products was hard to maintain in the face of modern competition and they brought no profit to the company. Russian artists were engaged to make more salable designs and a brisk trade was developed, chiefly in small ornamental pots for Mohammedan prayer ablutions.

The isolated location made it necessary for the company to have its own railway connections and machine shops, in which most of the needed equipment was made from the local iron and steel, excepting intricate machines such as locomotives.

The new smelting plants were at some distance from the old, and a whole town was created at the new site. Warm log houses, schools, churches, movie theaters and hospitals were constructed and furnished with as much modern equipment as the "fixed habits of the people would tolerate." Russian technicians were employed to a great extent and a technical school for training in higher skills was set up. Wages were 25 per cent above prevailing levels. Land was sold to the peasants on very low terms and in such quantity as they wanted. Although the previous generation of owners had been extravagant, the present Baron was dedicated to the interests of his people. All took pride in their model community. The Russians and the Americans got along with instinctive camaraderie.

The Kyshtim enterprise illustrated one virtue which has marked all Hoover organizations. As told by Will Irwin, "He never forgot the human factor. In entering a foreign country he always considered and humored its institutions, its customs, and its mental attitudes. He made the natives forget he was a foreigner; infused them with his own enthusiasm for the job. In Kyshtim, for example, he encouraged the population, from the exalted lord to the humblest muzhik, to look on this as their town enterprise. About the works, Russian hovels magicked themselves into substantial houses. There followed, actually, schools. The priests insisted that the new works must be blessed—they were going to mean so much to the community! There followed a colorful religious ceremony and afterward a fete."

The relations of Hoover and his group with the Russian people at Kyshtim and at the different enterprises in Russia with which he and other Americans were associated had early attracted the favorable notice of progressive elements in the Czar's government. In 1912, the Baron had informed Hoover that his group had been requested to develop some of the Cabinet Mines. These were the personal property of the Czar and included a rather large part of the mineral resources of Siberia. Very liberal terms were offered, with the request that other communities like Kyshtim be built up.

Hoover knew little of the location of these properties or their value but he had a vague memory of mines in Siberia that had been operated with political prisoners until the practice was halted by a spasm of reform on the part of the Russian government. This had been caused by a book exposing the maltreatment of the prisoners in these mines. On rereading the book, the engineer realized the probable value of the ore deposits in question. A small syndicate was organized for preliminary investigation and Amor Kuehn was sent to inspect the sites concerned and other workings.

The most promising property was in the Altai Mountains, 750 miles up the Irtysh River from Omsk, where mining had been stopped at lowered levels by metallurgical difficulties. Kuehn sent for diamond drills to reach the inaccessible ore. The first drill hole, 1,000 feet deep, he reported had either struck an ore body 150 feet in width or had followed a rich "stringer." Tests disclosed almost solid copper, lead and zinc sulphides—including a large amount of gold and silver! These amounted to such museum specimens that Hoover, skeptical from much experience in mining, put the incredible find temporarily out of his mind as a rich stringer and went about saner business.

A while later, Kuehn reported that a second hole of similar depth, drilled a thousand feet from the first one, passed through the same ore. Hoover and his associates sat up and began to calculate! The promise of treasure, which they had not dared to credit, was coming true.

These deposits turned out to be probably the greatest and richest single body of ore known in the world. Working capital was raised by some of Hoover's financial friends and he organized the mining development. The plants, delayed by World War I, started up in 1917, only a few months before the Bolshevik Revolution. When the Revolution broke, the American staff, terrified by mortal threats and reports of wholesale murder to the north, fled for their lives. With many Russian engineers and their families, they escaped into Mongolia and managed to reach China.

The happy community at Kyshtim was shattered, too, when the Bolsheviks took over in the 1917 revolution. The Americans there were offered a train to take them out—to Vladivostok, over 3,000 miles away. In view of the raging terror and murders, they accepted at once. The Russian technical and administrative staff was fiercely driven out and a large number were brutally treated. Many were killed as bourgeois. In a week, the works broke down and 100,000 people were made destitute.

Another phase of Hoover's work was in assisting individuals whose overextended financial and business structures were teetering or had collapsed. Among the cases he accepted was that of a civil engineer and contractor who had undertaken construction projects for oil interests, ranging from Peru to South Russia, for which he was to be paid from future oil production earnings or in company stock. Another financial puzzle that Hoover took on had developed from a project to rework creek-bottom gravels around the Klondike in Alaska for gold. These beds had already been substantially worked during the famous Gold Rush of 1898, but the promoters expected to recover large amounts of the precious metal through the use of modern dredges. Two other examples of his industrial doctoring were the bankruptcy of a British oil stock flotation which had holdings in California and the overextended business operations of two well-known families of San Francisco.

After two months of hard work, Hoover completed the reorganization of the latter undertaking on March 2, 1914. That same night he left for Europe, as a representative of the Panama-Pacific International Exposition, to obtain the participation of Continental countries in the Exposition, organized in San Francisco to celebrate the opening of the Panama Canal. Mrs. Hoover and their two boys, then six and ten years old, went with him, planning to return in August.

During the six years of free-lance engineering, from 1908 to 1914, the Hoovers traveled less continually and spent more time in the United States than during the Bewick, Moreing partnership, but the number of countries Herbert visited a year still averaged about six.

In 1909, Hoover gave a series of lectures on mining at both Columbia and Stanford Universities. These were based, in part, on earlier research and were compiled into a textbook, *Principles of Mining,* which has been reprinted many times. It is still used in engineering schools.

Three years later, Herbert Hoover became a trustee of Stanford University and spent about a month there to effect some much needed changes. He was instrumental in the promotion of Dr. Jordan to the chancellorship of the university and in the temporary appointment of his old professor, Dr. Branner, as president. He proposed to the trustees that Dr. Ray Lyman Wilbur should succeed Branner as head of the institution. Remembering his experience as financial manager for student activities, Hoover arranged that the university accounts should be published. With great regret, he realized that the policy of free tuition would have to be dropped if the institution was to grow. Students working their way through college, however, were permitted to sign ten-year notes without interest.

Hoover proposed to the students the construction of a building to serve as a center for student activities, eating clubs and other purposes, to be known as the Stanford Union. He followed this by the gift of $100,000 to build the Union, on the condition that the trustees lend $150,000, to be repaid to the university from the future earnings. The students personally raised still more money, and they have continued to enlarge the center over the years.

At Stanford, the Hoovers lived in the cottage they had acquired earlier. Their two sons went to the campus children's school, which provided an excellent education.

Among the families of the college faculty there were plenty of young companions with whom the boys ranged the surrounding hills and rocks, and there were many devoted friends on the campus to look after the boys when Mrs. Hoover went on trips with her husband.

When the Hoovers were in England, the Red House was their headquarters, except for a few weeks during the boys' summer vacations, when Mr. and Mrs. Hoover would sometimes take a country cottage at one place or another, including Stratford-on-Avon.

Hoover gave a lovely picture of Red House in a letter written to his wife after revisiting the place many years later. He told how he persuaded the butler to let him enter by means of a ten-shilling note sufficiently exposed. Then he continued, "To the left was the oak-panelled library with its fine fireplace and its leaded glass bookcases—the same as ever. I imagined again, sitting on the opposite side of the desk from you, with the manuscripts and reference books of Agricola, piled between us, as we worked over the translation of *De Re Metallica*. Again I saw 'Pete' at the little table in the corner, making marks and announcing that he was writing a book too; and 'Bub' clambering into his mother's lap and demanding to know what the book said."

Lou and Herbert Hoover had become interested in the project of translating *De Re Metallica* from the Latin. This work was first published in 1556. For the next 200 years it was the classic source book on mining, metallurgy and industrial chemistry. Up to 1912, it had never been translated into English, although attempts had been made to do so. It proved to be not only a linguistic problem but also one involving scientific detective work. For five years the Hoovers worked on this project in their spare moments while located all over the world. Their joint translation was published in London in 1912, in a handsome edition.

"The dining room," Hoover's letter continued, "was the same walnut-panelled room and evoked all kinds of memories of the multitude of happy gatherings which had filled it. The living room had been redecorated from its old neutral tints to modern white French and was a 'repellent stranger.'"

Will Irwin recounted that the Hoovers, unlike many Americans with foreign interests, never succumbed to social ambition while in England. Their guests included "great" people who, like the others at their dinners, were invited for their wit and worth, and not for their rank.

Red House was awaiting the Hoovers when they arrived in London in the spring of 1914—even to the century-old mulberry tree in the garden which they nursed for years with steel I beams.

Hoover went to Wales to look into a management offer of a large coal concern whose owners wished to introduce more modern American methods. He was deeply distressed by the low wages and poor living conditions of the working people revealed on that trip. He felt that the only way to raise wages was to install American machinery and methods and so increase the output per man. This would decrease the number employed at the start until larger sales could again provide jobs for all of the workers. He consulted local trades union leaders who argued that men in some other mines would then lose their jobs because of this increased competition.

Hoover, on the other hand, felt that, if the whole industry

were re-equipped, resulting in lower prices, Britain's coal export—her economic backbone—as well as total consumption, could be expanded and higher wages paid. One company alone, he was convinced, could not effect a change and he refused the offer. The difficulties, he realized, stemmed from "the same old philosophy which caused the riots against Whitney's cotton gin."

In London, Hoover was asked to do an industrial repair job on the overextended, world-wide holdings of a British promoter, whose "house of cards" had begun to fall. He did not wish any further English responsibilities but finally decided to take on the job as he felt he could salvage something from the wreck for the stockholders, provide further work for his associates and continue the jobs of the many people employed by the different companies. He became chairman of the concerns involved, placed Govette and Hamilton on the boards and his London and New York staffs in technical control.

Meanwhile, Hoover took up the matter of the Panama-Pacific Exposition with Continental governments which in general had refused to participate. In the various countries, he secured commercial and industrial support. A campaign among British industrialists, arranged by Hoover the year before, had succeeded in reversing the initial British decision not to participate in the Panama Canal Celebration. Hoover was making good progress. Then, suddenly, the attention of all Europe was turned to "matters more pressing for civilization than a public spectacle on the shores of the Pacific"—as the unpredicted result of a murder in the Balkans.

On June 28, 1914—Archduke Francis Ferdinand, heir to the Austro-Hungarian Empire, was assassinated in Sarajevo by a young native of the Austrian province of Bosnia.

At this catastrophic moment, Hoover would probably not have been in Europe—had it not been for the Panama-Pacific mission.

Stranded
Americans

CHAPTER 7

Herbert Hoover, on the eve of his fortieth birthday, had risen to be the foremost mining engineer in the world. He was headed for the largest engineering fees ever known. The acclaim of his fellow engineers was to become a long parade of honors. At the same time, he felt a growing urge for a role in American public life.

Will Irwin had met Hoover in Europe in 1912, and during a three-day wait for a steamer they had picked up the threads of the old intimacy. On the last evening, they talked about Hoover's future.

"I'm getting to the point," the engineer disclosed, "where I'll soon have an independent income—big enough."

"What's enough?" Irwin asked.

"Not a great deal, as money goes nowadays," was the reply, "but enough to live on comfortably and to be certain the family is secure and a margin to make sure."

"And then what?"

"I don't know exactly," the engineer continued. "I am interested in some job of public service—at home, of course."

When Irwin pressed him for details, Hoover gave his view that many of the world's problems could be resolved by common sense, honest intention and co-operation—the method used by a good engineer on any big job. And he felt that a man of his experience could find a place in such work, somehow, somewhere. He was moved too by the conviction that a man who had earned enough to insure himself and his family a comfortable living before the age of forty had the obligation after that to do something for his generation.

"It sounds to me a little like politics or government," Irwin commented.

"Well, I've always been interested in government and all that sort of thing," his friend answered. "You remember Stanford. I don't know yet what it will be—but something." Beyond this, he was vague, for Hoover.

Two summers later his undefined aspirations were crystallized into specific humanitarian action—with the coming of World War I.

For a while the assassination at Sarajevo on June 28, 1914, was wishfully taken as just another Balkan lapse into "barbarism." However, the Austrian Government held the Serbian revolutionary societies to which the assassin belonged responsible for the murder. An ultimatum was sent to Serbia threatening war unless all but impossible conditions were met. Diplomatic lightning soon flashed from capital to capital. All Europe developed signs of serious disturbance and alarm. Austria, Serbia and Russia gave indications of mobilizing. War fears mounted. Austria-Hungary declared war on Serbia on July 28, but there was still hope in England that the conflict could be limited to Eastern Europe.

In the rising panic, Hoover and his associates tried to appraise just what this war would mean in terms of human life and misery. How would it affect America, all the people they employed and their business? As the immediate market for their partially finished products had collapsed, Hoover cabled his agents all over the world to slacken production. He wired, too, his plans for taking care of their unemployed and their families if distress developed among them.

Economic breakdown thundered about their ears and by Friday, July 31, world markets were closed. That afternoon Hoover was advised by one of his banks to send over immediately for cash to meet the office payroll, as there might be a moratorium. Late that evening, the government closed the banks for Saturday and the Monday following.

For a long time, the Hoovers had been planning to spend that week end with their great friends, the Edgar Rickards, at Westgate. By Saturday morning, the war outlook had become extremely ominous, but, not wishing to disappoint their sons, the Hoovers motored to the country. That evening, they heard that Germany had declared war on Russia and that France was mobilizing.

Sunday morning brought the news that the bank moratorium had been extended and that Germany had demanded passage through Belgium for her army. The sale of petrol or gasoline was stopped in the country village of Westgate. Hoover's chauffeur had managed to buy a few tins just in time, so, leaving their hosts some of these, the Hoovers were able to start at once for London. Their route took them past Cowes, where they saw the British fleet in war trim—mobilized for action.

Hoover went to his office early the next day, to see what news had come by cable and try to pick up the pieces of his world-wide industrial enterprises, shattered by the economic earthquake. By telephone, he learned that Germany had declared war on France. Could England possibly stay out of the conflict?

Cables advised that his employees and staff officials in Russia were being taken into the army. Commercial transportation was disrupted and production had been suspended. Hoover's managers in other parts of the world asked for instructions as banks in Australia, Burma and South Africa were also closed. Ships carrying their cargoes of ore had been ordered to the nearest ports. New destinations had to be arranged. Cables were promptly sent by Hoover and his associates asking American smelters to take over the copper, lead and zinc which had been en route to German, Belgian and French smelters.

While Hoover was considering the desperate situation, late that Monday afternoon, the American consul general called him up. Robert P. Skinner, an old friend, revealed that there was a crowd of a thousand stranded American tourists milling around in the Consulate and spilling out in the street. All were penniless, as no money could be raised on travelers' checks or other documents of credit. London hotels were even refusing to accept American currency in the panic and would only give food and lodging to their old customers. Could Herbert think of anything to do?

Hoover went right over to the Consulate. He found Skinner beset by panicky and irate tourists who demanded that the United States government protect its citizens from such inconveniences. Among these tourists were many teachers whose plight touched Hoover deeply. They had pinched and saved to make the trip to Europe, in order to become better teachers and now, without supplementary resources, they were the hardest hit of all the travelers. However, although they were so very anxious, they were always polite.

After listening to the plaints of several commercial travelers and surveying the confusion in the Consulate, Hoover borrowed Skinner's telephone. He asked two of his American engineers to bring over the cash reserve drawn for the staff salaries, as well as all other gold and currency in the office. He then arranged to exchange British money for United States dollars at the usual rate. Loans of ten shillings on I.O.U.'s were given to those who had no American currency. When the consul announced this program, a faint cheer broke out. Many did not consider this a direct enough reprimand to Europe for inflicting the inconveniences of war on them!

The crowd was divided into five lines and interview tables were set up. In three or four hours, all the tourists had been taken care of for the night. Yes, they certainly would be back the next day to see what their government was going to do about the situation!

As the last petitioner left, Skinner called up the American Ambassador, Walter Hines Page, and informed him of the temporary solution to the tourists' problems. Mr. Page replied that he had a "mob" of his own and no money. He asked Mr. Hoover to come to see him right away.

The Ambassador, Hoover found, was in worse trouble than the consul. Thousands of Americans were rushing in from the Continent. In all there were between one and two hundred thousand Americans in Europe, the majority of whom were in a panic to escape the war. All British sailings to America had been canceled. German passenger ships had raced to the nearest nonenemy ports. Immediate prospect of transportation home appeared to be very dim.

At Mr. Page's request, Hoover attended a mass meeting that night at the Savoy Hotel, arranged to consider what could be done about procuring passage back to the United States. Between one and two thousand stranded Americans attended and elected a representative committee.

As the committee members would be leaving England as soon as possible, Hoover suggested toward the close of the meeting that he form an organization among the more permanent American residents and try to clear up the bleak and chaotic situation. The committee agreed to his proposal and disbanded in a few days. The thousands of dollars which they had collected for charitable uses was given to Hoover's group for similar purposes as soon as currency exchange could be arranged.

During the evening of the initial meeting, Hoover asked some American engineers, including Edgar Rickard, John

White and Colonel Millard Hunsiker, to meet him at the Savoy Hotel the next morning. Mrs. Hoover arranged for a committee of ladies to meet there, too. The hotel agreed to provide reception rooms, tables and chairs without charge. Hoover promised Mr. Page and Mr. Skinner that his group would be ready to take on all stranded United States citizens by nine the next morning. Coping with the plight of the American tourists helped to reduce Hoover's feeling of helplessness to do anything about the calamitous situation in the face of the world war. Even as he went home about midnight—England was brought into the conflict.

At the meeting the next morning, Hoover was installed as the chairman of the American Committee for Repatriation of American Citizens from Europe. All the banks were still closed but one of the American institutions where Hoover was known sent him a few thousand pounds to see the committee through the day. The staff was increased by volunteers from American business offices, mainly engineers, and the committee was soon in full swing. Further helpers were recruited from among the tourists and by evening there was a staff of 500. The methods of the previous day for assisting each citizen were improved.

Droves of American tourists came to the committee rooms at the Savoy. Financial help was required by many. Some only wanted to discuss the "approaching end of the world." All wanted passage home. The needs of each individual were carefully considered. In the financial department, keen young Americans sized up the applicants and divided them into three credit groups—those who "looked good," the doubtfuls and the temporarily destitute. Financial assistance was given the first two groups from a London bank account, guaranteed up to a million dollars by Hoover and nine other men. In addition to the funds from the first committee, money was raised for the destitute—often coming from other American travelers. Outside of this charitable assistance, over a million and a half dollars was paid out, with a final total loss of under three hundred dollars because of loans not made good. The interviewers had shown exceedingly good judgment, and the American travelers were very honest.

Hoover went to work with the same energy on the big problem of securing American and neutral ships to transport the stranded Americans back home. He set up branch committees in the main continental cities. These and American groups in other smaller cities channeled the tourists to London, where Hoover's committee found lodgings and steamer space for them. After the first rush of travelers came many of the Americans who had been living and working in Europe. The United States Congress appropriated a large sum of money to repatriate these people. The commissioner sent to accomplish this task "shed" his work onto Hoover's committee. They did the job without cost to their government beyond the actual outlay of funds to the destitute citizens. In all, the American Committee assisted over 120,000 compatriots.

For the first time, Herbert Hoover's friends, outside of his mining business associates, had a chance to observe him closely while at work. Will Irwin later realized that, compared to Hoover's big engineering enterprises, the work of the American Committee was almost child's play. "We marveled nevertheless at the smooth run of his improvised machine," Irwin wrote. "He concealed that machinery as he always does; gave human individuality all possible leeway; instead of commanding, he led."

The care of the women and children traveling alone was taken over by Mrs. Hoover's Women's Committee. A large part of its work was in consoling the frightened. To fill in the time of those waiting for steamer space, Mrs. Hoover organized sight-seeing excursions in London and, by train, to the cathedral towns, Shakespeare and Lorna Doone country.

There were many diverting episodes to lighten the general tension and gloom. One old lady utterly refused to sail unless provided with a written guarantee from Hoover himself that her ship would not be torpedoed in the Atlantic. Hoover complied. "I knew," he explained afterward with a chuckle, "that there wasn't one chance in ten thousand that her ship would be harmed."

A few adventurous Americans wanted to stay in Europe and "watch the show." One of these was a young girl from Lansing, Michigan, whose father had cabled the American Committee to find his daughter at any cost and send her home. Imperious telegrams from her father, forwarded by Hoover's organization, finally brought her to London. En route, she lost her five trunks. Her father cabled her five-thousand-dollars worth of credit, through the committee, to replace her lost wardrobe. Trusting Americans only at that point, she sent her purchases to the repatriation rooms at the Savoy. All packages of clothing addressed to the committee went directly to the old clothes department that had been established by Mrs. Hoover's group to outfit needy women and children arriving from the continent. These splendid "gifts" delighted the committee ladies and were immediately given to women of the proper size— dressing them beyond their most extravagant dreams! In due time, the young girl appeared to collect her new wardrobe— and the Women's Committee was in for a hard time!

By far the most picturesque American travelers to adorn the committee headquarters were the members of a wild west show —twelve American Indians and ten cowboys—all in full regalia. Stranded in Poland by the war, the performers and their manager had worked their way to Hamburg. There they had been adopted by a twelve-year-old boy who had landed on his way to visit his grandparents in Croatia just as the war broke out. Plans to meet him were disrupted by the conflict. Lost and alone, he was wandering the streets when he beheld a "vision of real America," complete with beads, feathers and chaps, and promptly attached himself to them. He had some money which helped the wild west group, whose first concern was repayment of the boy's loan, reach England. Steerage passage was arranged for the party and the boy's mother was cabled that he was being sent home under the good care of White Feather of Pawhuska, Oklahoma.

After two weeks, the American Committee for the Repatriation of American Citizens from Europe had been so well organized that its chairman could spend part of his time at his own office. The "whole fabric" of international finance was smashed. Since Hoover's bills for ore shipments were drawn on continental buyers involved in the war, the banks demanded collateral. His concern soon ran out of that but, on August 12, the Bank of England was authorized to take up all such documents on the government account.

In mid-August, Hoover asked the important lead and zinc producers to come to his office to consider resurrecting the old smelters at Swansea in Wales. Great Britain did not possess many sources of finished lead, zinc and copper, since the large amounts of these ores mined in the Empire had been sent to Continental smelters and refineries. Britain would need great quantities of these metals for war use, and Hoover was anxious to provide work for the men in the mines that he managed in various parts of the world.

Hoover booked and canceled homeward passage for his family and himself on five ships. Mrs. Hoover finally sailed with Herbert and Allan on October 3, as she had to hurry to Palo Alto to put the boys in school. Hoover learned of their safe arrival in New York through a cable from Herbert stating that he had eaten seven cream puffs in one day on the trip. This was merely his triumphant announcement that he had won out over seasickness, in spite of grim forebodings. To the British censor, however, it was a "deep and sinister" code. Hoover's explanation of the message failed to satisfy the official, who accepted it only with dark warnings of the dire fate that awaited spies.

Hoover himself had to linger quite a while longer to finish up his various activities. Toward the end of September, Edgar Rickard introduced to Hoover a caller just arrived from Brussels, in war-torn Belgium, which, by now, was overrun by the German army. He was Millard Shaler, an engineer, who, being an American neutral, had been able to come through the German lines with funds to buy 2,500 tons of food for Brussels.

This first step toward obtaining food for the Belgians had been taken by the branch American Committee in Brussels, instigated by Hoover. The chief members included Daniel Heineman, the chairman, Shaler and Hugh Gibson, secretary of the American Legation. They had set up a committee for Brussels and Heineman had secured verbal guarantees from the German military authorities not to seize imported food.

Shaler had bought the food from English merchants but was refused permission to export it to Belgium by the British authorities, on the grounds that the Germans would appropriate the supplies and that it was the duty of the enemy to feed the countries they conquered. Hoover suggested that the permit might be granted if the food were consigned to the American Minister in Brussels and distributed under his supervision.

Hoover then took Shaler to Ambassador Page, who was sympathetic but felt unable to intervene without authority from the State Department. Hoover drafted a cable which Page sent to the Secretary of State. However, Page took up Shaler's problem with Sir Edward Grey, British Foreign Minister, without waiting for a reply from Washington. To allay Grey's fears, a confirmation of the German promise to Heineman to keep their hands off was secured. Shaler soon received export permits for his food purchase but he was informed by the Foreign Office that no further permits would be given.

Hoover took up the plight of the Belgians with his friend, Melville Stone, General Manager of the Associated Press, then in London, suggesting that their desperate situation and that of the Northern French be publicized in America. Stone responded generously with press coverage in the United States and also gave directions to other AP men abroad to follow suit.

This accomplished, Hoover had no thought of further responsibility in the situation and again booked passage for home—this time for October 25, the first available date. Of his work for the American Committee, Ambassador Page wrote to President Wilson, "Life is worth more, too, for knowing Hoover. . . . He's a simple, modest, energetic man who began his career in California and will end it in Heaven; and he doesn't want anybody's thanks."

Other delegations from Belgian cities came to London, asking to be allowed to import food. Hoover suggested that they see Page by appointment, through the Belgian Minister in London. He continued to wind up his own affairs.

Just one week before his sailing date, Hoover received a request by telephone from Mr. Page to go to the American Embassy. There, with the Ambassador, he found Count de Lalaing, the Belgian Minister, and three men who had just come from Belgium. They were Baron Lambert, Hugh Gibson—and Emile Francqui, from whom Hoover had parted in China thirteen years before on "less than friendly" terms due to their disagreement over the management policies of the Chinese Engineering and Mining Company.

These men were discussing the desperate food needs of Belgium and the complex difficulties of trying to remedy the shortages. Page told Hoover that Secretary Bryan had authorized him to use his "good offices," but without obligating the United States. Hoover listened and said little.

Suddenly Francqui turned to him. "We must have leaders to organize and conduct this matter," he said. "They must be men of wide administrative experience and knowledge of the world. They must be neutral and they must be Americans. They must have the confidence of the American Ambassadors. We in Belgium and Northern France," Francqui continued, "are faced with life and death for millions of our people. You alone have the setting for this job. If you will undertake it, I will either serve under you or retire from any connection with it."

The Ambassador, the Belgian Minister and Hugh Gibson all joined in urging Hoover to accept the assignment of mercy. Describing the "bare bones" of the situation, Francqui asserted that Belgium produced its own food for only 30 per cent of the population. The cities were normally dependent upon imports. The Germans had seized part of the current harvest and thousands of cattle for their own use. Due to the British blockade, the enemy would still be short of food themselves and would do nothing to help. At Hoover's request, Francqui outlined the Belgian financial resources upon which the relief mission could depend. Page urged that there would be a great charitable response throughout the world if Hoover took charge.

Hoover replied that he must have a day to weigh the matter before reaching a decision. As well as the great difficulties to overcome in this undertaking, he had responsibilities of his own to consider.

Will Irwin was staying at Red House with Hoover at the time. He tells of hearing the "steady tramp" through the night as Hoover walked the floor above him, appraising all the factors.

Part of the relief project could be handled readily by an experienced engineer, but other phases of the relief work in pioneering the feeding of a nation would have to be improvised. He would have to find the major food supply for the Belgians, raise money to pay for it, get the food past warring navies at sea and occupying armies on land, distribute the supplies justly—and see that the enemy took no crumb of it.

To devote full time to the undertaking meant relinquishing temporarily the great business he had built up. His engineering practice extended over the United States, Canada, Mexico, Chile, China, Russia, Mongolia, Burma, Penang, New Zealand and Australia. The various enterprises with which he worked employed a total of 175,000 men. Could he give up his responsibilities to these concerns which were in trouble, due to the war? He consulted with his associates and cabled his principal clients abroad. The clients agreed that they would accept Hoover's engineering associates if they were placed in temporary charge, provided he gave personal assistance on critical matters.

At that time, described as the Golden Age of American engineering in foreign countries, Hoover had probably the largest earnings of any American engineer. Could he afford to give up his professional income, for any period, when the uncertain times jeopardized even the funds he had set aside for the future?

In addition, his concentration on base metals promised to pay off. Due to the wartime need, these metals would be as "gold." In the expansion of the postwar era, he could expect to accumulate a fabulous fortune, if he directed these operations correctly.

The following morning, Hoover joined Irwin for breakfast as usual. Bidding his guest good morning, he poured and sweetened his coffee. Then he looked up.

"Well, let the fortune go . . ." he said.

Hoover met with Page and Francqui and told them he would do the job on certain conditions. He was to have the over-all command. A universal charity campaign should be organized to raise funds and to create a world-wide opinion that would "keep the door to Belgium open through the blockade and keep the Germans from taking food from them." A central organization of Belgians should be set up, with Francqui as chairman. For himself, he would accept no remuneration. He could not ask others to sacrifice—without sacrifice himself.

So, suddenly, he took a leave from all his business connections and handed his enterprises over to his associates, in order to devote himself to public service in compassion for suffering people—in the best tradition of his Quaker faith.

When Hoover hurried to the American Consulate on August 3, he did not realize it, but his engineering career was over forever. He was on the "slippery road of public life."

On leaving his profession of engineering he later wrote:

"It is a great profession. There is the fascination of watching a figment of the imagination emerge through the aid of science to a plan on paper. Then it moves to realization in stone or metal or energy. Then it brings jobs and homes to men. Then it elevates the standards of living and adds to the comforts of life. That is the engineer's high privilege."

Feeding

a

Nation

CHAPTER 8

The next morning in his office, Herbert Hoover organized the Commission for Relief in Belgium with a group of "big-calibre" Americans, including engineers, a diplomat and a newspaperman from the Associated Press.

The job was to provide for the Belgians until the next harvests, eight months away, since it was thought that the war would be over the following summer.

"The knowledge," Hoover later wrote, "that we would have to go on for four years, to find a billion dollars, to transport five million tons of concentrated food, to administer rationing, price controls, agricultural production, to contend with combatant governments and with world shortages of food and ships, was mercifully hidden from us."

A program was set up to organize world charity and to rally world public opinion in support of feeding the Belgians. Plans were made to acquire an American volunteer staff to administer the Relief in Belgium. Those present decided that they must have Ambassador Page as an honorary chairman on the letterhead and all the other American ambassadors and ministers in Europe as well. Later, important neutral Spanish and Dutch officials were secured as patrons.

Lastly, John White remarked, "We are about to handle millions of dollars. Some day some swine will rise up and say we either made a profit out of this business or that we stole the money."

Rickard at once made arrangements with Sir John Plender of the leading firm of British accountants not only to audit the commission accounts but to actually keep the books with their own employees—and to countersign all checks. When such detractors did "rise up," they were confronted with independent auditors and the elaborate, infallible accounting statistics.

Ambassador Page readily agreed to serve as an honorary chairman and he added his support in enlisting other neutral sponsors. It was agreed that Hoover would set up his own direct relations with the belligerent government officials and that the ambassadors and ministers would help when things went wrong.

Belgian Relief committees were established by telegraph and cable all over the world. Melville Stone strongly backed the committee organized by Hoover's New York office. At Hoover's request, the governors of over forty states set up committees. The Duke of Norfolk headed a British Empire Committee and, with Sir William Good, added branches in Australia, New Zealand, South Africa and Canada. Other Relief branches were formed in the Scandinavian countries, Switzerland, France and, later, in most Latin-American countries and Japan. This charity organization and the world-wide support which it created for feeding the Belgians became the commission's "effective armor" against attempts of both British and German militarists to suppress or restrict its activities.

Among the volunteers who enlisted to serve in Belgium were fifteen American Rhodes scholars, studying in England. They were led by Perrin C. Galpin. Promising young men were also recruited by the New York office. The volunteers served without pay and only some received minimum traveling expenses.

With the aid of a patron, the Netherlands Foreign Minister, Hoover obtained 20,000 tons of wheat and other supplies in Holland, which were sent by canal to the larger Belgian cities. As this food was Dutch owned, a British permit was not required. The British blockade had not then been sufficiently perfected to control indirect supplies through neutral nations. Sir Edward Grey secured permits for the Relief to ship 60,000 tons of food from overseas directly through the blockade for the captive population. Thus the inhabitants of the Belgian cities were saved from starvation—for the moment.

Hoover went to Belgium by steamer via a Dutch port to build up the food distribution machinery. As he crossed the frontier from Holland on his neutral American passport he felt that he was entering a "land of imprisonment—" an impression which was strengthened by the rather rough search of his person by the German guards at the border. Enemy soldiers guarded every crossroad and street corner. Hoover saw no children at play. The faces of the Belgians were depressed and unsmiling. Industry had collapsed with the German invasion and half the population was unemployed and destitute. Food prices skyrocketed before the Relief was in action.

"The empty streets, the gaunt destroyed houses, the ruins of the fine old church of St. Pierre and the Library at Louvain," Hoover declared, "intensified the sense of suspended animation in the life of a people."

He soon realized with sharp despair that to provide the Belgians with even a minimum of 1800 calories a day and necessary supplements to children and special groups meant enlarging his ideas on quantity and finance. And even if he did manage to reach this minimum goal—the Belgians would still lead a desperate existence.

By early January, 1915, Hoover knew that failure was inevitable unless the Relief finances were more assured and better relations were reached with the British and German governments. To keep the 10,000,000 Belgians and northern French in the occupied territories alive, at least $12,000,000 a month would have to be spent on food for them. The C.R.B., as the commission was known for short, had exhausted the available Belgian foreign assets, which had proved disappointing. The charity gifts, which had been generous but totaled less than $2,000,000 at that time, had been used up. Hoover's proposal for exchange of Belgian currency into foreign money was not favored by the Allied governments. To assure the trans-ocean stream of food for the immediate future, he had incurred a temporary debt of $12,000,000 beyond the organization's resources. This was surely a case of Hoover's tendency in crises, as pointed out by Will Irwin, to think like a pessimist while behaving like an optimist.

To maintain the C.R.B.'s official existence, Hoover and his associates were walking a tight rope, the ends of which were anchored in the desire of the British and French on one side and of the Germans on the other to cultivate popularity in neutral countries. The committee's vigorously publicized demands for justice to the Belgians—caught between the millstones of a blockade and an occupying army—met with "limited" enthusiasm from both the British and German governments.

In reply to an English critic, Hoover described the undertaking as like "trying to feed a hungry kitten by means of a forty-foot bamboo pole, said kitten confined in a barred cage occupied by two hungry lions."

He decided to tackle the British lion first! He presented his views to the Prime Minister, Herbert Asquith, that the government should let the C.R.B. ships through the blockade on a definite schedule arranged in advance, facilitate the staff movements and consider financial support—all conditional on more effective guaranties from the Germans. The Prime Minister was sympathetic—except on finance.

Sir Edward Grey disclosed to Hoover that most of the Cabinet was opposed to feeding the Belgians. The military leaders considered that, if the enemy had to provide food for Belgium, it would make trouble for them and so help win the war.

Holding out little hope, Grey arranged a meeting for Hoover with a Cabinet committee. They discussed whether the Relief would continue and, if so, Hoover's proposals including the Belgian monetary exchange plan and acceptance of C.R.B. certifications for passport visas.

After listening patiently to Hoover, the Cabinet committee agreed tentatively to let the C.R.B. continue and accepted his proposals, all contingent, of course, on his ability to extract more effective food control in Belgium from the Germans. As to the subsidy—not a chance—even if the food leaks in Belgium were plugged. One of the committee, Lord Percy, was assigned by the Foreign Office to handle C.R.B. affairs. He became a staunch friend of the cause.

Hoover began negotiations with the Germans by cabling Secretary of State Bryan in Washington to present the Relief problems which he had outlined to the German Ambassador there. The Ambassador, he felt, would be especially sensitive to American reaction on the Belgian Relief situation. To make sure, he issued a press release stating the case frankly and bluntly to his "only court of appeal," public opinion in the United States.

The next day, Hoover left for Berlin. The American Ambassador there, James Gerard, arranged interviews for Hoover with high German officials and often assisted in person at the meetings. The Minister of the Interior, Theodor Lewald, head of the German food organization, was helpful. Due to visits in the United States on different missions, he was more conscious of the public relations situation than most of the others.

Among other "devilish habits," Hoover had found that the German army in the occupied country had levied upon the Belgian provinces heavy contributions of money which were paid in a compulsory new currency issue imposed on the Belgian banks. While respecting the guaranties they had given not to seize imported food, they requisitioned native food and cattle, giving this currency in payment. As a result, the Relief was forced to import more food and thus feed the Germans. The amounts were not great in actual proportion to the total supplies furnished but they provided ample excuse for complaints of the British Secret Service. German restrictions on their movements prevented the C.R.B. staff from keeping track of the situation.

As a result of Hoover's work, the Germans agreed to stop all appropriation of food from Belgium and Northern France, to allow his staff complete freedom of movement without search, to give definite instructions to submarine commanders to respect the C.R.B. markings on the Relief ships, to provide information on mine-free sea routes to Rotterdam, and to designate one officer with authority to deal with the commission in occupied Belgium and one official at headquarters in Charleville, to act as liaison for the Relief in all the four army zones. Through Gerard, they confirmed the agreements in writing and generally carried them out. The Germans promised to consider Hoover's proposals to abandon the forced Belgian contributions of money, which they never did.

Hoover's experiences in Germany convinced him that the war would not be over in the spring—rather that "it had not yet really begun." The top leaders there acted quickly and more effectively on decisions than the British, but he found something "indescribably automatic and inhuman" about their actions and thinking.

The only relieving laugh he heard came from Reich Chancellor Hollweg, when Hoover told him an American anecdote to illustrate the need for absolute instructions to submarine commanders to spare C.R.B. ships. The anecdote was about a man who insisted that his neighbor keep his bulldog under better control.

"Oh, he won't bite," the neighbor replied.

"You may know he won't bite," the man commented. "I may know he won't bite. But does the dog know it?"

As to finances, a tentative plan was reached whereby the Reichsbank would guarantee commission trade bills in the United States up to $100,000,000, secured by Belgian bonds and jointly guaranteed by Belgian banks. Hoover recognized that this was obviously a "kiting of paper" that would break down unless the war ended soon. But Belgians would be fed— and the offer might prove a lever with Allied governments.

Back in London, Hoover detailed his progress to Lord Percy. The Foreign Office accepted the new German guaranties to refrain from food appropriation and the other arrangements as good enough—except for finance.

Hoover had had a premonition that a German offer on finance might thaw out the Allied treasuries. The prospective exhibit before the neutral world of Germans saving Belgians, he had surmised, might even produce an explosion.

Percy arranged a conference right away with Lloyd George, then the Chancellor of the Exchequer, Lord Emmott and Hoover. The C.R.B. chairman announced the progress made with the Germans and reviewed the whole situation. Hoover was asked to submit a memorandum for the full Cabinet meeting the next morning. He prepared this during the night and had it in Lloyd George's hands before the meeting.

The same day, the chief finance minister asked Hoover to go to see him at the Treasury with Hunsiker, C.R.B. liaison with the British government. Percy, who was there, told the Belgian Relief head that the opposition had been overruled.

"We have agreed to give one million pounds a month to the 'Hoover Fund,' " the Chancellor of the Exchequer announced.

"You and the other ministers have taken a load from millions of hearts," Hoover replied.

Lloyd George responded, "You deserved to win out."

Next, Hoover approached the French government. His associate, Louis Chevrillon, arranged an appointment for the Chief with French Minister of Foreign Affairs Delcassé. Hoover cited to him the situation of the 3,000,000 northern French behind the German lines who were reduced to famine rations. The Relief was feeding 400,000 but unfortunately could not continue without depriving the Belgians whose needs were not even met by the British subsidy.

Delcassé listened with courtesy but spoke out violently on the obligation of the Germans to feed the conquered populations or get out. Feeling that his presentation had been inadequate, Hoover withdrew, discouraged.

Back at his hotel, Hoover was packing to leave Paris when M. Homberg, President of the Banque Union Parisienne, was announced. Homberg asked the American about his mission to finance food for the Belgians and northern French. Hoover explained the political, military and humanitarian arguments with which he was then so familiar that he repeated them in his sleep. He gave an estimate on the costs.

Homberg stated that he felt sure the problem could be solved and that Hoover need not postpone his departure. But the C.R.B. head stayed over in Paris briefly for further meetings with government ministers and learned that aid was arranged for the northern French.

After Herbert Hoover's return to England, a London bank official called on him at the London Relief Office about two days later, on March 27th.

The caller presented the C.R.B. chairman with two checks in sterling amounting to about $6,740,000.

Mr. Hoover asked to whom the Belgian Relief was to account these sums. The bank official disclaimed knowledge of the donor.

Since the Chief was aware that the funds must have been transferred through the exiled Belgian government, he questioned them on to whom to account for the money. He was told that they did not know but that "they had no obligations of repayment."

Hoover, of course, knew the source to be the French government, which did not want to recede publicly from Delcassé's stand on the German responsibility.

The "façade" for the food subsidies was continued by the French government, Hoover recounted, for about two years. The Germans, he declared, were not fooled. They well knew the exiled Belgian government had no such sums.

Under the requirements of the Allied governments, all food was the property of the C.R.B. until it reached the consumer's mouth. C.R.B. men were charged with its transportation, processing and storage, to safeguard supplies from the Germans. To kill the "black market," the Relief had to take over the farmers' surplus production. The commission was required to account to the Allies for all money.

The Belgian Comité National de Secours et d'Alimentation run by Francqui and Firmin Van Bree, the provincial and local committees and the French organization were all under the commission. The final stage of the distribution was in the hands of the local setups, run by burgomasters and mayors. The American staff sat on all committees ex-officio and served as channels of information, since the Belgians were not allowed to move freely. The American staff and the Belgian Comité National were located in an office building in Brussels.

Food rationing presented the problem of meeting the hundreds of variations in family and individual needs. To simplify organization and accounting, Hoover separated "Provisioning" of people completely from "Benevolence" to the destitute. In Provisioning, rations were sold by the local committees to everyone who could buy. From these proceeds, operation Benevolence purchased ration cards and gave them to those unable to pay.

From the sales of Provisioning, the commission performed many quasi-governmental services in keeping schools open and paying teachers, police and other officials. The major part of the sales of rations was absorbed by Benevolence. Total grants amounting to over $600,000,000 made it possible to maintain the soup kitchens, care for the destitute, provide daily "Hoover lunches" for two and a half million children and others, run hospitals and other public institutions, distribute clothing and aid the women lace workers.

A daily chore for Belgian children was fetching soup obtained by cards from Benevolence. The wartime symbol of Belgium might well have been a child carrying a bucket of the far-from-ordinary potage!

Over fifty thousand Belgians and French worked for the commission—mostly women—and the highest pay was free rations. They served with a zeal inspired by the chance to keep alive their national existence.

"Whether internal distribution, care of the destitute, or shipping were relatively the worst problems I could never decide," Hoover later said, looking back. "No day went by without a fight to keep part of the mechanism from breaking down."

All during the Relief operations, he had troubles with shipping. Chartering vessels in the face of sinkings by German submarines and surface raiders was always a "fierce battle." The Allied need for transportation constantly increased and the commission required about sixty cargo ships.

Hoover had secured the Belgian merchant ships but he had to charter the rest of the C.R.B. fleet from neutral countries at mounting costs. His plan to charter German cargo vessels, in refuge in neutral ports, was blocked by the French until too late. The Germans eventually realized that use of their ships would free other tonnage for Allied service and withdrew the agreement.

One time when Hoover was pressing a British Admiralty official for a permit to export some supplies, the official asked, "But what use would a permit be when there isn't a single ship available?"

"We've got the ship," Hoover replied, "and it's already loaded."

Difficulties in arranging charters arose from early British search demands and their insistence that the C.R.B. deliver no more than four weeks' advance supply of food into Rotterdam. Distribution schedules were continually upset by German army interruptions of rail and canal transportation. Food was purchased wherever it was cheapest—and often had to be shipped long distances.

Safety measures for the C.R.B. ships were arranged with the British and German governments. On every ship, a huge sign, lettered BELGIAN RELIEF COMMISSION, was stretched almost from stem to stern. This was visible for ten miles. Deck signs were also used and a C.R.B. flag flew at each main mast. The captains were wired current directions of the supposedly mine-free channel from the North Sea to Rotterdam, arranged for the Dutch. Prior to the end of January, 1917, the Relief lost nineteen ships, mostly from mines. Three were attributed to submarines, although the C.R.B. had been promised immunity from such attacks.

From the time of the German declaration of unlimited submarine warfare on January 31 of that year until the United States entered World War I on April 6, Hoover and the Relief had a desperate time. Nineteen of their cargoes were at sea, en route to Rotterdam, and only two reached that port before the required deadline. Two vessels were torpedoed, one with only a single survivor. The rest reached British ports. Their food cargoes began to deteriorate and 100,000 tons—a three weeks' food supply for the Belgians—had to be sold to the British.

Hoover notified the German government that the Relief would have to stop. The answer came on February 11, urging the commission to stay, with promises of protection and indemnity for the two ships sunk.

However, twelve more ships were lost, eight of these sunk by enemy submarines. Two other vessels narrowly escaped when fired on by submarines in the "safe" zone. The Dutch and Spanish Relief patrons protested to the Germans who declared the sinkings to be "mistakes" which would not be repeated.

Due to these losses and the food "stalled" in England, deliveries fell from 150,000 tons a month to under 25,000. Cardinal Mercier ordered special prayers throughout Belgium that the Relief should be sustained in its "fight for the lives of the people." The food supply was not restored until June, 1917.

Throughout World War I, the Hoovers' family life together was necessarily erratic. In the fall of 1914, after leaving the two boys in public school in Palo Alto under the watchful care of their professor neighbors at Stanford, Mrs. Hoover returned to London. Despite the dangers of the mine-laid North Sea, she accompanied her husband to Belgium on his second trip. That winter, they stayed at Red House, keeping it open as a general meeting place for their Belgian Relief associates. Mrs. Hoover was one of the leading organizers and the manager of the American Woman's Hospital at Paignton, England, which took care of thousands of British wounded men.

At the end of May, 1915, Mrs. Hoover went back to California to take care of their two sons. When her husband had to go to New York on Relief work in October of the same year, she and the boys rejoined him there and the whole family returned to England together.

Late that year, and on into 1916, Hoover wrestled with a divided mind, as to whether or not he should give up his engineering practice completely. The commission needed his undivided energies to such an extent that he was not giving any "adequate service" as an engineer and executive to his business concerns—even to those in London.

Due to wartime needs, tremendous business opportunities were opening up in connection with the raw material sources of the world. Hoover was in a position to build up an enormous fortune in view of his great knowledge of metal ores. To relinquish his engineering practice at that time meant the final sacrifice of his career. But for Hoover there was only one answer. He gave up fabulous wealth to serve his fellow man—not as a duty, but as a God-given privilege. To continue the Belgian Relief, Hoover resigned from every business connection except his directorship in the Burma Lead Mines.

Though her husband was often away, Mrs. Hoover remained at Red House with their sons. She continued her war work and the boys attended a small private school, acquiring a decided Oxford accent.

The Germans had begun bombing London from Zeppelins. One evening during a raid, a bomb exploded near Red House. Mr. and Mrs. Hoover rushed to the boys' room—and found their beds empty! After a frantic search of the house, Hoover finally located the boys on the roof. They were calmly watching the streaming searchlights and fighting planes. Their parents decided to join them—and saw a Zeppelin brought down in flames.

At dawn, the Hoovers went out in their car to search for the wreckage, heading for the spot where they thought the airship had gone down. Thanks to an understanding bobby, or London policeman, at the scene, both Herbert, Jr. and Allan acquired souvenirs of the dirigible which they cherished for many years.

Because of the raids and her husband's frequent trips to the Continent, Mrs. Hoover took the boys back to California to

resume their American schooling. This proved the last of the
happy times at Red House for the Hoover family and their
friends.

Many critical moments came up for the Relief, when its
very existence was at stake. In 1915, Hoover learned that he
had been accused by a discharged member of the commission
of violating the Logan Act in dealing directly with foreign
governments. He was informed that Senator Lodge was preparing an attack on him and the C.R.B. work as a violation of
the law and a "dangerous involvement" of the United States.
The maintenance of public goodwill and confidence in America, as well as around the globe, was the lifeblood of the effort
to save the Belgians and northern French. Unfavorable publicity would damage the Relief prestige and the flow of charitable gifts. Hoover sailed for the United States early in May.
With influential aid from Melville Stone, some Cabinet members and President Wilson, himself, the crisis was averted.
When Hoover went to see the Senator, the latter, he found, had
been "misinformed." On this trip, the Relief chairman visited
former President Theodore Roosevelt at Oyster Bay. He offered his aid in the situation, and became a loyal supporter of
Herbert Hoover.

One day in London, the Chief received a telegram from
Hugh Gibson, urging that he go to Brussels at once as disaster
confronted the C.R.B. The German General Staff at Charleville
had notified Vernon Kellogg, Relief liaison at headquarters
there, that the American C.R.B. staff was engaged in espionage
and demanded that the entire American personnel be removed
from Belgium and France. Hoover rushed to Brussels and
obtained a report from Colonel Marx, German liaison officer
at C.R.B. headquarters. One American of pro-German lean-
ings in the Rotterdam office had listened to offhand anti-
German remarks of C.R.B. men in Belgium and reported them
to the German Intelligence Service "with embroidery." Only
six other Americans were actually involved. This disaster was

ended by Hoover's returning the six men to America, while the
instigator was ordered to England, where he was arrested by
Scotland Yard and deported to the United States.

A great storm gathered over the 1916 surplus crops in the
German army zones of Belgium and France, as harvest time
approached. Under the C.R.B. agreements, when the German
army requisitioned and used farmers' surplus production in the
battle areas, the army was to replace the food from stocks in
Germany in an amount jointly agreed upon as fair by the army
and the C.R.B.

That summer, the German army's estimate of the amount
of food to be replaced to the commission from Germany
amounted to about $40,000,000 less in quantitative value than
the commission felt was correct, even allowing for produce
grown by Germans on the many abandoned farms. This dispute was aired in the Allied press. Hoover joined Dr. Kellogg
at Charleville but they were unable to resolve the matter with
the German quartermaster general. In the hope of making
better progress with the top officials in Berlin, it was agreed
with the general that a joint meeting with high government
representatives be held at the Esplanade Hotel in that city on
August 4.

Hoover and Kellogg kept the engagement at the hotel but
were not given the opportunity to present their case in person
to the Berlin officials. When the general and Major Von
Kessler, the liaison officer with the C.R.B., returned to the
hotel from the conference, the major announced the bad news.
There was to be no compromise on the food estimates. The
authorities had also discussed doing away with the commission
entirely. Most of them were in favor of this. Only Lewald had
spoken on behalf of the C.R.B.

Further conversation between the two Americans and the
two Germans disclosed that the general had been disturbed by
the publicity he had received in the neutral press for having
been responsible for the execution of Nurse Edith Cavell. He

said he had been "painted as a monster all over the world." As the Relief was apparently about to be abolished, Hoover decided on a last bold stroke. He made it clear to the general that ending the commission would mean death for millions of people, mostly children, and that, as the responsible official, the German officer would be pictured before the neutral world for this act as a "monster infinitely bigger and blacker." The general, softened perhaps by a personal tragedy he had suffered due to the war, or by the human appeal, gave in. He directed von Kessler to ask Lewald to take up the matter of the food estimates once more and settle it. A part reduction in the C.R.B. estimate was made to "save face," and Hoover and Kellogg left Berlin within the hour, lest the German army opponents force a change of terms.

The British growled at the compromise figures, but Lord Percy persuaded the military authorities to accept the new estimate. As it turned out, the C.R.B. received more food from the Germans than they, in turn, had been able to collect from the French farmers.

Hoover had many experiences in his travels for the Relief. He made forty crossings of the North Sea in all, to and from the Continent. The Dutch steamers, which made the trip from the Hook of Holland through mine-infested waters to England, were small and old. He was often seasick but he felt that this condition had one advantage—it made him "oblivious to danger."

Inspection search and delay at the various frontiers was reduced for Hoover and his associates by the use of special C.R.B. passports which he had arranged with British, Dutch and German authorities. This was accomplished on the basis of his pledge that C.R.B. officials would mind their own business. But the channel crossings and his trips on the uncertain Continental railways in wartime brought Hoover much enforced waiting about. To fill in the hours, in addition to reading, he wrote a narrative of his life up to that time for his two sons. He hoped they would follow his profession and become engineers, which they did.

On one North Sea crossing, Hoover read in a book by Andrew D. White, president of Cornell University, of his difficulties in reconstructing the objective story of the French Revolution, as so much of the "ephemera," or contemporary documents, had been destroyed. This complaint struck the initial mental spark that led to the establishment of the Hoover Institution on War, Revolution and Peace, at Stanford University. Hoover realized that he could be of unique help in documenting World War I, as he, probably alone of all Americans, could move freely across the frontiers of the combatants and visit the headquarters of the belligerents. With the aid of his Relief associates, he started collecting the primary source materials of mankind's first great total war. Grateful Belgians assisted in this invaluable work for posterity by smuggling furtively acquired German directives and underground publications to C.R.B. staff members.

Hoover's original project became known as "Operation Pack Rat," from a comment of Ray Lyman Wilbur, president of Stanford University. "Hoover is the greatest pack rat of all time," Wilbur said, "because whenever he leaves a ton of food, he picks up a pound of history."

In 1916, Herbert Hoover was invited to visit King Albert of the Belgians who was living at La Panne, a small beach resort. On the way there, Hoover experienced a German bombing attack in Boulogne. At La Panne, heavy shells, fired from the German front, whined over the royal cottage on the way to their objective, Dunkirk. The King had been urged to seek a safer refuge, but he insisted on living on Belgian soil. Albert asked Hoover anxiously all about the Relief and his people. He wished to bestow some decoration on the humanitarian, "just to assure you of our devotion," but he fully understood the American's democratic feeling in declining the proposed honor.

In September of that year, Hoover took the Dutch steamer at the Hook of Holland, on his way to England from Brussels. As required, he spent the night before departure on board, since the boat left at dawn. He was awakened at revolver point by a German marine. The steamer had been captured at daylight and taken into Zeebrugge Harbor, in occupied Belgium, where Hoover found it to be surrounded by German destroyers. An officer, on learning his identity, told him the ship would be allowed to proceed to England, after a search of passengers and mail. About thirty English passengers were taken off for internment. Five were civilians accompanied by their wives, and the wives were forcibly left on the boat. While waiting for the signal to depart, Hoover and an elderly Hollander watched the activities from an upper deck. There was a sudden explosion and the Hollander dropped at Hoover's feet. They were being bombed by a French plane, which had hit a barge fifty feet away on the first run. Splinters from the wrecked bow had slightly injured Hoover's companion. He, himself, suffered only a crick of the neck from his intense interest in watching the four further bomb runs of the plane. The steamer was not hit—but each time he expected the aim to improve!

The following January, 1917, Hoover took a steamer in Holland headed for Tilbury in England. On going aboard, he congratulated the steward on his escape from the sinking of the steamer *Queen* several days before. The Dutch kept only one boat in service at a time. As a vessel was lost, due to hitting an explosive mine or some other war accident, another was substituted and the surviving crewmen resumed their duties on the next boat. It was Hoover's custom to pay the steward for his meals and cabin at the end of the voyage. This time, when he was eating breakfast, the steward blurted out, "You must pay cash." Hoover protested that he had always paid generously, and that it hurt him to feel he had lost the steward's confidence.

"Well, ten passengers were drowned on the *Queen,* and they

owed me sixty-five guilders," was the steward's encouraging reply. "I can't take any more risks." Fortunately for Hoover's share in the channel-crossing risks, this proved to be his last return trip from Belgium during the war.

Early that year, he was notified by the British and French that they could continue their subsidies only a few months longer. Hoover went to New York to further negotiations for a loan on certain Belgian assets. The United States, he found, seemed headed for war.

In Washington, he called on Colonel Edward M. House, President Wilson's adviser, who had been helpful in C.R.B. problems. On the colonel's visits to London, Hoover had kept him informed on current political forces in the war. House asked the C.R.B. head about the possibilities for success of the President's renewed peace drive. Though pessimistic on the outcome, Hoover advised that Woodrow Wilson persevere in his efforts for a negotiated peace.

For many reasons, Hoover was opposed to the entry of the United States into the war. In the first place, he did not think America could change the political forces of Europe on a permanent basis. Then his Quaker training was naturally against war. He remembered, nevertheless, his militant Quaker uncle's precept, "Turn your other cheek once, but if he smites it, then punch him."

On the German declaration of unlimited submarine warfare at the end of January, 1917, the whole picture changed. As his country moved rapidly toward entering the war, Hoover was anxious to get back to Europe, to be on hand for trouble and to make plans for the Dutch and Spanish officials to carry on the C.R.B. if the United States did become involved. Passenger travel was suspended between North America and North Europe, but he finally secured passage on a Spanish boat for March 13.

While he was seeking passage, Hoover was called to Washington for conferences with Cabinet members on problems of war organization. At the President's request, he went to the White House to discuss the aid America could give the Allies in case of war and the important part food would play in the conflict—second only to military action. Wilson questioned Hoover closely on the war organization of economic matters in the various countries abroad and suggested that Hoover informally study the methods used on his return to Europe, in case the situation worsened. Secretary of the Interior Lane had already given Hoover a hint that he would be wanted in Washington if the country went to war.

On reaching Europe, Hoover found the Belgians were having a terrible time, due to the interruption of food deliveries caused by the German sinkings. He arranged that the neutral Dutch and Spanish patrons take over the Relief, if necessary.

On April 6, 1917, the day the United States declared war, Hoover received a message through Hugh Gibson, saying that the President wanted him to return to the United States to take charge of the food organization. He replied that he would need a few days to adjust the C.R.B. The American staff was withdrawn, and the Dutch and Spanish were installed inside Belgium. The commission continued as before outside the occupied land. As food organizer, Hoover was confident that he could solve the Belgian and northern French Relief problems.

Herbert Hoover has paid high tribute to the American volunteers who served with the C.R.B. One of them, Vernon Kellogg, wrote of his superior:

"Those of us who have lived through the difficult, the almost impossible days of Belgian relief . . . have come to an almost superstitious belief in his capacity to do anything possible to human power. . . . People sometimes ask me why Hoover has such a strong hold on his helpers. The men of C.R.B. know."

But his associates could not persuade Herbert Hoover to accept any share of the publicity rightfully due the successful pioneer of the first food administration in history of a whole nation. "Play up Belgian Relief," the Chief directed his press staff, "not Hoover."

A British journalist who worked under the Chief in the Relief later described him as having "an utter absence of 'side,' coupled with a very kindly and a completely unassuming manner."

When Hoover was in Brussels he tried to keep his presence quiet, but the news spread. To express their gratitude, on one occasion Belgians came to the legation door, singly or in twos, day after day, and left their cards. The tokens ranged from scraps of butcher paper with names scrawled on them to finely embossed calling cards. These soon mounted up in overflowing piles. As Herbert Hoover fingered these heart-warming mementos, he was filled with as much appreciation as he had felt when the Silver Medal was awarded him by the King and Queen of Belgium.

Herbert Hoover had emerged on the world scene—as a humanitarian.

"Food
Will Win
the War"

CHAPTER 9

Herbert Hoover arrived back in Washington on May 4, 1917. He reported to the President very promptly and Wilson formally requested him to organize food for winning the war. He accepted at once, with the understanding that he also continue as head of the Belgian Relief and that he serve without pay. He believed the war team post would convey more moral leadership if he were a volunteer.

At this meeting with the President, Hoover also delivered two urgent messages which he had brought from Admiral Sims in London. The first asked that more destroyers be sent abroad and that many more be built to oppose the enemy submarines. In the second, the admiral begged Wilson to demand that the British set up a convoying system across the Atlantic. Unless this was done, the Navy expert warned that Allied merchant shipping would be done for before the end of the year, at the current rate of sinkings—and the war would be lost.

As Hoover had told President Wilson a couple of months earlier, food was second only to military action in importance during wartime. Now he had his chance to mobilize his country's food resources. Within four days, the United States Food Administration was underway.

President Wilson favored boards and commissions to run all the new war agencies. Hoover had seen many such Allied organizations fail, dating back to the outbreak of hostilities in 1914. He was convinced that the Food Administration should be directed by a single executive head whose authority must cover every phase "from the soil to the stomach." He felt, too, that President Wilson had been influenced by the newspaper headlines dubbing him "Food Czar" and "Food Dictator" that had marked his arrival in Washington from abroad. The President, he knew, was also disturbed by possible conflict with the Department of Agriculture. Hoover assured Wilson that the Agriculture Secretary would agree to his plan, while pointing out that a division of authority, such as the President advocated, had caused friction, waste and "great failure" in every European country at war.

Hoover insisted that an individual could inspire a wealth of voluntary action which no impersonal board could secure. Voluntary methods, too, provided a guard against "Prussianizing" or despotic military rule of the country. He finally argued Wilson out of the board idea. His suggestion of the designation "Administrator" for his post was perhaps the deciding factor in the President's reluctant agreement.

In a few days, after he came to the capital, Hoover had recruited the men and women needed to start the organization. Many C.R.B. men joined. To meet the crises which arose daily, Hoover secured the best men and women with "know how," then told them to go ahead and solve the problems. Except for the clerical staff and accountants, the workers were all volunteers.

In describing how Hoover accomplished his great tasks of

creation and management in the war period, Will Irwin has written, "He believes that most able men are all-around men; given a chance, they will generate suggestions beyond the borders of their nominal jobs. Also, he knows how to delegate authority. On appointing a subordinate, Hoover gives him the general idea, makes him responsible for results, and, so far as possible, lets him alone."

Washington was, of course, jammed with people employed by the war agencies. The Food Administration started out in the Willard Hotel, then moved to a few rooms in the Interior Department. Next they took over an old hotel. The final move was to a building completed for the agency in ninety days through the efforts of General Kilpatrick. This wallboard structure accommodated an office force of two or three thousand. It was "abominably cold" in winter and hot in summer. But, happily, the enthusiasm of the occupants survived the temperature!

Unfortunately, however, Hoover was handicapped by the partial crop failures of 1916 and 1917 in this country. His problem was to "squeeze out" enough exports from the United States, Canada and the West Indies to relieve the large food deficits of the Allies and certain important and needy neutrals, all with the least possible disturbance to the American economy. Lack of shipping facilities prevented transportation of the food that was available in more distant parts of the world.

Ultimate success rested as much on increased production as on reduced consumption through voluntary food-saving measures. Hoover stimulated farm production by maintaining incentive prices at farm level in critical items such as breadstuffs, meats and fats, and extending limited price guarantees to farmers on selling their produce, as well as by guarding the farm labor force and machinery supplies—and appealing to the farmers' patriotism for superior efforts.

Amicable relations with the Department of Agriculture were readily established, and Secretary Houston organized the

Farmers' War Committee for the Food Administrator. Hoover selected the members for Wilson's Advisory Committee of Consumers, headed by Dr. Harry Garfield, president of Williams College. These committees fixed the stabilized price for wheat at $2.20 a bushel. President Wilson declared that "Mr. Hoover, at his (Hoover's) express wish, has taken no part in the deliberations" nor even "intimated an opinion" on the price figure. Later guarantees and prices were set for hogs, beans, peas and sugar.

Worried about the effect of the draft on the farm labor manpower, Hoover called on General Enoch Crowder, the draft head.

"Agriculture is really a munitions industry," Hoover began to explain. "The outcome of the war and the peace afterward may depend upon what we can produce, as well as what we can save."

"My boy, I know all that." The general cut him short. "I would even put it stronger than you do. You must have every needed boy on the farms. Leave it to me."

With the general's fine co-operation, in addition to harder work on the part of the older people and enthusiastic help from boys and girls of all ages, sufficient manpower was provided for sufficient farm production.

Hoover opposed rationing for Americans, to eliminate waste and reduce food consumption. Among other reasons, he felt this couldn't be done without the general requisitioning of all farm produce, since farmers needed no ticket to obtain essential food. In stimulating them to increase their output and enlisting their wives to save food, Hoover felt there was more to be gained than by irritating the farmers with tickets. From his European experience, the Food Administrator realized that issuing ration cards for staples to a hundred million Americans would involve a stupendous bureaucracy at an enormous expense, in addition to being an unneeded restriction upon the American individual rights.

He therefore organized farmers, housewives, owners of public eating places and distribution trades on a voluntary basis for conservation as a patriotic service. Almost all Americans can be led to make great sacrifices, Hoover knew. Under his inspired leadership, the program worked with great success.

To restrain prices, prevent profiteering and "black markets," Hoover employed a new method of stabilizing prices of raw food materials at the market point nearest to the farmer. This avoided retail ceiling prices, which Hoover had found to work unsatisfactorily in Europe to keep consumer costs down. In the war years prior to the United States' entry into the conflict, food prices had risen over 82 per cent in this country, due to Allied buying and the lack of war-emergency American government restraints. A continued rise threatened all economic stability—and survival.

To stabilize prices at farm level, the Food Administration Grain Corporation was created, under Hoover as chairman and Julius H. Barnes as president, with the sole right to purchase wheat—and later beans and peas—in the primary markets. A working capital of $150,000,000 was secured from Congress. Then the Sugar Equalization Board, headed by Hoover, was formed to buy the entire yearly crop of American, West Indian and Philippine sugar for resale to processors and exporters.

Hoover presented the sugar plan to Wilson on a single sheet of paper. After having decided on policy, Wilson was characteristically indifferent to detail. He read the plan, initialed it, "Approved W. W." and handed the paper back to Hoover without comment.

"The White House should have a copy," Hoover suggested, "since it involves billions of dollars."

Wilson grinned. "Would that get any more sugar?" he jokingly asked his highly trusted Food Administrator.

The purchase of all Army, Navy and Allies food supplies was channeled through Hoover or carried out with his approval through a deputy. To make certain that all the food was edible, he extended his agency's own inspection service to every item of military and civilian food not included under the check customarily made by the Department of Agriculture on food processing. He never had a complaint!

To implement price stabilization, the food organization controlled export and import licenses, for both Allies and neutrals. The food commodity exchanges were also under Hoover's regulation, to guard against speculation for hoarding but not to interfere with any regular trading.

"Ninety-nine per cent of American business," Hoover reported afterward to the President, "gave hearty co-operation." Restraints for those who did not co-operate in the price and distribution controls were set up voluntarily by the trades, themselves. Hoover arranged that each trade group form war committees, to cover processing, wholesaling and retailing and report any violations which they were unable to correct themselves. He assured the group representatives that these were strictly war measures, planned to end promptly with the conflict, without any lasting change to commerce and industry. The purpose was to win the war, not to alter the economic system of the United States. The Attorney General ruled that, as long as the war committees were acting for the Food Administration, any collective moves would not be regarded as Anti-Trust Act violations. The great majority in the trades were intensely concerned about the honor of their groups in the war effort, and even more anxious when given responsibility for the participation of their trades. They did an amazing job of self-discipline. In fact, at times the committees were felt to be too hard on violators, and Hoover's office had to intervene.

The many state and local Food Administration branches and the Washington enforcement division checked controls too, but the main purpose of Hoover's plan was to give responsibility to the trades and avoid a huge bureaucracy of unskilled persons. His plan succeeded. Many great sacrifices were made by all concerned in carrying out the national aims. Some few resisted the emergency measures, however. On one occasion, Hoover said, in a public statement to the press:

> One looming shadow of this war is its drift toward social disruption. We shall surely drift to that rocky coast unless we can prove the economic soundness and willingness to public service of our commercial institutions. With the gigantic sacrifice of life the world is demanding sacrifice in service.

On one occasion, due to difficulties arising from food policies, Hoover was attacked in the Senate. He and other associates were unwarrantedly charged with grafting money from the Belgian Relief. John White met this by a smashing reply in the press, disclosing that, from its start, the Relief had appointed an independent firm of auditors to check all accounts.

If the voluntary system of price and distribution control failed at any point, Hoover went to Congress to obtain the needed legal powers. He conferred with individual members and committees. It was his first close contact with a legislative body. He encountered some strong opposition but, under the leadership of Congressman Lever and Senator Simmons, the Food Administration legislation was finally "nursed" through. This covered the whole agency program.

The penalties—which Hoover considered too strong— were used only in a few cases of repeated willfulness. Mistakes and mild offenses were settled by donations to the Red Cross.

Great success in conservation and elimination of food waste came from enlisting housewives and the other groups closely concerned as "members" of the Food Administration. Each member signed a rules pledge and received a certificate. The rules were simple and encouraged use of substitutes for critical household items.

Twenty million members signed up. Food saving became a kind of national game. War gardens sprouted in season, and wheatless, meatless days were observed with spirit. Victory Bread was popular and "Serve just enough!" was admonished across the land at meal times. At one time, the people were over responsive when Hoover asked for a special saving of fats and butter. They saved so much that the industry was upset, the Allies were flooded and Hoover beat a retreat on that front!

To obtain the needed local co-operation in meeting the food problem in a country so large and so accustomed to local government, Hoover decided on intense decentralization. In line with this, state, county and municipal food administrators were set up to do the job of promoting conservation, production and reporting shortages and serious violations of the rules to Washington. Those appointed were leading men and women in their communities, who served as volunteers.

At the outset of the Food Administration, President Wilson had issued a statement on May 19, 1917, stressing the need for the public's voluntary co-operation and asserting that there need be no fear of a permanent bureaucracy, since the agency would be composed mostly of volunteers, nor was there any risk of legal and voluntary control of consumption, once the war was over. Hoover amplified the President's message in a press release which concluded:

> The whole foundation of democracy lies in the individual initiative of its people and their willingness to serve the interests of the Nation with complete self-effacement in the time of emergency. I hold that Democracy can yield to discipline and that we can solve this food problem for our own people and for our allies largely by voluntary action.

In World War II, the current administration met the country's food problems on a different basis, with mandatory food rationing and retail ceiling price controls, which were followed by all patriotic citizens. This method of handling the distribution of food supplies incurred a great deal of criticism and was, of course, extremely costly in comparison with Hoover's program.

In August, Wilson consulted Hoover about the confused coal and oil situation which the Food Administration and the Department of the Interior were hopelessly trying to correct with "co-ordinators." Hoover restated the need for a single-headed organization and suggested that the President appoint his old friend, Dr. Harry A. Garfield, as Fuel Administrator. Wilson finally sacrificed the board idea on the "altar of progress." Hoover secured Walter Hope, a lawyer, and Mark Requa, an oil engineer, from his staff and Henry Taylor, a coal man, to aid Garfield; and a successful fuel agency, similar to the Food Administration, was soon established.

Should a large American army be sent to Europe? Indecision on this major military strategy plagued the Allied governments during the last half of 1917 and on into the next spring. The British and French opposed the plan, as they believed the war could be carried on with the help of the American Fleet, the Air Force, engineers and ample amounts of munitions and food. General Pershing and the American military insisted that the war could not be ended quickly without sending large numbers of ground troops abroad. It was not possible to do this without absolute assurance from the British and French that they would provide ships for the transport of troops and supplies.

To these Allies, supplying all this tonnage meant giving up the long voyages to distant parts of the world for food and a resulting dependency for their sustenance on the United States and Canada. This involved great loss of foreign trade, too. In addition, they were afraid that America could not produce the necessary supplies. There was some justification in the latter view, due to the low prewar exports and the recent partial crop failures.

Moreover, the Allies were haunted by the German submarine sinking of so many available merchant ships. In April,

1917, more than 850,000 tons were sunk. Losses ran to over 500,000 tons of shipping monthly until August of that year, when the British finally adopted Admiral Sims' plea for Atlantic convoys. By November, losses were held to under 300,000 tons.

Hoover repeatedly advised President Wilson and General Pershing that, unless the British and French provided adequate protected troop transport facilities, it would be dangerous to send a huge army to Europe. From the response of the American people on food conservation and from the efforts of the farmers in production, Hoover was confident that the food needs of the Allies could be supplied, even with the meager 1917 crops and a growing surplus obtained from the 1918 harvests.

General Pershing was in accord with Hoover's solution of the necessary means to send a large expeditionary force across the Atlantic. He urged the Allies to make the changes the Food Administrator suggested and thus be able to give him the required ships. The British war leaders would not accept the estimates of sufficient food available, and the British Cabinet "flatly" announced in a mid-October dispatch that they would not furnish any considerable tonnage to transport American troops.

Hoover felt that the war would not be won by the food blockade, which had its impact on the enemy women and children, but by the blockade on military supplies and by military action. In addition, he was convinced that civilization could not be rebuilt with security on "stunted minds and deformed bodies" in the next generation. But his plan to send extra food, under proper neutral controls, to children and the weaker women in Germany was far from acceptable to the Allies.

On the other hand, to tighten the Allied naval blockade, Hoover was handed the problem of controlling the food supplies sold to Germany by the surrounding neutrals. By using food to make friends, he achieved the co-operation of the six small neutral nations in stopping leaks of meats and fats to the enemy. American relations with the neutral world were greatly improved under Hoover's policies.

On her husband's return from Europe in May, 1917, Mrs. Hoover had met him at the boat. In Washington, she located a furnished house which proved large enough to take care of forty leading staff members of the Food Administration until they found other quarters. Then she rented the Adams house on Massachusetts Avenue for her family. When it was available, she brought the boys, then fourteen and ten, on from California. Herbert Hoover had seen his sons for less than six months altogether during the three preceding war years.

The boys went to the Friends' School. In summer, Sunday picnics were planned at suitable brooks around Washington with other families of the Food Administration. Lunches were cooked over campfires and the grownups joined the children in building dams and canals in the streams. These resulted in waterfalls and pools, with water wheels and boats. In winter, expeditions were made to good snow fields or skating ponds.

The Hoovers often had guests at dinner. They were mostly staff members or people from other government agencies who were being consulted on common problems. It was also Herbert Hoover's duty to entertain visiting delegations from abroad. Marshal Joffre, Arthur Balfour, Jan Paderewski, Thomas Masaryk, Lord Reading and Fridtjof Nansen were some of the visitors who met American officials at the Hoovers' gracious, hospitable home for off-the-record talks. If social activity, "with a Big S," was current in Washington, the Hoovers were not concerned.

Under the leadership of Mrs. Hoover and other staff officials' wives, a Food Administration Girls' Club was organized where many of the women employees lived. Rooms and board elsewhere were provided for the remainder. The group of wives insisted that a large cafeteria was needed in the new Food Administration building. They ran this so well that they were nearly swamped at mealtimes by employees from other departments. When the serious flu epidemic struck in the fall of 1918, Mrs. Hoover and her associates arranged a special service of care for the sick Food Administration employees besides doing their share for the city in the flu crisis.

Hoover, himself, worked at a terrific pace, which often wore out associates ten or fifteen years younger. "Where he gets that inner strength," they said, "Heaven only knows!" Lewis Strauss told a story of his Chief's vitality. The two men had started work at seven-thirty in the morning and finished exactly twelve hours later. Strauss, exhausted, had a quick dinner and fell into bed. When he reached his office the next day, he found his desk had been unlocked and rifled of certain important, confidential papers. He was about to telephone the Secret Service when Hoover came in.

"I picked the lock of your desk after dinner last night," he remarked. "Needed some of those papers."

Hoover had worked until about one o'clock himself—but had not wished to disturb his secretary. "Fresh and bright-eyed," he plunged into the job again early the next morning.

During the first six months of America's part in World War I, the government "broke out with a rash of boards, commissions, and committees." For some time, the Food Administration stood alone—unencumbered by divided authority. By degrees, however, many of the other war agencies fell into disputes and "muddled" action. Some friction and jealousy developed between them and the prewar departments. One by one, single administrators were appointed to run the boards.

Building up teamwork among all the war agencies was an urgent, yet difficult matter. Based on his experience with all the warring European governments and, more recently, the involved situation in the United States, Hoover prepared a memorandum advocating a War Cabinet, to be made up of the heads of the permanent government departments concerned with war, the Secretaries of State, War, Navy and the Treasury, combined with the heads of the Munitions, Food, Fuel, Shipping, Railways and War Trade Administrations. He presented the recommendations to Dr. Garfield in the belief that Garfield could succeed in convincing President Wilson of the wisdom of this move, since he himself had failed to do so. Garfield was successful. The first meeting was called on March 20, 1918, and regular meetings were held thereafter. The group was known as the "War Council." This was the direct antecedent of the National Security Council, set up in World War II as a permanent government agency. In addition to the regular business of the advisory body, President Wilson brought more and more major military and international problems before the meetings.

The deteriorating military situation in Europe forced the British to change their view about transporting an American army. After compelling Bolshevik Russia to make peace on March 3, 1918, the Germans concentrated their armies on the Western Front. In late March, they smashed the British Fifth Army and broke through the battle lines. A minor disaster was the resulting loss of 100,000 tons of Allied food.

News of the German break-through brought to Hoover his "lowest spiritual point" during the American war years. From that day on, the members of his agency knew their job was cut out for them. With a tremendous effort, the food loss was replaced in thirty days.

The major result of the disaster was the realization by the British and French that the large American Expeditionary Force, upon which General Pershing insisted, was essential. At the time, there were less than 200,000 American combat troops in Europe. The convoy system had reduced the terror of the submarine. Of vital weight in the decisions was the Food Administration's steady performance in producing large shipments from a "statistically empty barrel."

Every day, Hoover anxiously pored over the information

on expanded farm production and the figures on food conservation.

As if he didn't have problems enough, a crisis—stemming from the American government—arose over C.R.B. transportation which threatened the very existence of the Belgian Relief! In the shipping shortage, the American military authorities decided that the 300,000 tonnage being used by the C.R.B. could be transferred to their use. Hoover suddenly "woke up" to the fact that they had the backing of their British and French colleagues and were on the verge of action to obtain use of the ships. Hoover protested to President Wilson. News of his protest was sent to Prime Ministers Lloyd George and Clemenceau, through the London and Paris offices of the Relief. The two Prime Ministers immediately sent word to Wilson that they did not wish the C.R.B. interfered with.

The problem of what to do about Russia caused dissension among the Allies. Because of his experience in the former empire, Hoover was consulted by President Wilson about an Allied proposal that Japanese troops be sent into Siberia. He was later asked about heading a food mission to Russia. He pointed out that it would not be logical to distribute food and supplies on the Western front while sending American troops to the Bolsheviks' Eastern front.

Early in July, 1918, Hoover brought before Wilson a need for tax action by Congress. In order to get high-cost manufacturers of food and other war supplies into full production, prices and margins had to be set at a level which resulted in very high profits to low-cost producers. Legislation was planned, with the aid of Senator Simmons, and a tax was enacted.

With summer, an abundant crop and the enormous savings of the "spiritually mobilized people" brought food relief. Ships remained the problem, however.

On July 11, Hoover sailed for Europe, to confer with the

prime ministers, food administrators and military authorities of Britain, France and Italy. Soon after his arrival, an Allied Food Council was set up, with Hoover as chairman. A re-survey of Allied and neutral food needs for the coming year was quickly completed, together with an estimate of available food sources and shipping. Their minimum figure for Allied civilians, including clothing and medical supplies, was 2,000,-000 tons a month.

General Pershing intervened. A wide-scale assault was planned on the Front in September and he cut the Food Council figures for imported civilian supplies by 800,000 tons for the next four months. This meant that the Allies would overdraw on the summer crops and their edible animals and a dangerous shortage would develop in the spring months of the following year. When the battle began, shipping space was cut to 700,000 tons.

Pershing was confident. Hoover could only "ruminate" that the military would learn something very tragic about civilian populations short of food—if the fall attack failed. He experienced a sinking sensation at the thought that lack of supplies might mean defeat, despite the brave assertions of all the American posters—"Food Will Win the War."

The American victories saved the situation. Germany asked for a truce on October 6, 1918. Five weeks later, the Armistice stopped the war.

During the operation of Hoover's agency, food exports from America, mostly to the Allies, were almost trebled. Adequate sustenance was provided to both the Allies and friendly neutrals—about 220,000,000 people. Transactions amounting to over $10,000,000,000 capably were handled with no charges of wrongdoing—not even a "ten-cent loophole" for criticism or suspicion. The total working capital of $155,000,000 was returned to the United States Treasury. Profits from trading, mostly with neutrals, amounted to over $98,000,000. Total overhead costs, including buildings and later European relief-administration expense, were less than $8,000,000. The Food Administration not only cost the American people nothing but it brought $90,000,000 of surplus to the Treasury.

Hoover paid great tribute to the loyalty and capacity of the men and women who composed the Food Administration. They became his lifelong friends—steadfast in times of defeat and grief.

In summing up the operations, Hoover declared that the assumption by the government of great economic powers was a necessity of war. Evil consequences therefrom were avoided by the "voluntary character of our staff and the building of our control measures through co-operation of the trades, together with our quick dissolution of them after the war."

This voluntary program, known as "Hoover measures," brought high esteem to its organizer, in contrast to the unpopularity incurred by European food controllers, due to their drastic programs. A new verb, meaning to conserve, became a household word—"to Hooverize."

Hoover's assurance that America could provide sufficient food to the Allies—successfully carried out—was his part in the victorious strategy of World War I. His share in the victory as Food Administrator was the reason for General Pershing's inscribing a note to him:

"For Herbert Hoover, whose contribution to the success of the Allied cause can hardly be overestimated."

"Food
Regulator
of the
World"

CHAPTER 10

F rom the day in October, 1918,
when the new German government asked for an Armistice,
Hoover and his associates started to adjust their food policies
onto a postwar basis—to meet the gigantic famine which he
had long been sure would inevitably follow the war.

On November 7, President Wilson requested Hoover to
transform the Food Administration into a new agency for the
relief and reconstruction of Europe. In the President's words,
"This service is second only to the mission of our Army in
Europe."

Herbert Hoover was faced with the problem of providing
or co-ordinating food, medical and clothing supplies for thirty-
two nations with a total population of about 400,000,000 per-

Top: Herbert Hoover at the age of five with his brother, Theodore. *Bottom:* Hoover's birthplace at West Branch, Iowa. This has now been restored to its original size and is a national shrine. A museum to house the former President's papers, documents, books and mementos has been built nearby.

Top: Hoover's geology class at Stanford University. He is second from the left. *Bottom:* Stanford football team, 1894, showing Hoover, as financial manager, not in uniform.

Top: Herbert Hoover in Western Australia. *Bottom:* Sons of Gwalia Mine at Mount Leonora, Western Australia. showing the plant installed by Hoover in 1898.

Courtesy Hoover Institution on War, Revolution and Peace

Mrs. Hoover in the White House

Herbert Hoover delivering his Inaugural Address

Former President Hoover with his two sons, Herbert, Jr., and Allan

Top: Herbert Hoover with Polish children in Warsaw, in 1946. (*Courtesy United Press International and Perrin C. Galpin.*) *Bottom:* Admiring members of Boys' Clubs of America surround former President Hoover, Chairman of the Board since 1936. (*Courtesy Boys' Clubs of America.*)

Top: President Eisenhower shakes hands with former President Hoover White House portico, July 21, 1953, after luncheon meeting on plans for partisan commission to study government operation. The former Presid became head of this second Hoover Commission. The work of the Commiss ended two years later with a Hoover report on water resources which urg drastic curtailment of federal power development and more opportunity private utilities. (*Courtesy Wide World Photos.*) *Bottom:* Former Presid Hoover is met by Prince Albert on arrival in Belgium, July 3, 1958, to repres President Eisenhower at Brussels World Fair. In Belgium July 5 was proclaim Herbert Hoover Day. (*Courtesy Anvers Presse.*)

sons—half of whom were short of supplies and the other half suffering from acute famine—while all were easy prey to pestilence. It was also his job to bridge over European economy until the various countries could resume production and support themselves. A break in the United States wartime guaranteed farm prices must also be avoided until the guarantees expired.

At some pre-Armistice meetings, certain Allied and American officials in London had planned "complete world controls" of the earth's economic life for some years to come. With the President's approval, Hoover cabled to these officials that the Americans considered themselves trustees of all their surplus production to benefit the "most necessitous and the most deserving—," and that the United States could not enter into any agreement by which control was lost over its postwar exports. In addition, no extension of any wartime functions of the Inter-Allied councils could be considered. In another message, he cautioned that, while co-operation would continue in existing Inter-Allied economic bodies, these bodies should not assume any permanent role in postwar world rehabilitation. Before the Peace Conference convened, all wartime restrictions on United States economic power must be completely lifted.

To speed food to Europe, Hoover arranged that the troop ships going over to bring our men back home carry supplies on their eastward crossings. The Grain Corporation was empowered to function abroad and assigned to keep the accounts with all the nations involved. The large surplus of army food and clothing in France was handed over to Hoover to distribute and the Navy agreed to set up organizations to help with supplies and relief problems in general at ports where needed.

Edgar Rickard was put in charge of the Food Administration in Washington. All control measures, except those affecting the guarantees to farmers, were dissolved at once and the staff was reduced. State and local units were disbanded rapidly.

Soon after the Armistice, Hoover arrived in London with his advisers, Alonzo Taylor and Robert A. Taft, Julius Barnes, who was the president of the Grain Corporation, and Lewis Strauss, secretary to the Chief. The glow of victory was starting to fade as the world began to survey the wreckage left by the first total war in history and especially to count the tremendous cost in human life.

Within a month, revolutions in enemy and liberated countries threw out the old leaders. Constitutional governments were adopted, with guarantees of personal liberty. Even as the world took the first steps toward recovery, the memory of the recent indescribable sufferings and the countries that had caused them surged back. Hate colored the demands for punishment and reparations.

Soon a growing fear of famine and pestilence enveloped Europe, with the realization that starvation would probably force the weak new governments of Central and Eastern Europe into anarchy. Then a far greater menace to liberty threatened—Communism, which had captured Russia. With Czarist gold, its agents fostered revolution in Europe and parts of Asia. Among starving peoples, the "infectious poison" spread like wildfire. Defeat of all for which America had fought loomed on the horizon.

When Hoover met with the Allied ministers, he soon discovered that they were still intent on the pooling of all Allied and American economic power, which was to continue long after the Peace. This pool was to be managed by a council of Britain, France, Italy and the United States, in which the latter would have only one vote, although contributing most of the resources. The ministers were also determined to reduce American food prices and to keep the blockade on the enemy countries, as well as on the neutrals and the liberated areas.

On being advised of the situation, President Wilson transmitted a plan for a single-headed administration of relief and rehabilitation, which would have an advisory committee representing the Allies, but would maintain the identity of the United States and control of all American resources. This plan was strongly opposed by the Allies, particularly by the British.

Hoover suggested that each of the four nations declare what resources it would contribute and that each should participate in the management in proportion to its contribution. After many wearing conferences, no progress was made. In a note to the President's special adviser, Colonel House, Hoover recommended that Wilson propose that the American government take independent action on its humanitarian mission immediately and invite the Allies to co-operate.

The terrible sufferings of the Allies, their tremendous economic problems and their animosity toward the enemy were all fully realized—but starvation does not wait.

Hoover opened offices in Paris on his actual authority, as United States Food Administrator, of representing the American people in this—their second intervention in Europe. He still held his jobs as chairman of the grain and sugar agencies and head of the Belgian Relief. The War and Navy Departments extended their services and the Secretary of the Treasury, Carter Glass, agreed to establish credits for the Allies, including declared new allies in liberated areas, in order to enable them to pay for supplies and transportation. Hoover thus had command of credit, food and some transportation with which to fight famine in Europe.

By mid-December, more than a hundred cargoes of food were arriving in Europe or on the seas. Admiral William S. Benson agreed with Hoover that the blockade on liberated countries, and even on neutrals, should be ignored. "Let me know if anyone tries to stop an American ship on these missions," was the admiral's forthright answer.

With careful distribution, these cargoes tided the liberated countries over until the organization of relief was in full operation. To meet the need in those liberated countries which could not qualify as allies for aid under the existing law, Congress provided an appropriation of $100,000,000 to be administered by Hoover under the American Relief Administration created to handle this grant separately. The blockade prevented supplying food to enemy countries, except for emergency supplies sent to Austria. The neutrals managed mostly on rations already allowed through the blockade—for the time being.

The gigantic problem of alleviating hunger, facing Hoover and his associates in the different countries, included not only food and other needed supplies but also currency, credit, coal, the reconstruction of ports and railways and communications. In addition, the job involved the "stiffening" of weak governments, the renewing of industry and employment and the rebuilding of economic departments and food administrations. In the midst of political chaos, it was up to his organization to see that food reached the people equitably and in sufficient quantity to save Europe from starvation and pestilence.

Hoover brought a few key men from Washington. He called former C.R.B. men from military and naval service and enlisted other personnel from the armed forces in Europe. With General Pershing's willing assistance, about 2,500 officers and men were detailed from the Army and Navy or were recruited from among those recently discharged.

The top Allied military men asked Pershing what Herbert Hoover's functions were. The general's reply to this question was, "Mr. Hoover is the food regulator of the world."

He quoted this in a letter to Hoover, then continued, "By this I mean to express my very complete appreciation of the enormous task that has fallen to your lot. . . . I shall always be ready to assist in any way possible."

Hugh Gibson, then First Secretary of the London Embassy, was appointed liaison officer with all the Allied foreign offices with which the relief had to deal.

An apartment house on the Avenue Montaigne, in Paris,

was rented for the organization offices. All overhead and travel expenses were paid by the United States Food Administration. Most of the civilian staff served without salary, on modest expense accounts. In addition to their service pay, the army and navy men received only travel money. Herbert Hoover, as was his practice, took no salary and paid all his own expenses.

As Hoover wished to live with his staff, some of them joined with him in renting a large house on Rue de Lubeck at their own expense. It was a little congested at times—with only four baths to thirty men! An army private who had worked for a former neighbor of Hoover's was installed to do odd jobs about the house. Hoover began to notice other privates and even sergeants around the place. The first private had had sixteen army friends transferred to work in the household on the grounds that "Mr. Hoover wanted them." But he had exercised some care in his selection—included were a tailor, a clothes cleaner, a bootblack, chauffeurs, assistant cooks and watchmen!

American missions of relief and economic specialists were dispatched into all the enemy and liberated countries, and representatives were sent to the neutrals. Staff and local office expenses were paid by the countries concerned. Some members of each group spoke the language of the country to which they were assigned. Their job was to establish the machinery of economic rehabilitation. They supervised the food distribution and saw that those with resources paid for their supplies. And they enjoyed their duties.

The work of these Americans displayed the "power of the American way of life." Many determined the fate of hundreds of thousands, always to the benefit of the hungry peoples. They demonstrated that the United States was primarily interested in humanitarian objectives—by pouring out millions in compassion.

After President Wilson arrived in Paris on December 15,

1918, he settled Hoover's status beyond any shadow of doubt. The Allied prime ministers agreed to his appointment as sole Director of the Relief and Rehabilitation of Europe, to be directly responsible to President Wilson, Prime Minister Lloyd George, Premier Clemenceau and Premier Orlando, known as the "Big Four." The advisory council proposal was approved as well. The major relief work, however, continued, as before, under Hoover as United States Food Administrator.

When the council convened, the pooling plan was immediately revived in the form of an international agreement which Hoover did not sign. He found that the council setup was a futile "chatterbox," and, on his recommendation, the group was dissolved by the Big Four in February, 1919. A purely co-ordinating agency, known as the Supreme Economic Council, was then established by a resolution written on the spot by Hoover in less than fifty words.

The relief worked hard to sustain the weak representative governments by providing them with food and supplies. Such weapons, Hoover felt, could do more than arms to preserve and strengthen the new parliamentary governments, in the current situation. It was a desperate race against time. Added to all the difficulties was the problem of Communism which made such progress among the hungry peoples that its adherents were able to take over a dozen large cities at different times and one central European country, Hungary.

During the period of the relief—October 1918 to September 1919—Hoover's organization handled over 27,000,000 tons of overseas supplies, as well as hundreds of thousands of tons in eastern European interchanges of vital commodities, mostly by barter. Financial operations, amounting to over $4,000,000,000, were handled by a staff of 4,000 Americans and a multitude of workers within the nations themselves. These operations were mostly financed by loans from the United States to European countries, including the Allies, of more than $3,200,000,000. Less than 6 per cent of this immense sum was ever paid back. The sale of supplies brought in more than $570,000,000. Over $50,000,000 was given in charity.

Other nations, joining with the United States, provided over 4 per cent of the tonnage and about 5 per cent of the credit. Most of these loans were later collected by these countries.

Beyond technical matters, Hoover's organization did not enter into agreements with the governments aided by the relief, except with enemy countries. As long as they received co-operation from a nation, the Americans did the best they could for its people. If co-operation was withheld, the relief was free to pull out. In this way, control over the distribution of supplies was retained.

The co-ordination of supplies in the world shortage proved a "shifting picture puzzle." Hoover was able to check on Allied food movements, not reported to him or under his control, through the American consular staff all over the world. The neutrals co-operated fully and often loaned supplies for emergencies on promise of future replacement in kind.

Solution of the supply problems in the liberated and enemy countries, Hoover found, was entirely up to him and his relief organization. On his skill and courage rested the future of millions of people.

Telegraph and telephone communications between Allied and enemy areas were all but impossible during the Armistice. A message sent from Paris to Warsaw sometimes took a week. At Hoover's request, Admiral Benson solved this difficulty by stationing an American destroyer or cruiser, equipped with a wireless, in all the important European ports. He established wireless offices for the relief in Berlin, Vienna and other key places. In addition to providing instant communication with the European capitals and ports, these stations handled the messages to the United States. In February, 1919, another system had to be contrived, as the Navy wished to withdraw most of its communication vessels.

Under the direction of Major Frank Fay, of the Army Signal Corps, a special telegraph system was set up for the organization. Twenty-six Allied, neutral, liberated and enemy governments assigned to Hoover telegraph circuits between capitals, ports and other important points. These were to be operated by American soldiers. To satisfy censorship, Hoover pledged that all messages would be uncoded and could be read by the various officials. All governments co-operated except France, which insisted that the regular system be used across the French frontier. Since this setup then involved delay, General Pershing had a line built from the offices in Paris to his headquarters in France, which had a direct line to Cologne.

The non-coding provision resulted in a lot of trouble. Hoover's representatives had to send him strictly confidential messages from government officials all over Europe and to give "candid opinions" on such officials. This presented a big problem. As an example, wires from Helsingfors to Paris passed through seven countries whose authorities could read every word. The relief men found a way out of this predicament themselves—by deliberate use of American slang terms and brief descriptions for names. Two European statesmen became "Mutt and Jeff," presumably due to their relative heights, and an American minister "Casey," because of his ability at bat. Current and revived slang, and phrases drawn from the popular terminology of baseball, football, colleges, stock markets, service clubs and armies, crackled over the telegraph system, full of double meanings.

The Peace Delegations realized the advantages of the relief circuits and Hoover was finally able to arrange that all the official government agencies could communicate with their delegates in code over his organization's wires. The State Department and the American press were also anxious to use the relief system. Press material, however, was carried uncoded. To handle these additional messages, a telegraph office was opened in Paris by Hoover's organization and rates were set up. Profits ran as high as $5,000 a month—all of which was put into the Children's Relief Fund.

Through General Pershing, courier service all over Europe was arranged to handle the relief organization mail. Special passports for the American staff were accepted by almost all the countries. A foreign officer at a frontier, it is said, would often salute when he read Hoover's signature on a relief pass. Even in distant parts of Europe, this name meant life-sustaining food.

Sea transportation of the relief supplies was a constant problem. The victorious nations, intent on recapturing their foreign trade, evaded assigning ships for these supplies. Up to the end of February, 1919, 80 per cent of the cargoes were carried by American ships, 10 per cent by Allied tonnage and the rest by neutral charters. The shipping situation threatened a total breakdown.

On the active intervention of the President and Henry M. Robinson, a member of the American Peace Mission and of the Allied Maritime Council, enough space was secured so that Hoover was able to manage—with the addition of the German and Austrian vessels alloted to the United States. In all, about 2,000,000 tons of shipping was handled by the relief.

Total railway disruption, particularly in Central and Eastern Europe, was an aftermath of war. From Germany to Azerbaijan, the lines were in chaos, compounded by the lately formed boundaries of all the recently established countries in these areas. The new governments would not allow rolling stock to go out of their territories, for fear it would never return.

Hoover sent an American railroad man to each of the liberated and enemy countries, to deal with the situation and to co-operate with their ministers of railways. The relief head was able to guarantee the return of cars to the different governments of their origin by stationing American Army officers

at border crossings, to check the cars passing in both directions. Most of the German locomotives and railway cars alloted to the American military at the Armistice and some
surplus rolling stock of the American Expeditionary Forces
were made available to Hoover.

To remedy the crippling shortages, Hoover worked to get
surplus railroad stock in one country sold to nations in critical
need. When there was no credit or good currency to use, payment was made in commodities. One time Hoover received a
telegram from Vienna which read, "Have arranged sell Galicia
ten locomotives for eggs. How many eggs go to a locomotive?"

"Does not matter," the Communications section wired in
reply. "We have no confidence in the age of either."

In spite of the careful planning and valiant efforts of Herbert
Hoover and his co-workers, the distribution situation deteriorated. Transportation was being used for political pressure.
Food piled up in the ports and coal movements slowed down.
Cities were starving and without heat and light. On March 5,
1919, the Relief Director put the crisis before the Big Four,
with a new plan to start internal transportation moving and
organize the exchange and distribution of local supplies, especially coal, under the direction of American Army officers. The
plan was adopted and Hoover was appointed Administrator
of the Railroads of Eastern Europe. In all, about 30,000 miles
of railways were managed by his organization.

The story is told that a relief train rushing supplies to Vienna
was halted at the head of the Adriatic. The American soldier
in command failed to persuade the armed guards to let the
train proceed. He then ordered the engineer to start up the
locomotive, and he covered the guards with his automatic revolver as the cars pulled out. When questioned about the incident after his arrival in Vienna, he announced that those
foreign kings and generals meant nothing in his life. He was
working for Herbert Hoover!

Months after the Peace, Hoover received a letter from "the

forgotten man"! It came from a lieutenant who had been assigned to count railway cars at a German-Polish rail crossing. His recall papers had apparently gone astray, and he asked plaintively to be relieved from the tab of cars passing the frontier.

Hoover also directed transportation on several thousand miles of waterways. The Danube River, which served seven states, presented particular difficulties. Hoover eventually set up his own barge system and these craft moved freely under the relief name. However, this arrangement had to be suspended during the Communist Revolution in Hungary.

Coal was as important as food and in Central Europe this vital fuel industry was in a complete upheaval. Undercover wars were being carried on for possession of the coal fields. Miners were unable to work efficiently from hunger and Communism was making great headway. Hoover finally secured a mandate from the Big Four to serve as Administrator of the Coal Mines of Eastern Europe.

General Pershing assigned Colonel Anson C. Goodyear to run Hoover's Coal Section. The colonel's first job was in the Duchy of Teschen, where he found the whole district on strike and a three-sided war being waged for possession of the coal. With "firmness, food and fair treatment," he soon had the district in productive action. Goodyear proved equally successful in the other coal fields of his area, and within a month he and his men had doubled coal production.

On one occasion, Colonel Goodyear telegraphed Hoover, "Sending $25,000. Send me that much tobacco."

Both the announcement and the request were new to the relief operations, and the "Chief" asked for more information.

In the coal area, the colonel had found bank holdings of American gold certificates with which he proposed to buy tobacco for the miners who had not had a real smoke in a year. "You know," he appealed to Hoover, "a miner cannot work unless he gets a smoke."

Hoover's mining and smoking sympathies were aroused. Tobacco was provided from army stocks and the colonel issued tobacco rations subject to increased coal output. The banks received local currency from the ration sales in exchange for the American certificates—and Goodyear got the coal!

In August, 1919, a violent local war broke out between Poles and Germans in the Silesian coal districts. Single-handed, the colonel "raced from one side to the other and finally stopped it." Despite the obstacles involved, 50,000,000 tons of coal were distributed by the relief.

In addition to coal, petroleum products, tannin, food and other necessary commodities were exchanged between countries—under American escort.

Throughout the liberated and enemy countries, there were millions of children in deplorable condition. Using the experience gained from child feeding in Belgium and Northern France, Hoover determined to set up a canteen system in each country, to provide all youngsters with one hot meal daily. The homeless and orphans, gathered in special institutions, were to be given three meals. Infants and other needy groups came under the program, which was financed by the American Relief Administration.

This relief work was confined to organizing and providing the necessary food, clothing and medical supplies. Local committees and volunteers did the rest. Hundreds of thousands of people in the countries helped became partners in the program. In Germany, the mission was carried out by the Friends' Service Committee, which worked with Hoover's experts and organized food distribution.

With the satisfactory harvest of 1919, the battle for the relief of Europe was thought to be won, but Hoover knew that another year at least would be required to aid the undernourished children. With President Wilson's approval, this extended program of health feeding was transformed into a private organization of Americans.

The child feeding operation—a free gift of the American people—touched the "heart of the populations at large" in Europe as much as any American relief activity had done.

Early in April, 1919, typhus began to sweep westward, on a line stretching from the Baltic to the Black Sea. All Europe was menaced. The Big Four referred the crisis to Hoover. He decided that his organization would have to find some solution. With the aid of General Pershing and the Army Medical Corps, a "sanitary cordon" was established along a "battle line" in front of the typhus area, extending for hundreds of miles. Traffic across this line was denied to all who did not have delousing certificates. Working eastward, the American soldiers extinguished most of the pestilence.

The unfortunate situation of the Russian prisoners in Germany was laid before the Big Four by President Wilson, at Hoover's urging. The Food Director finally arranged to provide supplies through the President's Personal Fund, as no other resources were available. Later on, the French army decided the prisoners should be held in Germany lest they join the Communist armies in Russia on repatriation. Due to this, the French agreed to furnish half the food until Peace was made.

Two other vital, interrelated problems claimed the Food Regulator's attention—the attempt to break the American war-guaranteed farm prices and the continued blockade of neutral, liberated and enemy Europe during the Armistice. Hoover's proposal, made on December 22, 1918, that the food blockade on neutrals be let down, was accepted, then reversed. This meant that the deliveries of fats to neutrals, just ordered, could not be made. Then the Inter-Allied "Fats Executive" canceled all their American orders. Due to increased production, storage space for these perishable foods was limited to under sixty days. A stop in purchasing could crack the prices. Wheat orders for Europe were also canceled, but this foodstuff, not being as perishable, could be stored.

Hoover went to work. With the assurance of Admiral Benson that the American Navy would help, he informed the neutrals that the orders they had placed in the United States with his approval would be filled, regardless of the blockade. France and Italy then renewed purchasing in January. They placed large monthly orders for pork and dairy products and asked that wheat shipments be continued. Hoover increased the Belgian Relief orders and had any surplus fats and wheat consigned to him in neutral ports. At one time, his consignment obligations for the relief and the Grain Corporation borrowing amounted to more than $550,000,000. But Hoover knew that the food blockade must break—"or all Central Europe would go Communist."

Thus the price break was stopped and the guarantees ran out—but Hoover had had apprehensive nightmares over the threatened economic collapse of the American farmer.

An article had been incorporated into the Armistice terms, stating that provisioning of Germany during the Armistice was contemplated by the Allies, "as shall be necessary," mainly at Hoover's instance. Austria, Bulgaria and Turkey were later included. This was strongly opposed by the major European Allies still influenced by war-inflicted sufferings, and nothing had happened. Hoover pressed for relaxation of the food blockade. The condition of the German people was deteriorating. By March, 1919, the situation was desperate. British occupation soldiers complained urgently about the half-starving children they saw, and wanted to be sent home because they could not bear to look on at such suffering. The Communists were making great headway and had seized Munich, Hamburg and Stettin. The feeble German government was on the point of collapse.

On March 8, after a fiery hearing, the Big Four ordered that Hoover's formula for feeding Germany be applied. A delegation was appointed to present the formula to the Germans at a conference, and, six days later, an agreement was reached in Brussels. Four months time had been lost, with repercussions to the Germans—and to the Allies. Francqui, representing the Belgians, sat with Hoover across from the Germans—but the tables had been turned on begging for food concessions.

Hate was still so "livid" on the Allied side and in some parts of America that Hoover issued a statement to justify his course. To him, the maintenance of the food blockade was a "crime in statesmanship and against civilization as a whole."

He diverted cargoes to Germany at once—fearful that they would be sixty days too late. It was a neck and neck race to keep ahead of the Communist movements that had grown out of hunger. By late March, 1919, the food blockade was let down for the other enemy countries through the efforts of Hoover and others deeply concerned.

Among the many countries that Hoover's relief organization assisted were the Allies—Great Britain, France and Italy; the neutrals—Norway, Sweden, Denmark, Holland, Switzerland and Spain; the liberated—Belgium, Poland, Finland, Estonia, Latvia, Lithuania, Czechoslovakia, Yugoslavia, Rumania, Armenia, Georgia and Azerbaijan; and the former enemy lands —Germany, Austria, Bulgaria, Hungary and Turkey.

The fight against starvation in many of the countries was desperate, particularly in those of Central and Eastern Europe and Germany. Against a backdrop of famine and disease, the "Hoover" men did a superlative job in the midst of human woe, intrigue, economic and political disintegration, war, massacre, anarchy and Communism. It was impossible to avoid dealing with the political and economic forces in each country aided.

Poland, which had suffered four separate invasions during the war, proclaimed her independence at once after the Armistice—"fortified" by President Wilson's assurances of national freedom for the Poles under the thirteenth of his famous Fourteen Points. Hoover's mission, which included Dr. Kellogg,

Colonel William Grove and Maurice Pate, found dreadful devastation in that gallant country. They poured in food, clothing, supplies and rolling stock and worked hard on the internal rehabilitation. Despite all this aid, Prime Minister Paderewski declared that the people were still in misery and an easy prey for the Communists. Red Armies were attacking on the Galician frontier. The famous pianist insisted the "tide could only be stemmed" by a show of backing from the United States, and he invited President Wilson to visit the country before his return to America on June 28, 1919, when the Peace Treaty was to be signed. The President could not accept, so he asked Hoover to go in his place. Paderewski joined in urging Hoover to make the trip. They had known each other since the American's college days, when his lecture bureau had arranged that recital by the pianist, which had not proved a financial success.

Accompanied by several generals and admirals, Hoover arrived in Poland in mid-August. He had a hectic tour, divided between conferences and official occasions. Honors were heaped upon him.

His reception at Warsaw by the Polish children touched him the most deeply. Ranging from five to twelve years in age, they had been brought by train from the soup kitchens where they were gathered in for meals. Many were dressed in rags. Fifty thousand strong, they marched past an old race-course grandstand where Hoover and the other officials of the various governments were stationed. Chattering and laughing, they passed in review, trying to keep some sort of marching order. At one point, a rabbit jumped out of the grass. The line dissolved as hundreds went after the elusive animal. He was captured and brought to Hoover. Darkness finally ended the touching parade. General Henrys, head of the French Military Mission, was so overcome by the children's tribute that he had to leave the stand. He told the guest of honor that there had never been a review of honor in all history that he would have preferred for himself rather than the one which had been given Hoover that day.

After declaring her independence in 1917, Finland had had to fight a civil war with domestic Communists. The internal conflict was put down with German aid and a brother-in-law of the Kaiser was made king. At the November, 1918, Armistice, a republic was set up under General Mannerheim. Soon after Hoover arrived in Europe, a Finnish delegation presented the dreadful plight of the people to him. Continued Communist disturbances, a bad crop, separation from Russia, which was a former source of food imports, and the blockade had reduced Finland to the starvation point. Hoover immediately diverted cargoes to the Finns and guaranteed to replace in kind emergency shipments ordered from Sweden and Denmark. The supplies were delivered under American naval protection.

A mission of American Army officers was sent to Finland, headed by Major Ferry Heath. Child feeding was set up as a gift from the warm-hearted American people. Hoover worked hard for the recognition of the Mannerheim Republic, which was finally granted on May 3, 1919, by the Allied Council of Foreign Ministers at the direction of the Big Four.

The other Baltic states—Estonia, Latvia and Lithuania— which were occupied by Germany at the time of the Armistice, fought for their emancipation under appalling difficulties, magnified by starvation. Afraid of complete chaos, the Allies asked the German forces to remain in the area temporarily. The spread of Communism was fanned by invading Red forces. Hoover's missions supplied food and worked for order in the midst of incredible conditions.

On June 28, 1919—the day the Peace Treaty was signed —many citizens of Riga, who had suffered horribly, as well as people from other towns, all with their children, came to the relief organization offices in thousands, bearing flowers. Tearful thanks were given the Americans as the bands played *Yankee Doodle.*

By January, 1919, frantic appeals for food had reached Hoover from Czechoslovakia. He dispatched a mission under Dr. Lincoln Hutchinson to administer the aid program. American experts on railways, finance, child feeding and coal were later added. The food problems included almost all the usual difficulties and, in addition, the Czechs had to be persuaded to export coal to keep the Austrian cities going. Hoover was given a great welcome in Prague on his way to Poland.

The new state of Yugoslavia had famine conditions in its Adriatic provinces which were relieved by imports from America. The food surplus in the Serbian areas was transferred to Hungary, Austria and Czechoslovakia, after difficult negotiations. Old animosities flared against Hungary and Austria. In January, civil war broke out in Dalmatia, partly instigated by the Italians. A junior American Army officer, on relief business, was caught in the crossfire above Cattaro. He made contact with the general of the nearest army, who accepted his offer to negotiate an armistice. The commander of the opposing army agreed to the armistice but neither side would surrender to the other. The lieutenant drew up papers of surrender to the United States but, fearful of involving his government, he hastily changed the wording and made over the surrender to Herbert Hoover, as United States Food Administrator. He demanded the swords of the two generals and confiscated the machine guns and artillery. There were about 300 men on each side.

Short of labor to unload a ship in the harbor of Cattaro, the lieutenant offered wages of flour and bacon to one of the vanquished forces for its help. He soon had both armies working—one on the day shift and the other on the night shift.

Anxious about his use of Hoover's name in the surrender papers, he later went to Paris to explain. The director listened with a straight face, then asked about the two swords. Accepting one as his due, he promised to say nothing. A week's leave was arranged for the lieutenant and Hoover wrote him a note, saying that he was of the "stuff that had made America a great country."

Armenia presented problems beyond description, and aid, in which the Near East Relief Committee took part, had to be continued there until 1920. The two neighboring republics, Azerbaijan and Georgia, needed only minor supplies. They went Communist in 1920, and Armenia was later absorbed into Communist Russia. These territories were all originally part of Czarist Russia.

In Austria, denuded of her supporting areas, the food operation was a race against "both death and Communism." In late March, 1919, when Hungary went Bolshevist, the possibility of a Communist crisis arose in Austria, but dread of hunger prevented a revolutionary uprising. On May Day, the Communists were expected to try to seize the government. At Hoover's authorization, proclamations were posted on the city walls containing his statement that "Any disturbance of public order will render food shipments impossible and bring Vienna face to face with absolute famine." The day passed by quietly.

In February, 1919, Captain T. T. C. Gregory, head of Hoover's mission to Austria and Hungary, sent word to his chief that the Communist revolution was imminent in Hungary. Hoover forwarded his urgent warnings to the Big Four. On March 22, 1919, power was seized by Bela Kun, a Lenin-indoctrinated Hungarian, who established a typical "Red Terror." At the time, the relief had a train of twenty-five carloads of food headed for Budapest. This was held at the Serbian border by the French military. Hoover was in a quandary. The shipment, mostly special food for children, had been paid for by the Hungarian National Bank. Through Clemenceau, the train was released. Hoover arranged with the Communists for distribution of the food under American supervision. Child feeding was continued during most of Kun's regime under precarious circumstances, due to arrests and some executions of the Hungarian committee members.

The discovery, through the relief, that Kun was buying arms from a few Italian army officers was reported to the Peace Conference. The Italian representatives had the gold turned over to the relief, to buy food for Hungarians.

Through Frank Polk, who represented President Wilson, the Big Four asked Hoover's advice on the desperate situation in Hungary. Hoover submitted a draft, which was issued, stating that the Allied and associated governments could do nothing in Hungary until a representative government was established.

Kun was overthrown on August 1, 1919, by trade union leaders, and a new government was set up. To fulfill Allied promises, Hoover immediately ordered large shipments of food sent to Hungary. But grave trouble developed from the continuing invasion of a Rumanian army which occupied Budapest and plundered the country. By a *coup d'état,* or sudden decisive stroke overturning the government, a Hapsburg Archduke was put in power. This frightened the liberated states nearby and, at Hoover's suggestion, the Big Four decided to inform the Archduke that his government could not be recognized, as it did not represent the people. They directed that the message be delivered through Gregory, the relief head in Hungary. In reply came the organization's most celebrated slang communication. "Archie on the carpet 7 p.m.," it read. "Went through the hoop at 7:05 p.m." A representative ministry was then organized. When the 1919 harvest became available, Hoover's mission was ended and he recalled his staff. The Rumanian army stayed in Hungary until forced out by the blockade of its homeland by the Big Four.

Rumania had suffered terribly from German and Hungarian plundering during World War I. Hoover's men had great difficulty in distributing food and rebuilding commercial activity. He enlarged the administration by sending Colonel William N. Haskell in with a large staff. Rumanian oil was sorely needed for Central European railways and for exchange by barter, but any action was painfully slow. The British aided with food and army stores, and the French sent army equipment. There were problems of every nature, but, by the end of April, the situation began to improve. Haskell advised Hoover that, "the dangers of Bolshevist insurrection have been greatly lessened if not entirely obviated by the arrival of our food cargoes. . . . It is, however, still the chief topic of conversation."

The relief organization officially ceased under American law on July 1. Possible continuance of the work was given up when the 1919 European crop proved good. Operations were carried on into September, when Hoover recalled his men from the field, with the exception of those who entered the employ of governments where they were serving. Child feeding was continued.

While administering the European relief, Hoover carried his customary tremendous work load. Writing of his glimpses of Hoover during that period, Will Irwin described the Chief as a "chess master, playing twenty games at once and most of them blindfolded."

From his own observation, Vernon Kellogg declared that the news that the humanitarian of Belgian Relief fame was back on the job in Europe "acted like magic in restoring hope to these despairing millions." Kellogg added, "It was owing more to Hoover and his work than to any other single influence that utter anarchy and chaos and complete Bolshevik domination of eastern Europe were averted."

For his work in Europe in World War I and during the Armistice, Herbert Hoover received many honors and tokens of gratitude. These included honorary citizenship of Finland, Poland and Reval, Estonia; Hoover Avenue and Hoover Park in Warsaw; Herbert Hoover Strasse, Steyr, Austria; testimo-

"Gaunt
Realities"

CHAPTER 11

H erbert Hoover was intimately
concerned, both through his work and as a member of President Wilson's Committee of Economic Advisers, with the making of peace. Constant, sometimes hourly requests were made to him and his staff for information. These inquiries came from Allied councils and committees, as well as from Americans taking part in the formulation of peace. He was often called before the Big Four for consultation and advice. His organization was in daily contact with what was happening all over Europe. He dealt continually with the "gaunt realities which prowled outside" the halls of peace.

But the director of European aid let nothing interfere with his job of relief and reconstruction. With a work schedule of twelve to eighteen hours daily, he was well able to take part in two worlds—the rehabilitation of Europe as well as treaty making. Even mealtimes were used to do business. Hoover also kept an apartment at the Hotel Crillon, where the American delegation stayed in Paris, as a meeting place with American officials.

Bolshevist Russia, Hoover declared, was about the worst problem in both the relief and the peace conference worlds— the "Banquo's ghost" at every council table. Checking the spread of Communism was a factor in almost all the relief operations.

The question of what to do about Russia plagued everybody. Military intervention was tried. In February Winston Churchill proposed united invasion by the Allies. On many occasions, Wilson asked Hoover's advice on Russia. On March 28, 1919, in a letter to the President, the relief director asserted that Russia could not be recognized, even remotely, without stimulating Communism in all Europe and without "transgressing on every National ideal of our own." He did not favor military intervention. Instead, he suggested that a commission be set up, similar to the Belgian Relief and headed by a man with an international reputation who came from a neutral country. United States' aid could be offered to this relief director, if the Bolshevists ceased military action beyond defined borders and refrained from agitation abroad. Hoover finally persuaded Fridtjof Nansen, a Norwegian polar explorer, to head the proposed relief. Under Allied approved conditions, the offer of food was radioed to Lenin. The reply accepted the relief but refused the terms. A tirade against the wickedness of capitalism was added. The French objected to the proposal and no further effort was made to establish the relief commission.

Food was also given to "White" Russia, in the northwest part of the country. On May 13, 1919, General Yudenich with a White Russian army left the Baltic states on an expedition to recapture Petrograd from the Communists. The State Department asked Hoover to undertake the feeding of the civilian population in the areas taken by Yudenich in his advance, and to be ready to provision Petrograd. The military expedition failed within a few miles of its goal, but 400,000 people in the recaptured regions were fed and given enough to tide them over until the next harvest. The report of Captain Miller, of Hoover's staff, on conditions in the territory reclaimed from the Communists, was a "terrifying document." Other food supplied to White Russia was handled through Allied troops and governments.

All during the European relief effort, Hoover continued as head of the C.R.B. and of the work in Northern France. With William Poland, the European director, he had visited Brussels soon after his arrival in Europe following the Armistice, intending to wind up the commission. Due to the urging of the Belgian and French governments, the C.R.B. was continued until July 1, 1919.

Within three months after the truce, most of the unemployed in Belgium and Northern France were back at work and the funds needed for the destitute were reduced accordingly. Drastic rationing, controls and shipping problems were ended. At the request of the two governments involved, the C.R.B. food prices were raised to equate the prices in unoccupied France. The commission became a gigantic grocery business with 10,000,000 customers.

To expedite the relief in Germany, Finland and other countries, extra stocks were bought by the C.R.B. The Germans paid in gold for their supplies—at the same prices charged the Belgians.

After accounts were settled with the governments concerned, the commission had a surplus fund of almost $34,-000,000, including some remaining charity funds. Hoover proposed that the Belgian Ministry take over the job of winding up the work, paying the salaries and expenses of the employees from the profits and disposing of the balances as they wished. The Belgians declined, declaring that the balances were the property of the commission. To express their gratitude for the C.R.B., they requested that Hoover allocate the surplus from the relief operations in the way he thought would best serve the Belgian people, thereby establishing a "living memorial" to the commission. The funds were used to endow ten educational and scientific institutions, nine of which were in Belgium and one, the C.R.B. Educational Foundation, was to be located in New York City. From the operations in Northern France, a balance remained of over $5,000,000. This was spent on charitable institutions for French children.

The commission accounts were audited and kept by the same firm of British accountants during its entire existence. They were balanced out to the last cent and the last grain of foodstuff. The overhead expense of the C.R.B. amounted to less than one-half of 1 per cent. In their final statement, the auditors declared that the commission's records were so maintained that all transactions could be fully verified, "thus preventing any charge being sustained against the integrity" of the C.R.B. management. The firm further certified that Mr. Hoover had never accepted any remuneration for his services, even for travel or related expenses.

When the auditors' final account was received by the French government, its officials are said to have waved it aside, saying. "We have tasks more pressing and fruitful than questioning the integrity of Mr. Hoover!" For his work in the relief of Northern France, the French Chamber of Deputies passed a resolution of thanks to Herbert Hoover.

The King of the Belgians found a way to thank the decoration-shy commission head. He created an Order—for Hoover alone—"The Friend of Belgium and Honorary Citizen of Belgium." The Belgian Parliament passed the necessary legislation at a special session. Hoover was required to attend and witness the unanimous vote. He was also given a passport marked "perpetual," in case, as the Foreign Minister laughingly suggested, he should ever need sanctuary!

He was awarded degrees from three Belgian universities. In Charleroi, a boulevard was named in his honor and the Freedom of the City of Antwerp and of Brussels was extended to him. In ancient times, the Freedom of a City carried with it free lodging and the right to secure merchandise without charge, but this part of the custom had apparently died out!

As a public expression of appreciation, the Belgians wished to arrange parades and receptions in Hoover's honor in the nation's cities. The plan to bestow the most important orders of distinction and nobility upon him was again proposed. But the Relief head declined to accept any of these honors. To Herbert Hoover, his most treasured rewards were the thousands of grateful letters he received from the children of Belgium.

To one biographer, the Belgian Relief undertaking was Hoover's greatest achievement of the wartime period, since he worked then as an unknown American citizen "pitting his naked talent against kings, principalities and powers."

Even as the Belgian Relief was being wound up, the project of documenting World War I, from which the Relief had stemmed, was rapidly growing. In 1918, the Hoover Library on War, Revolution and Peace was founded at Stanford University. With his "Operation Pack Rat" in mind, he had engaged collectors to gather printed and written items on the war, particularly of the "fugitive" type, in the capitals and principal centers of Europe, and asked that the material be held until peace was declared. Following the Armistice, Hoover brought Professor E. D. Adams to Europe, to organize the collecting, giving him a fund of $50,000 for the work. General Pershing detailed about fifteen assistant professors and teachers of history from the army to gather papers and records over the whole of Europe. The members of the economic missions assisted, also. Aid was requested from the heads of the liberated and enemy governments. Confidential source material was contributed by many of these new leaders. To them—the records of their deposed predecessors were not sacred! Leaders who had lost out in the upheavals also donated their papers— to put them in safe hands! At various European ports, carloads of documentary material were placed aboard empty food ships returning to America.

The European relief men were well qualified to select significant items. Beyond the primary purpose of relieving starvation and aiding reconstruction, Hoover's mission had borne extensive political implications. It was also his job "to shield the frail plants of democracy" from the possible unhappy aftermath of "unemployment, anarchy, or Communism."

To achieve peace, Hoover believed the one hope was to support representative government. Moreover, he felt that all governments weakened by famine and disease were in danger of falling into Communism.

Hoover's two worlds—the relief and peacemaking—were interrelated.

The rehabilitation director was one of the few who advised President Wilson against coming to Europe as head of the American Delegation at the Peace Conference on the grounds that his voice would be more effective from the White House.

On his arrival in Paris, Wilson was acclaimed as a "second Messiah" by the people of every country. It was at this time that he had established Hoover's position as relief head in Europe with the Allied leaders. Hoover advised the President of the adverse changes in the atmosphere of Europe. Woodrow Wilson's famous Fourteen Points, with the subsequent eleven additions, on which the Germans had asked for an armistice, were admittedly never part of the Allies' official policy. Wilson had little knowledge of the men with whom he was to deal and the secret war treaties proved another obstacle to his program. Deference to American views was growing weak.

At Hoover's instigation, the President's Committee of Economic Advisers was set up on the lines of the War Council. This committee counseled the American Peace Delegation on such economic matters as the war debts and warned on purposes inimical to America.

On April 11, Hoover sent a memorandum to President Wilson and the members of the peace mission, opposing continued American participation in the Allied commissions for many reasons. In his view, revolution in Europe was far from over and he felt that the United States should maintain independence of action as the "one great moral reserve in the world today." The President replied that he would "fight shy" of most commissions.

Early in April, Wilson became ill and when he recovered he seemed to Hoover to be a changed man. With the delays in preparing the Peace Treaty, the relief head was fully aware that the whole European situation, economic and social, was seriously deteriorating.

Hoover was awakened at four o'clock in the morning on May 7, 1919, by a worried servant, who reported that there was a messenger waiting with a document so important that he could give it to no one except Hoover. This proved to be the printed draft of the Peace Treaty—which was to be handed to the Germans that very day! Hoover read the draft immediately. Though many of the ideas were known to him, he had not previously visualized it as a whole. He was greatly disturbed. He felt that some of the conditions established by the document would prevent the rebuilding of Europe—and the coming of true peace. He feared that the economic consequences alone would topple Europe—and injure the United States.

Much alarmed, Hoover got up and went out to walk the deserted streets in the early daylight. He met General Jan Christiaan Smuts and a young British economist. In a flash of understanding, each realized why all three were walking about at that hour. Comparing notes, they agreed that the proposed treaty was dangerous and each promised to alert his own countrymen to the dangers.

Hoover summoned experts of his relief organization for breakfast, and they spent some time discussing the consequences of the proposed treaty. They determined to take up the most pressing matters with the peacemakers, while waiting to hear from the Germans. Through the forthcoming Allied reply to the German response, the peace terms could be amended.

The British made some "sensible" changes, instigated by General Smuts. Hoover called on President Wilson with some other men. They urged Wilson to make some revisions, too. Tired and on the defensive, the President did not seem enthusiastic but agreed to call a conference of American leaders in Paris when the German reply was received.

When it was proposed that the food blockade be restored, to compel the Germans to sign the treaty, Hoover protested vigorously to the President, on May 14. The Big Four directed that military force only could be used to bring about peace, if necessary. Marshal Foch mobilized his army about June 19, with great ostentation.

May 30 brought the German answer, demanding "more amendment than they deserved," as Hoover had foreseen. The reports of Hoover's men revealed very serious political degeneration in Germany. Communist riots and disturbances broke out with renewed vigor throughout the Reich and were subdued only with a great deal of bloodshed.

The President met with the American leaders on June 3, 1919. Major weaknesses in the Peace Treaty were pointed out to Wilson. Hoover's remarks drew "sharp replies" from the President. Two days later, at the request of Secretary of State Robert Lansing, Hoover drew up a memorandum on the whole subject of the treaty. A copy was given to Wilson by Lansing.

Soon afterward, Wilson sent for Hoover, to talk over the memorandum. This turned out to be their last important discussion on any subject for over two years. Nerves taut, the President "flashed angrily" at some of Hoover's comments.

Later, the President accepted some modifications. However,

his main hope of effecting needed changes in the war settlement lay in the machinery of the League of Nations which, through his efforts, was to be established under the peace agreement.

On June 28, 1919, the Peace Treaty was signed in the Hall of Mirrors, at Versailles. Hoover found it difficult to keep his mind on the ceremony—instead, it was traveling along the road toward the fearful consequences ahead.

Hoover was convinced by his experiences during this period that it was not possible for America to make a lasting peace in Europe. Differences in concept and practices of more than 300 years were too great—differences in representative government, in equality of opportunity, in freedom of economic systems and in knowledge of Old World rivalries and diplomacy.

Mrs. Hoover came to Paris with Allan to join her husband for a few weeks before his job was finished. In all of Hoover's 11-month stay, he had no time for theaters, museums or sight-seeing. Fortunately, during his engineering days, the Hoovers had made many trips to France, so he was familiar with the country's chief attractions.

Sight-seeing excursions were arranged for Allan and General Pershing's son, Warren, who were both about twelve years old. With a French woman to teach them the language and an American army sergeant, they toured the battlefields and explored Paris. Allan picked up weapons at spots where they had been used or had fallen, and he acquired quite a collection. One evening, a general inspected the arms and, with alarm, quickly appropriated an aerial torpedo, which he disposed of by having it dropped into the Seine. Allan did not take kindly to this safety precaution, and no explanation could convince him of the general's good character and excellence as a military man.

On the announcement of Hoover's intended departure for the United States in early September, 1919, he was deluged by letters and telegrams. Expressions of genuine appreciation came from government leaders of France, Britain, Italy, Belgium and all the other countries the relief had aided, and from his associates in these lands. Messages were received from His Holiness, the Pope, and the heads of the Greek, Armenian and Lutheran Churches. A particularly appreciative tribute arrived from Cardinal Mercier of Belgium. But to the relief director, as always, the most cherished tributes were the many volumes he received containing thousands of signatures of children he had helped—also illustrated by their own hands.

The last person Hoover went to see before leaving France was Prime Minister Clemenceau. He thanked him for his "undeviating support." The Tiger, as the rugged French patriot was known, was gloomy.

"There will be another world war in your time," he stated bluntly, "and you will be needed back in Europe."

Although Clemenceau's tragic prophecy proved accurate in later years, on the voyage home Hoover had his first chance in five years for complete rest—and to take satisfaction from the humanitarian work he had just completed, which was made possible by the unparalleled generosity of the United States. As summed up by the director, the relief and reconstruction operation had "saved the Allies millions of human lives; it saved the peace-making; it saved large parts of Europe from Communism; it saved millions from starvation, and restored at least 15,000,000 children to health."

One observer, John Maynard Keynes, whose economic path was later to sharply diverge from Hoover's, wrote of the relief director:

"Mr. Hoover was the only man who emerged from the ordeal of Paris with an enhanced reputation. This complex personality, with his habitual air of weary Titan (or, as others might put it, of exhausted prize fighter), his eyes steadily fixed on the true and essential facts of the European situation, imported into the Councils of Paris, when he took part in them, precisely that atmosphere of reality, knowledge, magnanimity and disinterestedness which, if they had been found in other quarters, also, would have given us the Good Peace."

Secretary
of
Commerce

CHAPTER 12

Hoover planned to take the first train for California, the moment the *Aquitania* docked in New York. He had been with his family only for a few hectic months since war began. Now they would be able to get out the fishing rods, drive into the mountains and "live again."

While still at sea, Hoover was informed by wire that the American Institute of Mining and Metallurgical Engineers was arranging a large reception and dinner in his honor in New York and he would be asked to speak. Making a speech was not a "treasured occasion" in Hoover's life, and preparing the text broke into his well-earned rest. His remarks reviewed his work abroad and warned of the forces of social disruption active in the world.

The banquet over, the three Hoovers sped west to rejoin Herbert Jr. and enter on the life together of which they had so often dreamed, far from the seething "chaos of Europe." They lived in their cottage on the Stanford University grounds and went off on long-planned camping and fishing expeditions in the mountains. Some years before, Lou Hoover had made plans to build a Hopi-style house on land they had leased on a nearby campus hill, overlooking the mountains and the bay. She brought out the preliminary drawings, and building was soon underway.

Just past his forty-fifth birthday, Hoover felt he could reestablish himself in his profession of engineering and recoup some of the fortune he had expended while helping others. But the plan for "blissful living" was soon disturbed.

Personal acclaim followed Hoover wherever he went. He was selected by a *New York Times* poll as one of the ten most important living Americans. Hundreds of letters reached him daily. Even in the forests and in the streams, he could not escape cables, telegrams and telephone calls. He was constantly asked by the press for statements and by magazine editors for articles. He was surprised at the American appetite for speeches. He was bombarded with requests for the use of his name on sponsor lists.

In self-defense, Hoover prepared a humorous statement of his own, saying he was spending a month with two vigorous boys. During that time, he would not answer telephone calls, read any communication over a page long, or accept the honor of making sixty-four speeches. The American people, he felt, would be "gratified to find a citizen who wants to keep still." This rule was for the "public good." But even these spoofing rules were subject to a provision that nothing turned up to irritate his conscience and peace of mind.

Many things did turn up. Hoover found that America was not a "quiet pool." The country was suffering from a postwar economic headache and was, itself, faced with a gigantic task of reconstruction. Conflict raged over ratification of the Peace Treaty and the League of Nations Covenant. Besides his con-

cern over the state of the country and the Treaty fight, there
was the necessity to carry on the Children's Relief in Europe
and to wind up the war organizations he had directed. He soon
gave way to his conscience and made plans to return to New
York and open an office there to take care of these obligations.

Before leaving California, Hoover participated in the arrangements for a state visit from King Albert and Queen Elizabeth of Belgium. Accompanied by their son, Crown Prince
Leopold, they were the first official guests of the United States
since General Lafayette had been asked to lay the cornerstone
of the Bunker Hill Monument, a hundred years before. Due to
President Wilson's illness, their planned week's stay in Washington was changed to a visit to California.

Hoover was able to borrow two large residences in Santa
Barbara to accommodate the royal party of forty for the visit
and took charge of the official parade and reception in San
Francisco. Mayor Rolph of the Bay City, up for re-election,
had asked Hoover's aid, as he feared the adverse effect of hob-
nobbing with the King and Queen on his vote in part of the
city. The sheriff explained to Hoover that the size of the crowd
could be regulated. If he held the public from crossing Market
Street for five minutes, a fair crowd would build up on the
sidewalks of this thoroughfare, which cut diagonally across
the "checkerboard" city. A ten-minute halt would ensure a
large crowd, he declared. Hoover decided on ten minutes.

Hoover met the King and Queen at the ferry building, and
the parade, with Army and Navy units and bands, escorting
the royal visitors to City Hall was impressive. The acting host
was shaken by a last-minute telephone call from Mrs. Hoover,
saying she could not join him as Allan had fallen out of a tree
and broken something inside him. As soon as possible, Hoover
called back, to learn it was his son's arm that was broken.

Just before the official luncheon at the Palace Hotel began,
Mayor Rolph came to Hoover, much troubled, with the Order
of the Crown glittering in his hand. He had just been decorated

by the King and was worried about his vote the next day if he appeared at the luncheon with this "display of feudalism" pinned to his chest. Hoover suggested that the mayor accept the honor for the City of San Francisco. Greatly relieved, at luncheon, Rolph spoke in glowing terms of this tribute to his city and held up the decoration for all to see. King Albert asked Hoover just what the mayor was talking about, but Hoover said he would explain later, which he did. King Albert was so interested that he asked that the election results be telegraphed to him. The mayor was retained by an unusual majority.

From October, 1919, to March, 1921, Herbert Hoover had a busy time. He was not spoiled by his great popularity. He knew that it was the painful experience of men in public life that the prevailing opinion in democracies can be fickle and heartless. The Hoovers lived in an apartment in New York and he had offices at 42 Broadway. In addition to many press statements, magazine articles and forty-six public addresses, Hoover presided over fifteen public meetings, testified at nine Congressional hearings and made four extensive reports. He received gold medals, among many other distinctions, and added to his growing roster of honorary degrees. Instead of the secluded dream house in Palo Alto, he felt that he was living in a Pullman berth!

Setting forth his views in speeches and statements, Hoover took part in the unsuccessful fight for ratification of the Peace Treaty and membership in the League of Nations—with reservations. Although aware of the Treaty's weaknesses, he felt that hope of peace lay in sustaining the new representative governments. The best protection from the "radical infections" spreading in America was disinfection of the disease sources in Europe. With former President William Howard Taft, Charles E. Hughes, Elihu Root and other leading Republicans, Hoover joined in a statement of confidence in the League— always with certain reservations.

The campaign by a few Britishers and Americans to secure

more billions of dollars in credit for European nations drew protests from Hoover. In public statements, he insisted that Europe must rely on private credits and that the American business world should provide such credits on a business basis, organized to prevent fraud, waste and loss. At a meeting called by the American Bankers Association in December, 1920, to consider the problem, Hoover was the principal speaker. In advocating a corporation for the purpose of making foreign loans for constructive purposes, he declared that it was far better "that these problems be solved by the process of business and individual initiative than that they be attempted by our government." Except for the humane purpose of preventing starvation, he continued, direct loans to foreign governments to promote commerce could lead only to a dozen "vicious ends," such as political pressure from foreign statesmen and their nationals in America, inflation, waste and intrigue. The American government could not higgle in the market to exact returns appropriate to the risks, and for collection of debt could appeal to no court—except a battleship. But this plan for extending private credit abroad did not materialize at that time. Hoover returned to the question of foreign credits later, as Secretary of Commerce.

The winding up of the American war agencies he had managed had high priority on Hoover's list of immediate tasks. Some ten billions of dollars were involved in the transactions of the Food Administration, Grain Corporation, Sugar Equalization Board and Belgian Commission, and in the Treasury advances for relief and Congressional relief appropriations. In accordance with their previously mentioned practice of leaving no loophole for attack, Hoover, and his associates, who were all men of "ability and scrupulous integrity," had insisted, from the beginning, on such complete records, independent audits and final certificates that any unfavorable criticism could be answered down to the "last red cent." Hoover's administrative branch was never investigated by Congress, as were some others.

It did not escape the "slanderous attacks" that seem to befall every large official activity in a representative government, but he and his co-workers, who included such men as Robert A. Taft and Lewis Strauss, were able to prove instantly that they had taken no dollar of salary nor stolen a dollar; that most had paid their own expenses—and all had sacrificed much through neglect of their own business interests.

In spite of Hoover's direct recommendation in the spring of 1919 that the Sugar Board full control be continued, as sugar production could not be resumed in Europe for another year, Wilson was persuaded by one board member to end the operation then and there. As Hoover had predicted, a sugar boom developed which later collapsed, with great financial loss to many. Ironically, although this happened after the liquidation of the Food Administration, unkind critics have often blamed Hoover for the sugar "orgy."

When Hoover was leaving Europe, Barnardo Attolico, the Italian food director, had sent him a copy of an old Graeco-Italian coin, along with a message describing the relief head as a man of driving power and *bonae voluntatis,* or good will in the Biblical sense, and expressing deep appreciation of the fundamental honesty of intention and the love of humanity which had been the basis of Hoover's unfailing success. The coin, Attolico explained, represented an era when wheat had been plentiful in Italy, and was being offered as a tribute now because it had been due to Hoover that Italy had not lacked wheat during the war. "My only wish," the Italian declared, "is that on the other side of the Atlantic Ocean also you may find your way to devoting yourself to the reconstruction of the world."

Hoover did devote himself both to continuing needed relief in Europe and aiding in the postwar reconstruction in the United States. He implemented the organization of the private American Relief Administration, established in July, 1919, on the termination of the government agency, to continue the canteen feeding of European children. Besides the surplus supplies of the official ARA, the profits made in liberated and enemy countries from the sale of food to those who could pay were turned over to the new child-feeding organization. Funds were also available from "food draft" sales and gifts. In May, 1920, it was realized that six or seven million children must still be fed for another winter. Hoover organized a European Relief Council of other interested agencies to join in fund raising. The drive was dramatized by banquets to the "Invisible Guest." The "visible" contributors were seated at rough board tables set with tin dishes. They were served food identical with the meal, known as Hoover Luncheons, given the children abroad. An empty chair with a lighted candle before it stood at the center of the head table—representing the invisible child guest. The most successful banquet was held in New York. General Pershing and Hoover, sitting on either side of the honored "guest," made short addresses. Three million dollars was raised through this dinner, including a gift of one million from John D. Rockefeller, Jr. The whole campaign brought in a total of almost $30,000,000.

The great want among intellectual groups in many countries was recognized too. With special funds and arrangements, over 200,000 doctors, lawyers, scholars, teachers, journalists and artists were given food and clothing.

Five countries in Europe needed further help, in addition to Armenia. Hoover helped obtain Congressional authority to supply them with surplus wheat on credit.

But additional need was to be met. In July, 1921, the Russian author, Maxim Gorky, appealed to American and European people for help in the terrible famine in Russia. This was partly due to freakish weather, Hoover asserted, but also "to a halt in agricultural production while the Soviets were communizing the Russian peasants."

The great humanitarian outlined the minimum conditions on which he could undertake the charitable feeding of these starving people, especially the children—freedom of all American prisoners in Russia; full liberty to administer relief, including travel; the power to organize local committees; nonpolitical distribution; and free storage, transportation and offices.

After tedious negotiations, Walter L. Brown for the American Relief Administration and Maxim Litvinov for the Soviet government reached an agreement. By September, more than a hundred Americans were released from Russian prisons, over eighty of whom had not been reported to the United States. Food distribution began on September 21, with nourishing meals served to the starving at food kitchens. Dr. Kellogg and James Goodrich made a report on the situation. This disclosed that fifteen to twenty millions would perish unless the aid program was greatly expanded.

At the request of Mr. Hoover, his former relief associate, Colonel William N. Haskell, took charge of relief in Russia with an American staff, and by mid-1922 food was being given to millions of persons in the Volga River Valley, the Ukraine and other starving areas. American shelled corn became the major food staple. Acute famine was ended with the Russian harvest of that year, but aid to children was continued for another winter. Relief amounted to about sixty-two millions of dollars. This total included a Congressional appropriation of $18,662,180 from the Grain Corporation surplus, medical supplies worth $8,000,000, American charitable contributions through the ARA and food remittances.

As a gift, about 700,000 tons of food, clothing and medical supplies were provided and sent from the United States to the suffering Russians. Distributed by the ARA staff, these donations saved about 20,000,000 Russian lives.

Besides the above aid, the Soviet government asked the United States to buy seed and paid for the purchase with $10,000,000 in gold.

The American people, Hoover related, were somewhat

reluctant to alleviate the starvation in Russia, due in part to the "communizing" program of the government there.

The situation was complicated by Communists in America, who set up an organization and solicited relief funds. Hoover felt there was no assurance of honest expenditure, so he advised the public to support the ARA or one of the religious groups associated with it. This brought down upon him the "usual left-wing abuse." The Dies Committee later revealed that, with the approval of the Soviet government, more than a million dollars raised by the American Communist "relief" drive was largely spent on Communist propaganda in the United States.

In 1923, Herbert Hoover received a scroll of thanks from the Soviet government "in the name of the millions of people who have been saved. . . ." In the meanwhile, however, he was accused in the Moscow press of having carried on the relief with the hope that "his mines in the Urals would be returned to him." This was proved completely false by Hoover, who demonstrated that he no longer held any interest in these mines. Many of the Russians who had worked on the local committees, often for their daily bread only, were arrested after the relief work was finished. The American relief staff were unable to get further news of them.

"My reward," Herbert Hoover has stated, "was that for years the Communists employed their press and paid speakers to travel over the United States for the special purpose of defaming me."

During his whole European experience, Hoover had tried to define the American system—the "promise of human progress and the force" which had led the nation to greatness. He insisted that spiritual and intellectual freedom could not exist without economic freedom. "If one died, all would die." He summed up the excellent points and marginal weaknesses of the national way of life in a book entitled, *American Individualism,* including as well a program for recovery and progress.

In the fall of 1919, President Wilson had invited Hoover to serve on his second industrial conference, called to seek a remedy for the growing conflict between labor and management. As the Secretary of Labor, William B. Wilson, who was the chairman, could give little time, Hoover was asked to serve as vice-chairman. He presided at most of the meetings and oversaw the preparation of the report. This recommended collective bargaining in industry, by agents of labor's own choosing. There was then comparatively little of this. The right to strike was supported, except in government and public utilities, and a plan was set up for the adjustment of disputes. Child labor was strongly opposed. A decrease in working hours, better housing and the development of plans for old-age insurance were supported and inflation control measures were advocated.

In 1920, Hoover became the president of the American Institute of Mining and Metallurgical Engineers. He was then elected president of the American Engineering Council, which was composed of the leading American engineering societies. He immediately organized an exhaustive inquiry into industrial waste. This survey disclosed that 25 per cent of the cost of production could be eliminated without reduction in wages or increase in work load. Under the title *Waste in Industry,* the report was published in 1921. Later when he was serving as Secretary of Commerce under President Harding, Hoover implemented the plan through voluntary action on a nation-wide basis.

He examined the situation of the children in "our own American house" and found great neglect in the national health and education programs for them. Speaking to the Associated Charities of San Francisco in December, 1919, he urged aid for children, to provide each child with an "equal opportunity to attain that position in the community to which abilities and character entitle him." At a meeting of the Child Hygiene Association, the following October, he proposed a national program of health inspection in schools, free noonday hot meals served in the schools in certain areas, more compulsory education—and prohibition of child labor. This was well received. As a result of this meeting, the very effective American Child Health Association was later established. Hoover served as chairman throughout the years of the agency's life.

As the 1920 Presidential election approached, support developed in both the major political parties for Hoover to become the candidate for the highest office. Although his background as a Republican was known to his associates under the Democratic administration, his "Democratic complexion" had been increased by his support of the President's foreign policies in the 1918 elections. He had believed that Wilson's influence would be weakened in the peace negotiations if a majority opposed to his foreign policies was elected to Congress.

Hoover-for-President clubs sprang up, although he had not declared his candidacy or party and tried to stop campaign efforts in his behalf. He had supported Theodore Roosevelt in 1912 and joined the National Republican Club the same year. While he opposed the views of some Republicans, he felt that the rank and file membership of the Republican party in the North and West, comprising the "majority of skilled workmen, farmers, professional and small business men," gave it a "core of true Americanism."

While in Washington, Hoover's opportunity to observe the Democratic party had "re-enforced" his Republicanism. He described the Democratic party as including an "ultraconservative Southern group," "political machines in many of the large cities," and a set of "greenback, 'free silver' agrarian fanatics and near-Socialists." He said "there were in the Democratic party men of the highest purpose and ideals."

Hoover's name, as the Presidential candidate, was placed in some primaries, both Democratic and Republican, although, except in the case of California, he had withheld permission, if he could.

Nathan Miller of New York placed Herbert Hoover's name in nomination for President of the United States at the Republican Convention in Chicago in June, 1920, to great applause from the galleries. Thirteen votes was his top score on the convention floor but his prestige with the Republican leaders was enhanced by his political showing.

Shortly after Warren G. Harding, the Republican nominee, was elected President, he invited Hoover to join his Cabinet as either Secretary of the Interior or Secretary of Commerce. Hoover chose the Commerce Department. This was considered the less important of the two offices but, to Hoover, it afforded the greatest opportunity for service.

He heard no more about the post for several months. His appointment was held up by two Republican senators who held quite opposite political views on many questions. At the same time, the two men were most anxious to have Andrew Mellon as head of the Treasury. Harding finally declared to these senators, "Mellon and Hoover or no Mellon."

In the meantime, an opportunity in the mining field was presented to Hoover that was of such magnitude he took a week to consider his decision on it. In January, 1921, Daniel Guggenheim made him an offer said to be a full partnership in Guggenheim Brothers, the largest mining and metallurgical firm in the world, with a guaranteed minimum income of $500,-000 a year. The glittering avenues to a vast fortune were still open to the mining expert. In addition to interesting work, this offer meant more personal freedom than public service permitted and immense wealth. But Hoover, guided by his deep-rooted Quaker principles of helping others, held to his decision to accept the Cabinet post—wrongly, he commented wryly, from the point of view of a "comfortable and untroubled life!"

Hoover was formally tendered the Cabinet position in late February and was confirmed by the Senate as Secretary of Commerce on March 4, 1921. He stipulated that he must have a voice in all important economic policies of the Administration. He co-operated with the Secretary of State in improving the foreign service relations between their departments and suggested to him the revision of outdated commercial treaties, some 100 years old.

In Washington protocol, the Department of Commerce ranked next to the bottom at official dinner tables—but it had a wide-open charter for Hoover's objectives of reconstruction and national development. According to one predecessor, the job required only two hours a day. It was said to be a mere matter of "putting the fish to bed at night and turning on the lights around the coast."

Hoover set about revitalizing the department. Work was his main and often sole recreation. According to one biographer, a Hoover organization resembled a living thing, rather than a machine. He established each undertaking on sound principles which always took the human factor into account, assembled a staff of able men who would use self-initiative, inspired his associates with loyalty—and eventually the time came when the organizer could step aside and let his creation function and grow under its own manpower.

Hoover soon had the Commerce Department operating on a regular basis. From some of the bureaus he removed politicians, who, he felt, were unqualified for their jobs, and promoted men from the technical staffs without inquiry as to their party labels. Certain branches of the department, he found, had been taken out of the Civil Service System, filled with Democratic appointees, then "blanketed" back under Civil Service, all by Presidential orders. President Harding removed the personnel involved from Civil Service, then had the Civil Service Commission select their successors. By delegating the direction of some bureaus to two associates, Hoover freed himself from routine administration to devote his time to the goals he had set.

The Congressional Committees concerned gave support for

new activities in the Commerce Department but declined to add to Hoover's personal staff. He employed two secretaries and three assistants at his own expense. This amounted to more than his own salary as a Cabinet officer—but it all was in line with his determination never to take any salary earned in public service for his private use.

The depression of 1921–1922 was the first serious postwar crisis, and measures to relieve unemployment were considered at the Economic Conference, chairmaned by Hoover, in September, 1921. In his opening address, he stated, "There is no economic failure so terrible in its import as that of a country possessing a surplus of every necessity of life in which numbers, willing and anxious to work, are deprived of these necessities. It simply cannot be if our moral and economic system is to survive."

Nation-wide committees were set up to look after the destitute, public works were increased, industry was asked to apportion employment and undertake renovation and new construction and foreign trade was expanded. By the following spring, recovery was well underway, and the country was soon over the unemployment hump.

From his studies of recuperation from previous great wars, Hoover concluded that recovery depended on increased per capita productivity. His reconstruction program included elimination of industrial and commercial waste, with emphasis on improved railways, expansion of electrical power, simplification and standardization in manufacture, uniform specifications in government purchasing, reduction of seasonal operation of industry, arbitration of trade disputes, oil conservation, readjustment in the coal industry, elimination of waste in the Federal bureaucracy and of human waste in accidents and research in pure and applied science.

As an example of simplification, the number of standard sizes of automobile wheels was reduced from eight to five, and types of paving bricks from sixty-six to five. As a voluntary action under standardization, uniform thread for nuts, bolts and pipes was agreed upon and adopted by all manufacturers. Standard specifications resulted in great savings in government and industrial buying.

Under both the Harding and Coolidge Administrations, study was given to the vital question of oil. At Harding's request, the Commerce Secretary looked into the need for petroleum reserves. With support from Secretary of State Hughes, Hoover urged the oil companies to look to South America and elsewhere for new resources. This was done, and large holdings were acquired in Latin American countries. Domestic conservation recommendations were also made, based on expert knowledge.

In Washington, during the war, Hoover had noted the "amazing duplication, overlapping, waste, red tape, tyranny and incompetence" in the government bureaucracy. In the interests of better government, he "took a dash at this windmill," beginning in 1921. Four years later, he admitted the windmill was still "unharmed." Almost every item in his program met with opposition from some vested official or disturbed some vested habit. Reform would not be attained, he was certain, until Congress authorized the President, some board or a committee of its own members to do it. Years later, Hoover, himself, was to head two such commissions.

In addition to the work of the department to bring about a reduction in the number of accidents in mines, at sea and in the air, Hoover organized the first National Conference on Street and Highway Safety. This association has functioned effectively ever since.

While Secretary of Commerce, Hoover greatly enlarged the research work of the Bureau of Standards, the Bureau of Fisheries and the Radio and Aviation Divisions. In 1926, he organized a committee which raised from industry a million dollars a year for pure science research. This money was distributed by the National Research Council. In an appeal for this fund, Hoover emphasized that pure science research was the raw material for applied science and declared the genius in science to be the most precious of our citizens. We are realizing the far-seeing wisdom of his words with a special impact today.

Through the Carnegie Corporation, the Stanford Food Research Institute was established, to work on a scientific approach to the national food problems. A grant of $70,000 yearly for ten years was made, with the later addition of a large endowment.

Hoover found that opposition to his methods of reconstruction and increasing efficiency arose, not from employers and labor, but from a group of intellectuals and professors of mixed "socialist, fascist and antique ideas." In answer to their allegation that he was producing technological unemployment, Hoover declared that "for every man in the livery stable yesterday there are twenty in the garage today, at double real wages." The American Federation of Labor and the United States Chamber of Commerce both passed resolutions of endorsement for Hoover's entire program. Britain, France and Germany sent commissions to study the work of the Commerce Department.

The Secretary of Commerce received excellent co-operation from President Harding, who encouraged him in everything that he wanted to do and always kept his word. The tragedy of Harding, Hoover declared, was that he was betrayed by a few of his trusted friends—who were later proved to have betrayed their country, too.

Of the initial Cabinet members, Secretary of State Hughes, Secretary of the Treasury Mellon, Secretary of War Weeks, Secretary of the Navy Denby and Will H. Hays, Postmaster General, stood out in Hoover's estimation. He was grateful to them for the extra trouble they took to further his work. With Hughes' aid, he had succeeded in having Harry M. Daugherty, the Attorney General, rescind an injunction against striking railway workers.

Hoover did not find Harding's "play mates," including Daugherty and Albert B. Fall in the Cabinet, congenial and had only formal contact with them.

In June of 1923, the Hoovers were invited to join the President on his forthcoming trip to visit Alaska. The guest list, which had first consisted mainly of some of Harding's special cronies, had suddenly been changed. The President, as he confided to Hoover on the voyage to Alaska, had begun to find out about the wrongdoing of some of his alleged friends, but he gave the Secretary no particulars.

Warren Harding was taken ill on that trip. He died in San Francisco from a bad heart attack on August 2, 1923—broken in spirit by the betrayals.

Calvin Coolidge, the Vice-President, was at once sworn in as President. He asked Hoover to continue in his Cabinet post. The scandals of Teapot Dome and the California Naval Reserve Oil and other exposures soon broke. Fall and Daugherty were indicted in connection with the scandals and Fall was convicted. Daugherty's trial ended with acquittal.

The integrity of the leaders not involved in the indictments was clearly emphasized by contrast.

President Coolidge, Hoover found, was not taciturn with his associates, as he had been pictured, and he had an excellent, dry wit. His tight hold on government expenditures and constant reduction of the public debt were a "fine expression" of his New England thrift. He was not fond of many of Hoover's water development proposals because of their probable cost. Hoover and Dr. Hubert Work, Secretary of the Interior, had difficulty in persuading him to recommend construction of the dam across the Colorado River in Boulder Canyon.

Export and import trade was revived and greatly increased by the Department of Commerce. Hoover spent a great deal of time successfully combating foreign trade combinations against the United States. He inaugurated a new balance sheet, giving the real volume of our international trade, which was published annually. One British statesman is said to have burst out, "We have to fight not only American foreign trade but the American Department of Commerce."

Foreign loans, Hoover insisted, should be made only for productive purposes and with full investigation of their probable security. He warned publicly on foreign financing of which future repayment was doubtful.

Hoover was convinced that a great social need was more and better housing. He developed a comprehensive program to implement this, including the volunteer organization, "Better Homes in America," which had about 30,000 members who were mostly women. This organization supported the department ideas. The need for zoning and better city planning was emphasized and a standard building code formulated. Campaigns were started to encourage year-round construction and lower financial charges. Julius Rosenwald experimented in lending second mortgage money at greatly reduced interest rates.

Under voluntary organization, the yearly average of new housing units was nearly 750,000, while later, Hoover asserts, under the "planned economy" of the New Deal, the average fell to 320,000 new units a year.

Work for Better Children was mainly continued through the American Child Health Association, of which Hoover was the director. Among its activities was the publication of a report on health facilities in eighty-six cities, which resulted in greatly improved conditions. May Day was established as Child Health Day by Act of Congress. As the Communists had previously appropriated this ancient festival day for their demonstrations, Hoover took special satisfaction in providing this particular competition. Child labor was opposed and better schools were advocated for backward areas. To stimulate public interest, a great many publications were issued, including Hoover's *Child's Bill of Rights,* which circulated widely. During the

years of the association's existence, $5,000,000 was raised for
its support. When Hoover left the White House, he was no
longer in a position to secure the funds from private sources
and the association went out of existence in 1933.

With the co-operation of the Secretary of Labor, Hoover
and his department took an active interest in labor relations.
He worked for the unsuccessful Constitutional amendment to
abolish child labor. Through the work of the Child Health
Association, many states were induced to pass better laws pro-
hibiting child labor, and years later, at the end of Hoover's
own Presidential term, the evil was confined to only a few
states.

Early in 1922, Hoover undertook a campaign to reduce
working hours in certain industries. Armed with facts, he
initiated efforts, supported by President Harding, to lower
the work hours in the steel industry. The news that the industry agreed to the reduced work week reached President
Harding on July 3, at Tacoma, Washington, while he was en
route to Alaska. Hoover inserted the announcement in the
President's Fourth of July speech. When Harding came to
Hoover's added paragraphs, after speaking on the American
Eagle, he stumbled over the different vocabulary. During the
applause that followed Hoover's contribution, he asked, "Why
don't you learn to write the same English I do?"

As handy man of the Administration, Hoover was called on
to settle the railway shopmen's strike of 1922. This was accomplished only after some bitter lessons. Out of conferences
arranged by Hoover, the idea of the Railway Labor Board was
developed, to settle railway labor conflicts by voluntary media-
tion. With slight changes, this measure was passed by Congress
in 1926 and kept peace in the railways for the remainder of
Hoover's service in Washington.

The Secretary of Commerce felt that progress was hopeless
if labor and management—both producers—were set up as
"classes," fighting each other. He continued support of col-

lective bargaining but opposed the closed shop and feather bedding as denials of human freedom.

In 1925, he commended the American Federation of Labor, stating that "the forces (Socialism and Communism) of the old world that would destroy our institutions and our civilization have been met in the front-line trenches by the Federation of Labor and routed at every turn."

Hoover found many ways to aid the commercial interests of farmers, despite objections from the Secretary of Agriculture, Henry C. Wallace. Among other instances, the Commerce Department looked into export markets for American farm surpluses, and requests from farm organizations and exporters for assistance regarding these increased a hundredfold. Hoover opposed the McNary-Haugen Bill for federal price fixing of farm products, promoted by Wallace. Coolidge vetoed this. Urged by several farm organizations, he offered the agriculture post to Hoover after Wallace's death. Hoover declined, feeling he could be of more help to the farmers as Secretary of Commerce. William M. Jardine was then appointed. He paid public tribute to the Commerce Department for its service to farmers.

Another part of the department's program was better utilization of the nation's water resources. Plans should be made, Hoover felt, in terms of a whole river system. The federal government should bear the expense of navigation, with contributions from local governments, and should assist in flood control, irrigation and reclamation. He was convinced, however, that the federal government should not go into the business of generating or distributing electrical power as a general policy, as he was firmly opposed to the government entering into any business whose major purpose was competition with our citizens. He hesitated to contemplate the country's future "if the preoccupation of its officials is to be no longer the promotion of justice and equal opportunity but is to be devoted to barter in the markets."

Among the projects on which the Commerce Department

worked was the Colorado River Basin development that affected seven states. Hoover was chairman of a commission set up to deal with this undertaking. After extreme difficulties over a period of seven years, he managed to have a compact for equitable use of the waters ratified by the states concerned. Federal legislation for the building of the dam at Boulder Canyon was passed in 1928, with President Coolidge's aid. Power was to be sold to municipalities and utilities on a 50-year contract, which would repay the cost of the dam, including interest. Some vigorous opposition had previously grown up, even among a few engineers, to the proposed construction of this highest dam in history on the grounds that it would be impracticable, unsafe and subject to earthquakes. Hoover and Dr. Work selected a group of outstanding engineers to review the plans. They asserted that any fears of the dam's bursting were nonsense. "It will stick as long as the mountains around it stick," commented one engineer.

Hoover worked on plans for other great drainage systems, such as the Columbia River Basin, but was blocked in some by Coolidge's opposition to the costs involved.

When the unprecedented Mississippi River flood broke loose in 1927, the Governors of the six menaced states asked for federal help—and asked for Hoover. He went at once to Memphis, Tennessee, and mobilized state and local authorities, militias, Army Engineers, Coast Guard, a Navy air unit, the Weather Bureau and the Red Cross. The area which eventually became flooded stretched from Cairo, Illinois, to the Gulf of Mexico, a distance of over a thousand miles. After the first rush to set up relief operations, Hoover's organization was able to keep up with the speed of the oncoming crest of flood waters and act ahead where needed. Some million and a half people were driven from their homes but, once the rescue and safeguarding work was started, only three lives were lost and one of these was an overcurious sight-seer. When the supply of motorboats proved insufficient, Hoover arranged for the river sawmills to construct a thousand rough boats in ten days. Engines to run them were rented from manufacturers. When the count of motors to be returned was taken, however, many were missing—apparently gone with the flood waters! Financing was provided through a Red Cross drive, conducted by radio from the flood area. The United States Chamber of Commerce set up a nonprofit organization to make low interest loans for rehabilitation. The Rockefeller Foundation contributed a million dollars, to be matched by the affected counties, for the postflood sanitation campaign described earlier. Problems included the building of a high cement wall around the grave of Longfellow's "Evangeline," and, on occasion, moving a whole town's population—who just would not believe the flood could reach them—when the inevitable waters came.

Will Irwin, who reported the disaster for *World's Work,* said of Hoover's able management, "It was like seeing a master play billiards. You may not know much of the game, but you recognize supreme skill when you see it." He described Hoover standing on the tottering Melville levee, as he saw the Chief on a May morning in 1927—"his airplanes scouting overhead, his mosquito-fleet scurrying below, a group of prominent citizens about him listening to the wise, quick, terse directions that were bringing order out of chaos. It symbolizes the man, that scene—'The one tranquil among the raging floods.' " As Irwin was writing about this in 1928, he did not know of the raging floods ahead!

When an earthquake struck the Near East, Will Rogers thought it strange that Hoover was not called in to straighten things out. "Bert was only resting between calamities," he remarked. But Bert was not resting after the completion of the Mississippi Flood relief. He proposed a complete revision of the government flood-control measures. These were adopted by President Coolidge. Ten years later, in another major flood —from Cairo, Illinois, to New Orleans, Louisiana—the surging Mississippi River was held in check.

Finding no government interest in developing commercial aviation—in the very country where the airplane had originated—Hoover set out to do something about this foolish indifference. Over four years later, Congress passed legislation creating an aviation bureau, and the Division of Aviation was at once established under Hoover's agency. During the next three years, enormous progress was made in commercial air development.

Radio was little more than a ship-to-shore telegraph system when Hoover became head of the Commerce Department, which had jurisdiction over the infant industry. He called radio the most important new instrument for intellectual communication since Gutenberg invented printing from movable type. Along with the enthusiastic American boy radio operators and their crystal sets, the department played an important role in radio's astonishing development into a vital force in American life. To preserve the wave lengths for the people, Hoover declared, was "just as important as to keep our channels of navigation open for ships."

Following his precept of government by co-operation, Hoover called a conference in February, 1922, to consider the problems of the mushrooming radio situation. The meeting agreed that Hoover should serve as umpire of the ether waves until needed legislation could be devised. As Secretary of Commerce, Herbert Hoover issued the first broadcasting license—to Station WBZ, in Springfield, Massachusetts.

In February, 1927, Congress finally passed the radio legislation recommended by the Commerce Department, and President Coolidge asked Hoover to select the members of the commission to administer the act.

Through the State Department, Hoover called an International Radio Conference, held in Washington in 1927. He presided at the meetings which were attended by delegates from seventy-six countries. The Radio Treaties signed then have lasted through the years—except in Communist countries. Among radio's chief assets, Hoover counted the private ownership of broadcasting. Its defects, he warned, include the fact that radio "lends itself far more easily to propaganda than the press."

"Putting the fish to bed" ceased to be a joke after Hoover succeeded in having the Alaskan salmon industry saved through legislation. He made great progress in the conservation of the nation's fisheries, in arresting pollution of streams and coastal waters and in reinforcing game fish stocks. As President of the Isaak Walton League, Hoover was the nation's Number One amateur fisherman, and a wise, witty address he made to the league was widely circulated. "Man and boy," he declared, "the American is a fisherman." The pursuit of happiness obviously includes the pursuit of fish—"But it is too long between bites"!

At a meeting of the Committee on Business Cycles and Unemployment, which had been appointed by the 1921 Economic Conference, Hoover had warned: "Booms are times of speculation, overexpansion, wasteful expenditures in industry and commerce, with consequent destruction of capital. . . . The obvious way to lessen the losses and miseries of depression is first to check the destructive extremes of booms." This committee studied and made recommendations on the nation's economic movements. Feeling the necessity of further investigation, Hoover organized a Committee on Recent Economic Changes in 1927.

Statistics was a field in which the department could take positive action. Comprehensive industrial figures were made available, from which it was hoped that the business world could better detect the approach of booms and slumps. Hoover reiterated his warnings on excessive swings in the business cycle.

Other interests of the versatile Secretary of Commerce and his department related to water transportation, the merchant marine and working with trade associations on voluntary codes of business ethics.

Hoover's multitudinous activities in the commerce post have perhaps been best depicted in the cartoon by Ding, titled "The Traffic Problem in Washington, D.C.," which shows a crowd of Hoover images, each bearing the tag of one of his activities, pouring across a street, while the automobiles of Congress and other Cabinet figures are held up. A policeman named "Cal," representing President Coolidge, is trying to halt the rush and give the others a turn.

Firmly opposed to the government's entering into any business of which the major result or purpose was competition with private enterprise, Hoover constantly sought to determine the line between proper governmental action in the regulation of commercial activities and in operations which were beyond the capacity and purpose of business—and that which would be destructive of individual initiative. "Fundamentally," he declared, "this problem involved the destiny of the American scheme of life."

Hoover's inherent feeling for social betterment coupled with his engineer's training for increased efficiency and the elimination of waste were also important factors in establishing his policy of reconciliation between free enterprise and the right scope of government activity in the best interests of the people.

Some special participations of the Secretary of Commerce in the foreign field were the settlements of World War I debts, the Washington Conference for the Limitation of Armaments of 1921–1922, the appointment of the Dawes Commission on German Reparations and the nonrecognition of Communist Russia.

In the rising boom, which began in 1927, and the orgy of speculation which followed, President Coolidge was anxiously urged to take action against the dangers to the national economy by Hoover and others. Coolidge was by nature reluctant to make a move before the "actual explosion of trouble," so he rejected and side-stepped these warnings. One of the President's favorite maxims was, "If you see ten troubles coming down the road, you can be sure that nine will run into the ditch before they reach you and you have to battle with only one of them." But on this occasion, when that tenth trouble reached him, he was unprepared and the trouble had acquired such momentum by that time, it spelled disaster. However, when he left the Presidency, the country was still enjoying "Coolidge prosperity."

During Herbert Hoover's two terms as Secretary of Commerce, he and his family lived in Washington, in a large colonial house at 2300 S Street. Mrs. Hoover ran the establishment with her customary charm and economy. She transformed the garden and built a porch at the back of the house, where the family had their summertime meals out-of-doors. The Hoovers kept constant Open House. There was scarcely a meal without guests, including breakfast. Except for about ten days in Palo Alto in summer and a week's deep-sea fishing in Florida during the winter, Hoover had no rest from his official duties.

Herbert, Jr. and Allan attended the Friends' School in Washington, and the Western High School and the Palo Alto High School in California, before going to college. During vacations, Herbert, Jr. took jobs at manual labor—to his father an invaluable part of a boy's education. In 1921 he entered Stanford University and graduated in the class of 1925. Allan, four years younger, was greatly interested in animals, and he had many pets. He attracted countless birds with food, water and gourds hanging in the trees for lodging. Two dogs and two cats were the very minimum in household pets in his opinion. For a while, he had two ducks which he trained to sit on the front porch to the surprise of passers-by. A present of two small alligators made a welcome addition to his collection of land turtles. The rest of the family were not as enthusiastic—particularly since Allan was convinced the alligators must be bedded for the night in their bathtubs.

Among the domestic crises graciously met by Mrs. Hoover was the time that two senators and their wives were announced for dinner when she and her husband were already in the middle of the meal with a few close friends. The Commerce Secretary had invited the two couples and overlooked telling his wife! Under Mrs. Hoover's direction, he steered the new dinner guests into the library while the dining room table was reset with four more places and extra food provided by the cook, including a reserve Virginia ham. The original guests then made their appearance from another room, in which they had been quietly waiting, and the whole company sat down to the second dinner. The food went around safely—due to careful holding back on the part of the host and hostess and the first guests!

An incident which Mrs. Hoover found disconcerting occurred one evening when Senator Peter Norbeck was dining at the house on S Street. The Senator, busy talking on political matters, overlooked the small Belgian lace doily on his dessert plate when removing the finger bowl. He placed his helping of ice cream on the doily and then ate the desert—and the lace, too—before anyone realized what was happening! Fortunately, the Senator suffered no ill effects.

Mrs. Hoover assumed the presidency of the Girl Scouts of America soon after moving to Washington and gave that fine organization a great deal of her energy and time during the twelve years the Hoovers lived in the capital. She raised over $2,000,000 for its work and helped build it into a strong, constructive force for good, with the enrollment increasing from less than 100,000 girls to nearly 1,000,000 throughout her association with the organization.

In Washington, following strict official protocol, the custom of making formal calls was carefully observed. Mrs. Hoover rebelled at spending so much precious time in this ineffectual fashion. By securing an agreement among the other Cabinet ladies, she ended the practice.

The work of the Commerce Department was never out of the family picture, and two or three evenings a week Hoover worked at home, with secretarial assistance. To his colleagues in the department, he has paid much tribute. One of these men, Lawrence Richey, has the distinction of having suggested J. Edgar Hoover for director of the Federal Bureau of Investigation, in answer to a query from the Attorney General.

As Secretary of Commerce, Hoover made great strides toward the goal set by his social conscience. In his speech of August 11, 1928, formally accepting the Republican nomination, he summed up the more than seven years of economic progress—including an increased standard of living—in which his department had played such an important role: "To me the test is the security, comfort, and opportunity that have been brought to the average American family. . . . One of the oldest and perhaps the noblest of human aspirations has been the abolition of poverty. . . . We in America today are nearer to the final triumph over poverty than ever before. . . . We have not yet reached the goal, but, given a chance to go forward with the policies of the last eight years, we shall soon with the help of God. . . ."

When the domestic and European economic hurricanes struck the country, this speech was, of course, often thrown back at Hoover—but he never lost his faith that this goal can be attained, if the country sticks to those principles upon which the Republic was founded and on which it has grown to greatness.

Orphan
to
President

CHAPTER 13

While reporting on the progress of the Mississippi Flood Relief, as seen from the official train, Will Irwin found that Hoover was willing to be a candidate for the Republican nomination for President, provided that Calvin Coolidge did not run for re-election in 1928.

He remarked to the Chief, "My hat's in the ring for you, on one condition."

"What is that?" Hoover asked, his face set. In practical politics a condition coupled with a pledge of support usually meant a request for office.

"That you never offer me a political job!" Irwin replied.

President Coolidge did not ever explain the reasons behind his famous "I do not choose to run" statement of August, 1927, which led to unceasing curiosity and kept the Republican Presidential possibilities in considerable doubt as to their own campaign plans.

In February, 1928, Hoover informed the President that he was being urged to enter his name in the Ohio primaries by twelve Ohio Congressmen, including former Senator Burton, and asked Coolidge if he planned to allow his name to be filed in the primary.

"No," declared the President.

In regard to Hoover's filing, Coolidge responded, "Why not?"

Governor Lowden of Illinois was the other leading Republican candidate. There were also some active contenders in the Senate. In a Washington political column, Charles Michelson declared that the Republican Old Guard of the Senate, concerned over who would win the next Presidential nomination, did not like or understand Hoover and were doubtful of their ability to deal with him. Coolidge was at least a politician, thinking their language, even if he did not speak it much, while Hoover revolved in a "different orbit."

Hoover was attacked because of his long business stays in London—being dubbed "Sir Herbert" for this—and through the suit brought by Chang Yen-mao in the British courts, which was aired in the American press and in the *Congressional Record*.

A cartoon that appeared soon after the Coolidge pronouncement showed a G.O.P. elephant salesman trying the "Presidential Shoes" on Hoover and declaring them a fit. His personal popularity grew. Hoover clubs sprang up in various states. By mid-May, 400 delegates were counted for the "people's choice."

A "Stop Hoover" movement was launched but, by the time of the Republican Convention, the issue was no longer in doubt. Herbert C. Hoover was nominated on the first ballot at the convention in Kansas City in June, 1928.

In accepting the honor, Hoover disavowed the feeling expressed in the notice of his selection—that he had earned the right to the Presidential nomination—in these words:

My country owes me no debt. It gave me, as it gives every boy and girl, a chance. It gave me schooling, independence of action, opportunity for service and honor. In no other land could a boy from a country village, without inheritance or influential friends, look forward with unbounded hope. My whole life has taught me what America means. I am indebted to my country beyond any human power to repay.

Continuing, he warned of the new era and new forces affecting the nation's economic life and world role, which demanded constant study and effort in order to maintain prosperity and peace. If elected, he promised to advance the moral and spiritual welfare of all the people and uphold the traditions of the Republican Party.

Herbert Hoover had learned about political campaigning on a stumping tour for Calvin Coolidge in the middle and far West during the 1924 Presidential race. He knew that campaigning consisted of visiting with local committees and making speeches at luncheon, dinner and large evening meetings almost daily, with an overnight train trip in between. Fried chicken and peas he had found to be the universal and almost exclusive campaign food.

Among the crises he had encountered was the occasion when a meeting chairman, overcome by the chance to address a radio audience embracing the whole West, took up most of the half hour of radio time engaged for a major speech by Hoover. Repeated pulls on his coattails by others on the platform produced only a random backward kick from the runaway speaker. This struck the lady chairman on the shins. She did not applaud when the chairman finally stopped to present the main speaker!

But the 1928 Presidential race was a different matter for Hoover. His was the final responsibility. The full use of radio for the first time in a Presidential Campaign necessitated a new, original speech for each major broadcast. No longer could a good speech be repeated with small variations, delivery be improved by practice and eloquence enhanced by repetition. As Mr. Hoover always refused to use a ghost writer, his preparation of new speeches required a tremendous amount of time, as he took two or three weeks for each.

Besides the campaign desk work, the 18-hour day meant a "pneumatic drill on one's brain of personalities, committees, crowds, messages and incidents." At train stops, the assembled thousands must have short speeches. The local committees then came aboard and rode on to the next stop, to have a chance to talk over their favorite issues with the candidate. Thousands of babies had to be greeted by shaking their chubby fists. This candidate, who had saved millions of children from starvation, did not wish to make a bid for favor by kissing babies for their parents' votes.

Painful problems sometimes arose in the candidate's efforts not to offend those who expected to be personally remembered. In a Chicago reception line, a lady asked Hoover, "Don't you remember me?" and confidently waited for his delighted word of recognition.

"I am sorry, madam," he replied, always wishing to be honest, "but I would like to and no doubt could, if you will tell me where we met."

"Why, I sat on the end of the third row when you spoke in Indianapolis, and you looked right at me," came the quite indignant response.

Autographs proved a trial, too. With a possible half million in circulation, Hoover felt there was inflation in this issue!

After his nomination, Hoover strove for unified action from all groups in the Republican Party. He met with a single failure, Senator George W. Norris of Nebraska whom he described as a devoted socialist.

When speaking in New York, Hoover paid tribute to the

Democratic candidate, Governor Alfred E. Smith. The Governor had come up from the pavements, as had Hoover from the grass roots. Throughout the campaign, neither said anything in the way of accusations or misrepresentations which prevented the two men from remaining good friends after the election. On some other levels, in typical campaign fashion, such integrity was not displayed.

Among the topics debated in the campaign were the broad principles of government, various needed reforms, national defense, foreign relations, agricultural and labor policies, business regulation in support of the competitive system, prohibition, use of water resources, tariff and the approaches of "collectivism."

Speaking on the Eighteenth Amendment, Hoover described it as a "great social and economic experiment, noble in purpose." This, he owned, was an unfortunate phrase. It pleased neither the extreme drys nor the extreme wets and was easily turned into derision as a "noble experiment." The majority of the country, however, favored giving the prohibition law further tryout.

Hoover determined that the Republican party should unequivocally define the issue of the American system as opposed to all forms of "paternalism and state socialism." In an address in New York, on October 22, he warned that some proposals, in particular those of federal entry into the power business and the agricultural price-fixing plan, urged by the Democrats, would be a "long step toward the abandonment of our American system and a surrender to the destructive operation of governmental conduct of commercial business. . . . Free speech does not live many hours after free industry and free commerce die.

"The very essence of equality of opportunity and of American individualism," Hoover continued, "is that there shall be no domination by any group or combination in this republic, whether it be business or political. On the contrary, it demands economic justice as well as political and social justice."

Hoover, who deplored campaign dirt, was again attacked through the old Chinese lawsuit as allegedly having robbed a Chinese. This boomeranged when Tong Shao-yi, Prime Minister of China and one of the principal owners of the company involved, stated in the American press that the accusations were "dastardly."

As a tenant of a London house, regardless of nationality, Hoover had been required to pay local rates or taxes. Rate-payers were automatically placed on the voting rolls and this fact was used in an effort to misrepresent him as a "British subject."

Another attack concerned the false charge of employing only Asiatic labor at a ranch near Bakersfield, California, named for him because he had helped the owners in its purchase. This charge was denied by the Kern County Labor Union leaders. The "smear" lived on, however, for later re-use.

The corruption in the Harding Administration was much noised by the Democrats.

The Republican standard bearer was greatly disturbed over the religious issue that was raised in the campaign because Governor Smith was the first Presidential candidate of the Catholic faith. Hoover tried to keep this issue out of the contest, declaring,

"I come of Quaker stock. My ancestors were persecuted for their beliefs. Here they sought and found religious freedom. By blood and conviction I stand for religious toleration both in act and in spirit. The glory of our American ideals is the right of every man to worship God according to the dictates of his own conscience."

When the religious question was brought up against the Governor, Hoover indignantly opposed the attacks. He repeatedly stated that he wanted no votes on that score.

When the election results were counted, Hoover had swept the country, aided by the general prosperity, carrying all but eight states. He broke into the Democratic Solid South, with four state victories there which have been attributed in large measure to the prohibition and religious issues as well as to that of Tammany Hall.

In the newly elected House of Representatives, the Republicans led by 100 seats and the party had 17 more senators than the opposition.

As President-elect, Hoover undertook three major tasks, a trip to Latin America, assembling his executive staff and formulating the major policies for his Administration.

He made arrangements for the trip to Central and South America, which he described as a Good Neighbor Tour, since he believed that improvement in the relations between the United States and the nations to the south was imperative. Too strong an interpretation of the Monroe Doctrine by the United States had created suspicion and antagonism which, in turn, he felt, were increased by "dollar diplomacy" or promotion of some commercial business affairs of our citizens through diplomatic action. Foreign influence played on these antagonisms as part of trade war propaganda. Looking to the future, the peoples of the Western Hemisphere shared not only mutual interests—but common threats to those interests.

The battleship *Maryland* was assigned to the President-elect for the voyage from California southward to Chile. Besides Mrs. Hoover, who spoke considerable Spanish, the party included Henry P. Fletcher, former Under Secretary of State and very popular as a diplomat in Latin America, John Mott of Californian-Spanish descent, and about twenty press correspondents, among whom were Mark Sullivan and Will Irwin.

Each morning the Hoovers breakfasted in the admiral's cabin with the official party. Irwin and Sullivan were always invited, and, between ports, diplomats and other officials frequently joined the group. Irwin tells of fascinating discussions on government and politics that took place these mornings at sea. Among the topics reviewed were the dangers involved if the military faction in Japan should gain control and embark on a career of conquest, and the necessity to stock-pile tin, chromium and rubber at the first sign of war. Another discourse was on the habits of whales. At times, Hoover monopolized the conversation with captivating firsthand stories of Asia, Australia and Washington.

Honduras, Salvador, Nicaragua, Costa Rica, Ecuador, Peru, Chile, Argentina, Uruguay and Brazil were visited on this Good Neighbor Tour. In addition, Hoover had a meeting with Bolivian government leaders on the *Maryland,* off Antofogasta, Chile.

The feeling of hospitality and welcome for the distinguished visitor was expressed by parades, banquets, receptions and speeches. Everything possible was done to please Hoover's party—and all with extreme politeness.

Telling about the practice of giving him anything he admired because he was a high American official, Hoover declared, "In San José I ate a native melon and remarked how good it was. When I got to the ship, the sailors were putting aboard a bargeload of melons, with the compliments of El Presidente!"

In order to stop a civil war in Nicaragua, President Coolidge had indirectly promoted a presidential election conducted by United States Marines. The incumbent president had been defeated at the polls. On Hoover's arrival in that turbulent country, he learned that the loser was allegedly not going to give up his office peaceably. He invited both the Nicaraguan president-elect and the outgoing leader to lunch aboard the *Maryland.* Both came, as neither wanted to refuse. One of the naval officers described the meeting: "They stepped around like fighting cocks, making dog-eyes at each other." Hoover found them most interesting men. Their government problems were discussed and both were invited to visit the United States. There was no further revolution for a time.

The President-elect and the official party left the *Maryland* at Callao, Peru. At the end of the west coast tour, they traveled by train from Santiago, Chile, across the Andes Mountains and the Pampas to Buenos Aires, Argentina. On the last morning of the trip, shortly before they reached Buenos Aires, Irwin met Hoover in the observation car at the rear of the train. Hoover showed him an English-language Buenos Aires newspaper which gave a sensational account of the arrest of an anarchist. The man had a very large bomb in his room and a map that marked the spot on Hoover's route where he intended to plant the bomb under a culvert, triggered to explode when the train passed over the detonator set on the rail. This plot was discovered in a police cleanup of revolutionary radicals, conducted in order to prevent any such incident.

Hoover tore the front page off the newspaper and crammed it into his pocket. "It's just as well that Lou shouldn't see this!" he remarked.

Soon the train stopped at a station where a crowd was gathered to greet the future American *presidente*. Hoover went out onto the observation car platform. Two secret service men immediately stepped into place behind him, eyes roving about the people for any false movement. "I wish so many of them didn't have their hands in their pockets," one secret service man murmured.

President Irigoyen of Argentina met the Hoover party at the station in Buenos Aires. Three lines of police protection had been set up along the platform to prevent Communist outbreaks and hold back the spectators. However, the platform soon became a seething mass as many of the people pushed past the guards. Irigoyen's coat was ripped in the commotion, but the United States Naval Aides managed to keep the Hoovers from being crushed. After their safe arrival at the American Embassy, one of the secret service men reported to the Buenos Aires chief of police that his wallet had been stolen, to which the chief replied, "Well, they got my wrist watch."

At Montevideo, in Uruguay, the Hoover party boarded the

battleship *Utah* for the voyage to Rio de Janeiro. After four festive days in the Brazilian capital, the *Utah* prepared to sail at four o'clock on a Sunday afternoon. This was specially planned by Hoover so that the battleship would reach Hampton Roads two weeks later, on Sunday morning when a formal greeting ceremony would not be scheduled because of church services. As an example of the extreme respect in which he held the Presidential office, he wished to avoid the implied discourtesy of any official welcome while his predecessor still occupied the White House.

It was not too convenient, therefore, when President Luis of Brazil radioed Hoover to delay sailing until five-thirty, so that he might see the illumination of Rio from the bay. At last, the *Utah* moved out along the line of the Brazilian fleet and twenty-one-gun salutes were exchanged. Sudden darkness fell and an unequalled display of fireworks lighted the sky. As the ship came to the gates of the harbor, a succession of colored crowns burst over Sugarloaf Mountain. In response, the captain trained his searchlights on the Brazilian Flag flying from the summit of Sugarloaf and kept them there while the battleship was within range. The mountain erupted with hundreds of rockets as the *Utah* passed out into the darkness of the open Atlantic. Mrs. Hoover was frankly weeping and her husband's eyes brimmed with tears as they went below and the ship was set on its course, carrying the President-elect home to the United States and to another milestone in his career of public service—this time in the highest office in the land.

In his Latin American speeches, Hoover emphasized the Good Neighbor theme and proposed a better exchange program of intellectuals, particularly students and professors. He took up the question of inter-American aviation and from this initiative Pan American Airways was later developed. From government officials of Peru and Bolivia, Hoover gathered the information which became the basis of the compromise he later offered in his successful arbitration of the Tacna-

Arica dispute between these two South American countries. Another result of his trip was the withdrawal of American troops from Nicaragua and Haiti.

The President-elect's second task, the assembling of his administrative staff, was first of all the selection of his Cabinet. The members he chose were: Secretary of State, Frank B. Kellogg until June, 1929, then Henry L. Stimson; Secretary of the Treasury, Andrew Mellon; Secretary of War, James W. Good; Attorney General, William D. Mitchell; Secretary of the Navy, Charles Francis Adams; Postmaster General, Walter F. Brown; Secretary of the Interior, Ray Lyman Wilbur; Secretary of Agriculture, Arthur M. Hyde; Secretary of Commerce, Robert P. Lamont, and Secretary of Labor, James J. Davis.

Herbert Hoover has paid great tribute to all the men and women who served in his Administration, to their integrity and their continuing loyalty and friendship through all the ordeals they faced together.

He came to the White House determined to carry forward the reconstruction and development measures in which he took part as Secretary of Commerce, to undertake reform and progress and to reorient foreign relations with the aim of advancing peace and international progress.

March 4, 1929, was cold and rainy. According to tradition, Herbert C. Hoover took the oath of office as President of the United States outdoors at the east side of the Capitol, and then delivered his Inaugural Address.

The rain turned into a downpour as the new President and the official party started for the White House for luncheon. The waiting crowds were willing to be drenched if they could have a glimpse of the Chief Executive, so the Hoovers rode to their new home in an open car and arrived thoroughly soaked. It was not an auspicious start.

In his address, Herbert Hoover had warned that there was no short road to the realization of American aspirations and that ill-considered remedies for the country's faults only brought penalties afterward.

"But if we hold the faith of the men in our mighty past who created these ideals," he concluded, "we shall leave them heightened and strengthened for our children."

Seeing that the top on the Hoovers' car was lowered, the Vice-President, Charles Curtis, and his sister, Mrs. Dolly Gann, who acted as his hostess, also rode in an open car from the Capitol to the White House. They, too, reached their destination well drenched. Mrs. Gann discovered then Mrs. Hoover's great kindness and consideration for others. Busy as she was, on assuming the responsibility of running the White House that very day, the new First Lady sent Mrs. Gann's hat and coat out to be dried during lunch so that she would be comfortable, in addition to being well dressed, when the official party went out to see the Inaugural Parade from the reviewing stand on Pennsylvania Avenue, in front of the White House.

When President Hoover took his place to review the parade, he folded his overcoat and put it on the floor so his granddaughter Peggy Ann could climb on it to get a good view of all that passed by. It was a thrilling sight as Army, Navy, Marine and other units marched before the thirty-first President, while Army and Marine bands played *Hail to the Chief* and planes and dirigibles flew overhead in aerial tribute.

At this pinnacle in his life, the President had not overlooked those who had been good to him in his modest childhood. Among his supporters who had journeyed to Washington for the Inauguration was Herbert Hoover's first teacher back in West Branch, Iowa. Mollie Carran, who had wanted to adopt the orphaned Herbert, had a reserved seat in the reviewing stand to watch the honor paid her former pupil.

Battle
on a
Thousand
Fronts

CHAPTER 14

In addition to the magnitude of Herbert Hoover's multi-job as Chief Executive, Commander in Chief, Chief Magistrate, adviser to Congress, foreign policy maker and leader of the Republican Party, he faced other political and personal problems. He found succeeding a member of his own party to be a handicap, as there was little patronage with which to reward his own supporters, particularly since most of Coolidge's choices were able public servants. Also, he was unable to blame his predecessor for any inevitable mistakes, because he had inherited their responsibility from a fellow Republican!

Hoover had difficulties within his own party, too. The older Republican elements in Congress were not reconciled to his election to the Presidency and, at times, busied themselves politically at cross-purposes to the Administration. On the other hand, some party members wanted to show by "grasshopper bites" that they were more liberal than the President—and did not wear his often caricatured high, starched collar!

As to Congress, Hoover felt that there had been an increasing ascendancy of the Executive arm over the Legislative since the country's early years. He felt that the independence of the Legislative branch should be strengthened and he, personally, had little taste for forcing Congressional action or engaging in battles of criticism. He did not wish to appeal frequently to the people, lest Congress be discredited.

Hoover had been willing to assume the Presidency in the hope that he might take a leading role in forwarding progress in the United States. He was anxious to ease strains of growth due to new discoveries and inventions through reforms, and to aid in warding off the dangerous political infections which had arisen in Europe. He believed too that he could contribute to strengthening the principles and ideals which had given such abundance to the American people—and a way of life transcending all others in history. He had achieved the highest office in the land through his proven executive ability, his faculty for getting things done by voluntary co-operation, the help of his devoted friends and his integrity. He had not reached the top by way of the political ladder, so had not had the schooling of the rough-and-tumble precinct politics. He had not had, either, the experience of dealing with partisan politics on all planes.

A White House colleague affirmed that Hoover was more successful with men high in industry, business and labor than with those in public life during his term. Hoover's temperament and training did not accommodate themselves to "the peculiar rules of the great game of politics." Both his friends and his foes could agree on one point, though to different degrees—he was "no politician." One long-time associate felt that the Chief was out of character in the political arena. A partisan foe classed him as an amateur in the art of politics—one who did not know how to chart the process of overcoming opposition in this field.

The lack of political mastery and dexterity handicapped Hoover in carrying on his Presidential responsibilities. His work was hampered by his seeming inability to act with political sensitivity. It in no way helped that these political flaws stemmed from his finest qualities.

During the preconvention campaign, Hoover often kept important callers waiting, and sometimes refused to see them when he had work on hand he considered more pressing. This was a constant worry to his associates. One day he let an important political caller wait in the outer office, finally giving him only a few minutes on the way to an appointment. Arch Shaw was delegated to do something about this "tactlessness." Carefully, he explained how visitors expected to be treated by a man seeking office. This impressed Hoover. He paced the floor, thinking. Finally, he turned abruptly to his friend, saying, "All right! But I'll kiss no babies."

Mr. Hoover never liked the clamor of crowds or superficial social contacts. He never made pretensions to oratory, and long continued to be terrified at the opening of every speech.

As President, Hoover experienced the greatest difficulty in interpreting himself and his acts to the public. An innate Quaker reticence seemed to freeze him in the presence of a crowd. This factor, combined with his sensitiveness and modesty, constrained him from dramatizing himself and his program. Earl Reeves, describing Hoover as Secretary of Commerce, wrote: "He does not 'dress up' his statements or his acts; he is not on dress parade before correspondents. . . . A 'press agent' would say that he overlooks a million chances no politician should overlook." One biographer has remarked that Hoover seemed not to have the least appreciation of "the poetry, the music, and the drama of politics."

His friends often tried to convince him of the need for publicity and vote-getting build-ups. Early in his political career, his backers prepared a newspaper release, giving a dramatic account of the Chief's role in the Tientsin siege during the Boxer Rebellion. The account told of his rescue of a child trapped in the line of gunfire. The text was shown to Hoover before release to the papers. This was a mistake! Hoover read it with a frown, then slowly tore the paper into bits and dropped them into a wastebasket.

"You can't make a Teddy Roosevelt out of me," he announced quietly but with finality.

Since he shrank from presenting his personality and playing up his achievements and his selfless struggles in behalf of the people, the public's image of Hoover was left to his enemies with disastrous results. A myth developed in which his best attributes were somehow turned against him. His modesty and reticence were inverted to "callous indifference" and the "do-nothing" accusation. In sustained partisan emotion the achievements which could not be conveniently distorted, such as his great humanitarian work in saving millions in Europe from famine, were retroactively blotted out.

Herbert Hoover tackled his new job as President with his accustomed energy and dedicated, hard work. Determined that his Administration should maintain a rigid integrity and avoid the "slightest color" of yielding to any special influence, he gave a great deal of attention to government housekeeping, and its efficiency.

Immediately following inauguration, the new Presidential family began getting settled in the White House. Hoover restored to its original function the upstairs sitting room used as a study by all presidents from John Adams to William McKinley. To accommodate their large family, the Theodore Roosevelts had transformed it into a bedroom. In this study the Emancipation Proclamation and the document granting the freedom of Cuba had been signed. By examining a contemporary painting of the Emancipation signing, Mrs. Hoover identified in the attic some of the actual furnishings of the Lincoln Study at that time and brought them back to the historic room.

She moved her family's own belongings into the upstairs apartments where the Presidential occupants lived and made the rooms most attractive and livable.

The distinguished East Room had been refurnished by President Monroe, following the burning of the White House during the War of 1812. He had obtained Empire pieces from Paris, most of which survived, although now scattered from attic to basement. Mrs. Hoover brought these pieces back to this large formal reception room, thus restoring its former character and importance.

The Hoovers retained all the White House domestic staff, including the cook who had promptly disclosed her support of Governor Smith. Ironically, she lost out in the succeeding Democratic administration.

The White House annual receptions proved to be an assembly line of thousands of handshakes. Good wishes from a few thousand were an encouragement, but greeting all the people who came was exhausting. Hoover's right hand was often so swollen after a reception that he could not write with it for days. A bad cut he received on one occasion from a turned-in diamond ring on a well-wisher's hand brought the ceremony to a sudden end.

New Year's Day receptions were inaugurated by President John Adams, and 135 persons had wished the Adamses a Happy New Year at the first one. Nine thousand people came on January 1, 1930, to wish the Hoovers well. Some had waited since midnight to keep their places in line. Mrs. Hoover, particularly, felt that thousands of people would be disappointed if they could not come to the White House, and this would reflect unfavorably on the current occupants, so as many as possible of the customary formal receptions were held.

One advantage of being President was the privilege of terminating all interviews, conferences and social occasions. Hoover chose ten o'clock as his curfew hour for the evening parties, which were held to a minimum. He rose at six and also liked to catch up on some of his important reading during the night.

In the White House office, there were many time-consuming customs. One of these, which Hoover found he was too busy to continue, was a noon reception six days a week, when any caller passed by the F.B.I. could shake hands with the President. Under President Coolidge, the public callers averaged between three and four hundred a day. Hoover found himself devoting a whole hour each day to greeting from 1,000 to 1,200 callers.

Ding's cartoon on this change showed Hoover busy in a kitchen, preparing the Nation's needs, while the stream of citizens declared,

"That's all right, Mr. President. We can shake hands with ourselves."

Among other innovations was a delegation of power to Cabinet officers, so that they might do much of the necessary paper signing for him; also the installation of a telephone on the President's desk.

The problem of daily exercise for the President was resolved by a medicine-ball game with some of his colleagues on the White House lawn, every weekday morning at seven. The players gathered after the game for fruit juice and coffee.

To escape the well-known summer heat in Washington and remain near enough to the capital for work and emergencies, Hoover bought land at the headwaters of the Rapidan River, 100 miles away. Mrs. Hoover laid out and superintended the building of a series of log cabins, to provide enough room for the family and about fifteen guests. Hoover later gave this property to the Shenandoah National Park, incorporated during his Administration, for future use by the White House or by the Boy and Girl Scout organizations alternately. When the Democratic National Committee charged that the property had been paid for by public funds, Hoover had to make a public denial, proving that he personally had paid for the Rapidan camp—land, buildings and furniture.

President Hoover could not devote his term of office wholly to his program for the country. The Depression of 1929 started in the eighth month of his Administration and the primary need was to try to assure economic recovery and employment as speedily as possible. He labored toward this end unceasingly.

In spite of the serious handicaps, much was accomplished in national development, often in conjunction with relief measures.

Hoover was able to realize as President many of the dreams for the betterment of his country which he had had while he was Secretary of Commerce. With the co-operation of the governors of the states concerned, he prepared to carry out great multiple storage dam projects, to irrigate private and public lands, give flood protection, help navigation and provide a by-product of hydroelectric power to be sold to municipalities and power companies so the federal government would not go into the business of generating and distributing power.

In June, 1929, the Colorado River Compact was ratified by the Senate and, after the years of labor and negotiation by Hoover's commission, development of the great river was begun. Under the legislation authorizing the dam construction, the power had first to be sold and Secretary of the Interior Wilbur negotiated the largest power contract in history. Signed in April, 1930, this provided for the sale of the falling water, as a raw material, to private companies and municipalities, in a way which protected the public interest and guaranteed repayment to the government of its outlay in the entire cost of more than $400,000,000. The end of Hoover's term found the dam three-quarters completed. It was then the largest structure of its kind. Following the custom of naming large federal reservoirs for presidents, it was officially designated by Congress as the Hoover Dam.

The President directed the Reclamation Service to prepare engineering plans for the Columbia River project. Those for the Grand Coulee Dam, on that river, were so near completion at the end of his four years in office that the next administration was able to start building very shortly after the Democrats took over. The engineering work on the California Central Valley project had progressed so far that the best locations were blueprinted and much of the necessary information for the construction of the dams on the Sacramento, Kings, San Joaquin and American Rivers was lined up in 1932.

Preliminary engineering work for the Cove Creek Dam, in the Tennessee River Valley, was started by President Hoover in 1930, as a measure for flood protection and the development of water resources, under the same arrangements in regard to the sale of power and the return of construction costs with interest to the government, that had been made for the Hoover Dam. The federal government would thus cooperate with state and local authorities in putting the question of the Tennessee River development in the hands of the people primarily concerned—to their permanent benefit.

Controversy developed over the Wilson Dam at Muscle Shoals, on the Tennessee River, which had been built as a war measure. With the Governors of Alabama and Tennessee, Hoover appointed a joint commission to study the Tennessee River drainage. In November, 1931, the group reported their findings on the river development and also recommended leasing the Muscle Shoals power and fertilizer plants to private business under government regulations of retail rates and restrictions on usage.

The Administration was unable to get authority from the Democratic-controlled Congress which took office in December to proceed with the Cove Creek Dam on the power leasing, repayment basis advocated by Hoover, because Senator Norris and others planned to turn the project into a federal power distribution and fertilizer scheme. Hoover refused to agree to this "piece of socialism" and vetoed their bills as harmful to the American system.

As the public utility industry became more intrastate in character and larger companies developed, Hoover decided the time had come for federal regulation, in addition to that of the various states already existing. He requested a strong Federal Power Commission in his first message to Congress, in December, 1929, and again in his message the following year, but was not granted effective regulatory power.

In December, 1929, the President outlined plans to Congress to create a unified trunk-line system of interior waterways, both north-south and east-west, which would connect with the North Atlantic by way of the Great Lakes and the St. Lawrence River and with the Gulf of Mexico by means of the Mississippi River. A uniform depth of nine feet was set, and completion of work at this level on the Ohio River, undertaken while he was Secretary of Commerce, was dedicated by Hoover at Louisville, Kentucky, in October, 1929. On his recommendation, Congress passed a bill authorizing a large program of river and harbor works and approving the co-ordination of the systems into a national network.

By December, 1931, these improvements, speeded by relief appropriations, were progressing rapidly. In that year alone, the amount of material moved to carry out these projects equaled the entire removal during the construction of the Panama Canal.

The Mississippi waterway system was largely completed, including the flood control plan below Cairo, and in full operation in 1933. Many other waterway projects in different parts of the country were also completed or in progress. Over $700,000,000 were spent on river projects during Hoover's Presidential term, advancing them further in those four years than they had progressed in the previous thirty. In addition to the commercial benefits derived by the people, the through waterway system has been credited with saving the whole internal transportation from collapse during World War II.

While Secretary of Commerce, Hoover had been Chairman of the St. Lawrence Waterway Commission, which had completed most of the preliminary plans for this important waterway project. On becoming President, Hoover resolved the few remaining difficulties and a treaty with Canada providing for the construction was signed in July, 1932, subject to approval by the United States and its northern neighbor. This was shelved by the Senate following Hoover's defeat in the 1932 election. While recommending the treaty to Congress, President Roosevelt did not push its ratification, although he had a large Democratic majority in both houses. The scenic values of Niagara Falls had already been saved through a treaty with Canada, initiated by Hoover and approved by the Senate in 1930. The majestic cataract was thus preserved for the admiration of honeymooners!

Another major aim of President Hoover was conservation. Shortly after taking office, he set up a program of total conservation of government oil by refusing leases on government oil land and canceling those on which requirements had not been met. He initiated efforts to repress excessive drilling and consequent waste of gas pressure in new oil pools. Five of the major oil-producing states adopted conservation measures and the sixth acted later. Agreements on control of oil production were obtained among owners in the larger oil pools where the government also held property. After a taste of government dictation under part of the New Deal National Recovery Administration, later declared unconstitutional, the former President declared that the oil industry adopted the "Hoover principle" on production control, through state governments.

Much conservation work was also devoted to the western ranges, forests and national parks.

The development of radio, aviation and the United States merchant marine were continued and encouraged under

Hoover. Freedom of the airways was jealously guarded by the President.

Through needed revisions of the airmail postal contracts and the aviation laws, commercial air routes were consolidated into a national system, the character of planes used was changed from a purely mail-transportation function to large passenger- and express-carrying aircraft, and the speed and safety of air travel was increased. Under Postmaster General Brown's direction, airmail cost per mile to the government dropped from $1.26 to about 26 cents. Passenger travel rose from 165,000 persons to 550,000 in 1933. National defense was immeasurably strengthened by the attendant increase in plane manufacturing capacity and the numbers of trained personnel available.

A start was made on a modern merchant marine, which was to become an economic and military necessity within the decade.

The Chief Executive's care in establishing the proper boundaries between the airmail and ship subsidies and the airplane and shipping industries reflected his constant questioning of the role that the federal government should play under the free enterprise system, without endangering individual initiative and productivity. On the other hand, he sometimes found it difficult to reconcile his engineer's instincts for the elimination of waste and duplication with free individualism which sometimes proved uneconomical. He felt his way cautiously between the two, endeavoring to achieve the best conditions for the country's economic and political freedom.

The President's development program also embraced government buildings, the San Francisco Bay Bridge, national housing, highways and child welfare.

At Hoover's insistence, a National Conference on child health and protection was held in Washington during November, 1930. It was attended by more than 1,200 delegates. The cost, including publications, was met by a $500,000 fund, raised by the President from private sources. This meeting resulted in the distribution of many printed reports and recommendations and the establishment of a permanent staff to continue the conference aims. A Children's Charter was adopted. Written by Hoover and revised jointly by him and Secretary of the Interior Wilbur, the Charter begins:

> For every child spiritual and moral training to help him stand firm under the pressure of life.

Due to the public's response to depression needs, the nation's children received better care during Hoover's term than in the preceding normal years.

Great attention was paid to the problems of agriculture—financially out of balance with the rest of the country's prosperity. A Federal Farm Board to aid agriculture was one of the planks of the Republican platform, and legislation to create the board was proposed at the special session of Congress called by Hoover in April. After delays caused by the unsuccessful effort to amend the bill with the McNary-Haugen proposal for federal price-fixing of farm products, the legislation was passed and Hoover signed the Farm Board Bill in July, 1929.

Law enforcement, the Executive Branch of the government, veterans' affairs, the tariff, business regulation in support of private enterprise, social reforms—all these came under the President's careful study. Reorganization and reform were undertaken where needed. In addition to domestic matters, foreign affairs demanded a great deal of the Hoover Administration's time.

Prohibition was a troublesome question throughout Hoover's term in the White House. He advanced federal enforcement of the Eighteenth Amendment, as he was required to do in upholding all the provisions of the Constitution. But the Chief Executive was greatly disturbed by the corruption and defiance resulting from the Prohibition Act and the growing disrespect, not only for the Eighteenth Amendment, but for all laws as well. The Wickersham Commission, appointed by Hoover to investigate and recommend action on the whole crime and prohibition situation, first came out against repeal of the liquor law, then subsequently demonstrated the futility of this measure. However, public sentiment was swinging toward repeal.

Carrying out campaign pledges, Hoover finally achieved passage of the Smoot-Hawley Tariff Act in June, 1930, with some increases mostly on farm products and flexible tariff provisions for needed revisions to be administered under a bi-partisan commission. This bill proved to be very controversial and Hoover granted that, despite any benefit that resulted, it was a political liability.

The story of Herbert Hoover and his Administration is inevitably that of the early years of the Depression. Following the stock market crash of Black Friday, October 23, 1929, the President was absorbed in the desperate struggle to cushion the shock and ward off panic. He gave immediate priority to the speeding up of economic recovery and the increase of employment.

During Hoover's term, the country was turned back five times from imminent crises, each of which threatened to produce the destruction of acute panic. On each occasion, the tide was turned mainly through the battles fought by President Hoover and his associates—only to be reversed again by new perils. The first crisis resulted from the Great Crash.

Ironically, considering the blame unjustly heaped upon him for the Crash and the Depression, Hoover, beginning in 1926, was one of the few who had warned publicly against the dangers in the growing orgy of stock speculation and promotion, including real estate.

When further expansion of credit, through the Federal Reserve System, had been proposed in 1925, to save the European economy from the inevitable financial consequences of World War I, Hoover was active in opposing the policy. Such a program, he felt, meant inflation for the United States, with inevitable collapse bringing the greatest calamities upon farmers, workers and business. And no such credit poultice would cure the difficulties of Europe! The credit expansion policy was checked for the moment.

In July, 1927, the economic situation in Europe had grown more perilous and a successful attempt was made by several leading European bankers to win the Federal Reserve Board over to the policy of credit expansion, not then needed by American business. By open market operations and the lowering of the discount rate, the program to inflate credit was continued through to the end of the year. Hoover, as it happened, was in the South, directing the Mississippi Flood Relief at the time, and he did not learn of the board's secret action to expand credit until his return. He immediately protested to President Coolidge about this move.

Although injections of credit were stopped in early 1928, the speculative fever, once underway, continued to spiral upward. Further restraining action by the Federal Reserve Board had little or no effect, to the alarm of its members.

When Herbert Hoover entered the White House, the market boom was his first concern, and he immediately set to work to put brakes on the speculation through the Federal Reserve System. Money rates for speculative purposes went up to 20 per cent but failed to deter those intent on rubbing the Aladdin's lamp of sudden fortune. He had no federal authority to make any restraining or needed changes in the New York Stock Exchange, which came under state law. At his instance, caution was urged on the public through newspaper editorials, statements from public officials and conferences with some financial leaders. The Department of Justice was instructed to stop tipsters and bucket-shop operators from using the mails to stimulate speculation.

Concurrent credit inflation in Europe had spread the speculative boom world wide. By the summer of 1929, there had been market collapses in some European countries, and depression had started in different places around the globe. All this took place before the collapse in the United States.

Hoover felt the credit inflation policy was largely responsible for the late-October, mid-November market crash, with secondary causes including overproduction due to completing postwar reconstruction and increased national efficiency.

After the first shock of the Crash, a flood of reassuring statements was issued by economists, bankers, the press and labor. The President was not impressed by the optimism. He felt the situation was honeycombed with weak spots. In answer to urgings from the press, he made a short statement on progress in production and the long-range strength of the country. As President, he could not make things worse by stating his own misgivings in the midst of the Crash, but he firmly declined to discuss the value of stocks. To head off the panic, he began that grinding, brutal work schedule of eighteen to twenty hours a day, sometimes extending to around the clock. This concentrated labor was to continue while he remained in the White House—and for it he would be rewarded with the infamous legend that he "did nothing"!

Herbert Hoover was the first President in United States history to take federal leadership in mobilizing "the economic resources of the people, and in calling upon individual initiative to accept definite responsibility in meeting the depression." His pioneer leadership, within Constitutional powers, was without Presidential precedent, except for a few "helpful gestures," such as a little currency relief and Grover Cleveland's announced support of the gold standard. In asserting federal responsibility, he had to buck opposition.

He went into action within ten days after the crash began. To cushion the resulting shocks, federal departments were directed to speed up all public works, in order to give employment, and the Federal Farm Board was instructed to support wheat and cotton prices in the growing panic. A committee was created to promote state and municipal construction work, and the help of almost all governors and many mayors was promised to him. In a series of meetings in the White House, he conferred with business, industrial and labor leaders and was able to secure their voluntary co-operation in solving the difficulties of stability, employment and the pledge of industrial peace. He directed the Postmaster General to expedite contracts of subsidies for ship construction, to increase available jobs. In his first Annual Message to Congress, he recommended increased public works and reduction of non-essential government spending and some reorganization in the banking system.

By the middle of February it was evident that the danger of a general panic had been averted. With the aid of the Federal Reserve Banks the stock market loans had been liquidated down to $3,000,000,000. The index of employment had recovered to within half a point of the October level. Unemployment distress was being met by measures taken by private and local authorities.

In a speech to the United States Chamber of Commerce on May 1, 1930, the President said, "I am convinced we have now passed the worst and with continued unity of effort we shall rapidly recover." This optimism was shared by economic leaders. Hoover never said "Prosperity is just around the corner," a phrase coined by the opposition in attacking the President. He owned, however, that his encouraging statement was a political mistake as it opened the way for such an attack if things went wrong—which they did.

The constant need to meet new emergencies caused Hoover to say of the Presidency, "The office in such times as these makes its incumbent a repair man behind a dyke. No sooner is one leak plugged up than it is necessary to dash over and stop another."

The next serious "leak" to break out was the great drought

which spread over the mid-West in August, threatening the farming states. The President immediately arranged for the railroads to transport feed for the starving animals from other regions at half-rates and stepped up federal works in the areas to provide employment. With the aid of the governors of the states affected and the Red Cross, measures of relief were set in motion which prevented acute suffering. Seed loans were later secured from Congress.

Immigration was curbed, on the grounds that it contributed to unemployment, directly or indirectly. There were some exceptions, such as tourists and students.

In late September, Hoover found that the Soviet government was selling large quantities of wheat short on the Chicago Board of Trade, and he had the transactions stopped. Shortly afterward the Soviets dumped wheat in European markets, causing the price of this commodity to fall. The Soviets made considerable profits from their short sales in Chicago. A vice-president of Amtorg, the Soviet commercial agency in the United States, resigned. He stated publicly that the purpose of the Soviet government was to create disorganization and disturbances among the farmers in different countries by operations such as this one, managed through Amtorg.

William Green, president of the American Federation of Labor, paid tribute at their annual meeting, in 1930, to Hoover because of the great influence he had wielded in maintaining wage standards and preventing a general reduction of wages. As the country emerged from distressing unemployment, the value of the service Hoover had rendered wage earners and industry was better understood and appreciated.

But the President, fearful of the increase of unemployment and human distress during the winter, organized the President's Committee for Unemployment Relief, under Colonel Arthur Woods as chairman, and about 3,000 nonpartisan member committees were set up in states, municipalities and counties to see that no one went cold or hungry.

In the 1930 Congressional campaign, the Democrats largely blamed Hoover for the depression and, as a result, they won a sweeping victory in the House of Representatives on Election Day. The Senate was about evenly divided, but it presented an effective opposing coalition to Hoover. He was forced to battle the incoming 72nd Congress from the time it convened over a year later until the end of his term.

December, 1930, brought a slump in Winnipeg and Liverpool wheat prices, the failure of a fairly large bank and an increase in unemployment. In midwinter, Hoover announced that unemployment totaled about 4,900,000 persons, which was a real figure of about 2,900,000, after deducting those between jobs and unemployables. Despite all this, there were encouraging signs, too.

In January, 1931, although the number of jobless had increased, Colonel Woods was able to announce to a Senate Committee that his relief organization could take care of any distress and suffering during the winter. A survey at the end of the month showed that relief measures had been ended in 120 cities, as they were no longer needed.

Senate Democrats, aided by Senator William E. Borah, demanded direct government doles to those in distress, although the relief committees and the Red Cross reported that such action was not needed. In a statement issued early in February, 1931, Hoover asserted that the sole question was how best to prevent cold and hunger. He felt this should be through voluntary mutual assistance, backed by responsible local and state aid, with the federal government stepping in only when it became absolutely necessary. Direct federal aid to individuals, he was convinced, would bring an "inevitable train of corruption and waste." If the voluntary agencies and the local and state governments proved unequal to the job, he pledged himself to use every resource of the federal government to prevent any American from going hungry.

A Veterans' Bonus Bill, authorizing a cash loan of 50 per

cent of the deferred World War I bonus, passed Congress and was vetoed by the President on February 26, 1931, on the grounds that loans should be limited to the small percentage of destitute and unemployed veterans, plus the fact that the government must borrow the vast amount authorized through sale of the bonus reserve fund securities or impose further taxation, since there was not a penny in the Treasury to meet such a demand. He felt, too, that this payment might delay improvement in the economy. Sick and disabled veterans were currently being cared for at an annual expenditure of $800,-000,000. The Bonus Bill was promptly passed over his veto, nevertheless.

Recovery started in the spring of 1931, with upturns in all the business indexes, including sharp rises in employment, at the end of March. The American depression, to all appearances, "had run its course" and Prosperity *was* just around the corner. But, as Hoover had warned in his December message to Congress, the major forces of the depression then lay outside the United States. Fear of a panic in Europe haunted the President and those who were aware of the dangerous situation there, due to World War I and the economic consequences resulting from the Peace of Versailles. Apprehension of a panic overseas became a reality in late March, 1931, with the impending financial collapse of Central Europe, touched off by financial pressures accruing from the announcement of the German-Austrian Credit Union. By mid-May the Kreditanstalt, the largest private bank in Austria, was in financial difficulties. The United States was thrown back into what was to be the *Great* Depression by the economic earthquake in Europe.

In the immediate world-wide apprehension, security and commodity prices in the United States began falling, and Hoover directed the Department of Commerce and the Treasury to investigate. Steady European selling of American securities in United States markets, some flight of capital from

Europe to this country due to lack of confidence in currencies abroad and a sharp decrease in export orders were reported.

The decline in world markets continued and on May 6, the American Ambassador to Germany arrived in Washington on an urgent mission. He informed Hoover of the German Chancellor's disclosures on the disastrous financial crisis developing in Germany. There was danger of a Communist revolution, as well as threats from the Nazi elements. The military were rallying to Hitler.

The President at once directed that a full survey of the financial condition of Central Europe be made by the State and Commerce Departments. The International Chamber of Commerce was then meeting in Washington, and a canvass was made of the delegates' views. Not one delegate mentioned the growing panic in Central Europe!

As the strain in all international finance increased alarmingly, the President asked Secretaries Stimson and Mellon to suggest some way to relieve the pressure of the vast World War I reparations payments and war debts.

During the rest of May and into June of 1931 the crisis developed even more acutely. Bank troubles in Austria threatened the government and were patched with English and American bank loans. Heavy selling of American securities by European owners continued. The European survey disclosed that there were large sums from France and other parts of Europe on deposit in the United States and that Americans held large amounts of European short-term commercial debt. Wheat prices declined further on Russia's announcement of continued wheat dumping. Leading Democrats blamed Hoover for the falling prices of commodities and securities, and the Bonus Bill, passed over his veto, took over $750,000,000 from the Treasury. Unemployment continued to increase. The situation in Germany deteriorated dangerously.

Working at an eighteen-hours-a-day pace, the President had been preparing a rescue plan of his own behind the silent walls of the White House, in addition to all his other commitments. He felt that American leadership might save the situation. One evening, he was busily writing in his office when Theodore Joslin, his secretary, came in to make a report. Without stopping, the President asked him to wait. As often happened when Hoover was working on something especially important, he pressed on his pencil too hard and broke the lead. Tossing it aside, he took another, then another, repeating the process.

Finally, he looked up, saying, "This is perhaps the most daring statement I ever thought of issuing." And he read to Joslin the original draft of his proposal to all governments for a moratorium of a year on all intergovernmental payments.

The plan was suggested to Secretaries Stimson and Mellon and Under Secretary of the Treasury Ogden L. Mills on June 5. Both Stimson and Mills approved the idea. But it could not be presented to the countries concerned without assurances from the leaders of the opposition party that it would be ratified by the Senate in December. Hoover had commitments for speeches in the mid-West and he dared not cancel the trip for fear of disclosing the crisis in Europe and creating fear in the country. He therefore arranged to meet mid-West Congressional leaders on the train during the trip.

On his return to Washington on June 18, the President found that Secretary Mellon, then in Paris, had changed his views on the moratorium. Now in accord with the President, he was telephoning urgently that action be taken at once to protect American financial safety. Hoover also received an official appeal from President Von Hindenburg to save the Weimar Republic from collapse. For long hours, Hoover interviewed and telephoned Congressional leaders in both houses. Senators Garner and Robinson declined to take a stand but the approval of Senator Glass and other important Democrats was obtained. As soon as enough votes were assured, the Secretary of State was instructed to transmit the proposal to the governments involved.

Due to a leak of the plan to the press in a garbled form, the President was forced to make the proposal public earlier than he had planned. A news conference was called for 4:30 P.M. on June 20, 1931, and the President went over the announcement for the last time. As this was Saturday, when the President did not customarily meet the press, the correspondents knew something big was about to break. They poured into his office on a signal from Joslin. Standing beside his desk, the President read his moratorium plan to them. Joslin tossed the press copies onto his own desk and the reporters put on a football rush to get them for release the next morning. The President was criticized for this forced early release on the ground that he showed a lack of international courtesy.

The American press hailed the proposal, known as the German Moratorium, with great enthusiasm. The economic situation improved at once in the United States and men were called back to work. The upturn was world-wide. The French Ambassador, André François Poncet, has stated that, "Only an intervention 'in extremis' by President Hoover and his proposal for a moratorium saved Germany." The editor of a large London newspaper described the plan as the greatest thing since the signing of the Armistice.

Within a week, fifteen governments had accepted the proposal. The only important opponent was France, still activated by the German war wrongs. France delayed over two weeks while, as a result, the financial situation worsened. After much consultation, aided by use of the trans-Atlantic telephone, the President informed the French government that widespread support for the moratorium warranted going ahead without France. The next day, July 6, the French Cabinet accepted the plan. There was a momentary lift in world conditions—but it was only to last a few days due to renewed panic abroad.

Monetary drains on Germany, Hungary and Eastern European countries had depleted their gold reserves, but Hoover felt that something worse must be impelling the crisis. By July 15, practically all the banks in those areas had closed. Investigation revealed that the "explosive mine" was the vast amount of short-term commercial bills floated world wide by Germany, Austria, Hungary and other Eastern European countries, then thought to amount to $5,000,000,000, not including other German debt. These obligations could not be met, at least at the time, and renewals were being refused. This, Hoover felt, was one result of the expanded credit policy adopted in 1927 which had in effect postponed the inevitable European financial collapse from difficulties arising from the war. The borrowed money had been used for reparations, reconstruction and budget deficits.

"I don't know that I have ever received a worse shock," Hoover later wrote. "The haunting prospect of wholesale bank failures and the necessity of saying not a word to the American people as to the cause and danger, lest I precipitate runs on our banks, left me little sleep." The President realized he would again have to try to stave off collapse abroad and at home.

Calling in Acting Secretary Mills and Acting Secretary of State William R. Castle, Jr., Senator Dwight Morrow and Charles G. Dawes, American Ambassador to England, Hoover outlined his plan for a "standstill agreement" among all bankers everywhere to hold German and central European short-term obligations. They approved highly, and the proposal was cabled to Stimson and Mellon for presentation at the meeting of German, British, French, Italian, Belgian and Japanese government leaders, to be held in London on July 20, 1931.

Meanwhile, the President refused to participate in any loans to Germany. Presentation of the plan was delayed for fear of seeming American dictation. Hoover then took the step of publishing the proposals around the world. The conference adopted the plan the next day and delegated the Bank for International Settlements at Berne to carry it out. The report of the International Bank a year later disclosed that the total amount of short-term debt had been $10,000,000,000. Ambassador Dawes, in his account of the crisis, accredited the President with again having saved a world crash.

This European hurricane cost the United States the gains made during the early part of 1931—and more. But with the adoption of Hoover's two emergency measures, there came a short breathing space with the momentary checking of the crisis and a start at recovery.

As the President had said in an address at Indianapolis on his mid-West tour:

> This battle is upon a thousand fronts. . . . Some . . . people . . . demand abrupt change . . . in our American system. . . . Others have indomitable confidence that by some legerdemain we can legislate ourselves out of a world-wide depression. Such views are as accurate as the belief we can exorcise a Caribbean hurricane by statutory law. . . .

Against
All
Odds

CHAPTER 15

At the time, the American people had little or no understanding of the desperate battle their President was waging in their behalf, to stave off global economic disaster. His policy of working in silence was in the main the cause of this lack of understanding—both of his fight and of the world situation involved.

In times of emergency, it was Hoover's practice to take any action necessary and never talk about the business at hand until it was finished. Even then, he would only reveal as much as he deemed appropriate. Although sometimes imperative for public good, as was then the case in this threatening world-wide calamity, his policy of silence often caused him trouble and was "close to the root" of many antagonisms he encountered during his term. In addition to keeping the American public mostly in the dark about the tireless and ceaseless efforts he was making against the depression in their behalf, this "secrecy" policy made it hard to obtain necessary support from the public and Congress for Administration measures and programs.

Without question, these times were often so critical that broadcasting the impending crisis might have "pushed the nation over the precipice." Even publicizing lesser dangers in advance probably would not have been in the public interest just then. However, there were many occasions when Hoover might have talked but did not do so. When friends urged that he dramatize his actions, he replied, "This is not a showman's job. I will not step out of character."

This policy of silence naturally raised difficulties with the press, with whom Hoover had been on excellent terms when he was Secretary of Commerce. It also created some enmity in Congress. The Administration felt that it was not advantageous to publicize the preliminary steps taken to meet critical situations. When attempting to reconcile some key member or faction of Congress to the passage of legislation essential to his program, the President chose confidential talks, instead of summoning the person or persons involved to the White House to be interviewed in full view of reporters assigned to cover the Executive Mansion.

Hoover was equally convinced that secrecy should cloak the early development of all Administration plans involving business, labor and farm leaders. At crucial moments, when it was necessary to consult with important men whose very presence at the White House might lead to wild rumors, Hoover resorted to the telephone and unreported meetings. Some top-secret visitors were brought to the White House at unusual hours of the day and the night, when press representatives were not on guard—even at midnight. In international relations too, out of fairness to foreign governments, it was often vital not to reveal current discussions until basic conclusions had been reached. News conferences therefore were often canceled for different reasons, as the President would not countenance any cover-up statements. But his public relations secretary, Theodore Joslin, a newspaper man himself, has said that Hoover had a very keen nose for news and he could have solved the press relations problem perfectly satisfactorily, had he only had the undistracted time to give to it.

The President made many speeches to reassure the people and instill confidence. Writing all these addresses personally was hard work for him. He built his talks as he would "drive a mine shaft or construct a bridge," testing each word for stress or strain in expressing his exact thought and combining them with a network of lesser words, like the "web of wires on a suspension bridge." A first longhand draft, lined and interlined, was typed by a stenographer acquainted with his writing. This was reviewed by the President and then set up in type. Next the printed drafts were revised. Sequence was arranged by cutting up one of these into paragraphs, spreading them out on a large table, and fitting them together in the order desired, like a jigsaw puzzle.

But, beyond his own circle of devoted followers, the President lacked the magnetism to put his vital material across to large audiences. Perhaps because he always read from the manuscript in an even voice, instead of using the emphasis that marked his private, informal conversations, he failed to inspire the people as a whole to follow him unquestioningly in the bad times. He was stiff at public appearances and his quiet, effective humor and charm seemed to disappear in front of a microphone. He was at his best in putting over ideas in conferences in his office, in the Lincoln Study or before the fireplace in the "town hall" at the Rapidan camp. That was how he influenced many a political opponent.

The President found it hard to appreciate that the average individual likes to know personal details about the Chief Executive. Sometimes it seemed to him as if the public preferred to read about the President's wardrobe and whether his collar button was improvised rather than about the fundamental principles and causes for which he fought!

Hoover was widely qualified to serve in adversity. His wide experience with poverty, unemployment and the relief of human misery had been firsthand. Due to his earlier work in government, when the crash came he either knew the pertinent facts about the country's economy or where to get them.

Bernard Baruch has said that facts to Mr. Hoover's brain were as water to a sponge. They were not only absorbed, they were assembled, action deduced and brought about. Dr. Ray Lyman Wilbur has told that Hoover had the capacity to turn his mind like a searchlight from subject to subject. This gave him the very wide range needed during the day of a President.

He had a card-index mind and has been described as a walking encyclopedia. He did not need to make extensive notes at conferences and almost never had a secretary present to take down the discussions. He carried the whole subject in his head, complete with details. On leaving his office, some of those who have conferred with him have been heard to say, "Why he knows more about my business than I do myself!"

Not a moment of time was wasted when Hoover was President. Even between callers, he would write a sentence or two of a letter or a speech. During his term in the Commerce Department, Hoover sometimes sketched geometric designs on a pad while in conference. These nationally known "doodles" disappeared in the depression crisis.

The driving pace at which Hoover worked while he was President has not been realized, even now, by the public. A typical day began at six. Hoover liked getting up at this hour no better than the next man! On arising, he put on old clothes for the seven o'clock session with the "medicine ball cabinet." Then he dressed for the day, had breakfast, glanced at the morning papers and was in his office before eight-thirty. The first half hour was alloted to the preparation of an address or message, or to urgent correspondence. Reports were made and newspapers studied for the next hour. Appointments began at eleven but important officials and members of Congress assembled earlier on matters that could not wait. The average number of conferences a day was twenty-two, not including meetings at breakfast, lunch, dinner and at night. At twelve-thirty came the public receptions which replaced the hand-shaking ordeal. The President had his picture taken with different groups of visitors on the "shooting range" on the White House grounds.

He would exchange a few words of greeting with each group, sometimes asking, "Are you seeing everything you want to while in Washington?"

"Yes," was the usual reply.

"If not," the Chief Executive continued, "let me know. I am pretty well known around here. Perhaps I can fix it up for you." This always brought a laugh from the visitors. Seeing these friendly people provided a welcome change from the demanding routine and acted as a tonic.

Back in the office, Hoover looked over new information gathered by the secretaries during the morning before going to the house for lunch between one-thirty and two o'clock. With few exceptions, guests were the rule, often men with whom the President wished to confer for from half to three-quarters of an hour. Without visitors, lunch was a mere formality. The afternoon was spent in meetings with officials and others whom the Chief Executive wanted to see and in writing, planning and even plotting! He did not leave the office until six, often nearer seven. The first to arrive in the morning, custom decreed that the President must be the first to leave. Since none of the staff could go until his departure, this meant that they must stay on long after customary office-closing time.

Following a nap, the President and Mrs. Hoover had dinner with various guests at eight, and he would often confer with the men in the Lincoln Study afterward. Other groups, when scheduled, came at nine for meetings which lasted until late at night and sometimes into the early morning hours. Retiring usually at eleven or twelve o'clock, Hoover would sleep for two or three hours, then wake up and read for a while.

As an index of the increased work load that Hoover faced, Presidential telephone calls were 560,130 in 1932 in comparison to 153,840 in 1927. But the burden during the depression was, of course, immeasurable, and the trials of the harassed people haunted him from late October, 1929, on.

After Theodore Joslin had been with him two weeks, the President asked him how he was getting along as public relations secretary.

"That desk out there," Joslin answered, "is comparable only to the office of the managing editor of a metropolitan newspaper at edition time on election night."

"There is only one worse desk in the world," Mr. Hoover replied with a laugh, "and that is this one."

Although overwhelmed by world-shaking problems, the President could enjoy a smoke while he worked. He remembered to give instructions about White House domestic details and often planned the small attentions that made guests of the Hoovers feel so at home, realizing that a White House visit may prove a trying experience to anyone! He frequently saw personally that flowers went to the sick and that those in distress were aided.

The President did not feel that it was suitable for him to take any vacation when the country was in trouble but, once in a while, when a change was absolutely imperative, he would slip away for a few days' yachting trip down the Chesapeake or in southern waters. He was even reluctant to spend his week ends at the Rapidan camp. Wherever he did go, his work was always with him.

Because of the press of business, the Chief Executive could not take the time to visit his friends or associates, so people came to him. During his Presidential term, the Hoovers had guests the greater part of the time, staying at the White House, invited for meals there, or with them at Rapidan and on the few

trips taken away from Washington. To be exact, they numbered 9,769, and most of them were people who could aid the
nation in some way.

One time when the Chief Executive was so exhausted that
every bone in his body ached, his public relations secretary
suggested to Mrs. Hoover that he could get more relaxation
on his next trip to the Rapidan camp if only his family went
along.

"Oh, no," Mrs. Hoover answered, "that would not do at all.
He always wants to have people around him. The more he has,
the happier he is. Why, he would not have a good time at all,
if he went up alone. He would come right, straight back home."

At camp, interludes between work permitted the Chief Executive to indulge his one hobby of fishing. The drive to Rapidan took three hours from Washington and there were always
important messages waiting by the time the Presidential party
arrived. With unhappy frequency, acute depression problems
developed over the week ends when the Chief went to camp in
the forlorn hope of getting a little rest and recreation. A Marine
sentry would be waiting for Hoover's secretary when he reached
Rapidan. If the President planned to fish and the calls could
wait, Joslin postponed the messages until Hoover returned from
the trout stream in an hour. But work resumed the moment the
fishing rod was put away.

The public impression that Hoover devoted himself entirely
to fishing while at camp was erroneous. Announcements of
trout fishing given out by Joslin to protect his Chief in the
crucial work he was doing ironically contributed to this fiction.

In addition to all the President's other difficulties, the Democratic National Committee set up something new in between-
campaign party strategy. A publicity director named Charles
Michelson was hired in June, 1929. He was pledged an ex-
pendable fund of about $1,000,000. A Democratic reporter,
Frank R. Kent, wrote in Scribner's magazine of September,
1930, that Michelson's objective and sole goal was to run

down Hoover and his Administration. "It has been his pleasant task to minimize every Hoover asset and magnify all his liabilities . . . to obscure every Hoover virtue and achievement. . . . His employment is to get into the daily and weekly press of the country as much stuff putting Hoover and the Hoover Administration in an unfavorable light as he can. . . . His game is to 'plant' interviews, statements, and speeches with Democratic members of the Senate and House of sufficient standing and prominence to make what they say news. . . . Every move Hoover has made is followed by the firing of a Michelson publicity barrage."

This political agency, which was known as Michelson's Mills, more than any other, helped to mold the public mind in regard to Hoover. It is "an illuminating illustration of the amazing power of unopposed propaganda in skillful hands. . . ." Through radio, too, the products were broadcast in every direction. Contrary to the usual procedure, the Democratic National Committee began soon after Hoover's inauguration to work for victory in 1932.

With respect to decency and regard for his office, Hoover felt a President could not reply to "such stuff," and that some of the old guard Republican leaders were remiss in their traditional duty to counterattack and expose misrepresentation.

This Democratic propaganda, unopposed by the Republicans, went a long way toward filling and distorting the news vacuum created by necessity in the critical times and by the policy of silence that enveloped the Hoover Administration. It was suggested that the President was reluctant to encourage more publicity lest some writers portray him on a white charger of wrath, with a flashing sword of slogans. To him, the safety of the nation lay in the infinite drudgery of determining fact and policy and in patiently co-ordinating the minds of men toward a common objective.

In his successful campaign, the President had been presented as a miracle man. When trouble developed and did not end right away, some people, not knowing the enormity of the task, grew uncertain of his ability and became unhappy. It is to be wondered how much the white charger would have helped?

Following the rescue of Germany, the economic storms spread to England. Due to the withdrawal of over $1,000,000,-000 in gold and foreign exchange since July, 1931, the Bank of England defaulted on gold payments or international exchange. This had drastic repercussions in Europe and America. Practically all the world was driven off the gold standard with England, except France and the United States. In this country the gains resulting from the victory over the Central European panic were mostly canceled out.

During this nightmare, the President went by special train to Detroit, to ask the American Legion, then in annual convention, to abandon support for a cash bonus. He pointed out that sick and needy veterans were being aided, and he urged the servicemen to avoid this increase in government expenditure and help maintain the stability of the United States—"the first stone in the foundation of recovery and stability . . . in the world." After hearing the President, the meeting refused to endorse the proposal. But the plan was to be revived when Congress met.

The following day, the President held an off-the-record news conference. In view of the gold hoarding then in progress, he asked the press for its utmost aid in keeping the country "steady in the boat." The press co-operated helpfully in their news reports.

During the summer, a nation-wide survey of unemployment and relief problems was initiated by Hoover. In August, he enlarged the Relief Committee to meet the increased load. Unemployment was then estimated at about 8,000,000, including the between-jobbers, those not wanting work and around 1,000,000 idle being provided for by employers. Walter S. Gifford became chairman of the revised organization. Surveys proved that those in distress were being cared for and that relief requirements for the winter could be carried by state, local and volunteer aid. A national drive for relief funds successfully raised large sums.

In answer to European criticism that the United States was sucking up the world's gold supply, President Hoover announced that there had been no great increase in our own monetary gold stocks but about $3,000,000,000 in foreign gold was on deposit in this country.

Due to fear for the dollar after the British collapse, drains had started on the foreign gold. The threat of further withdrawals of this precious metal from abroad endangered the whole credit system. Domestic hoarding, as a result of the European hurricanes, had risen to $100,000,000 a week, causing many bank suspensions. Over-all prices had fallen sharply since April and unemployment swelled following the renewed panic set off by the British difficulties. Japan's seizure of Manchuria further unsettled world conditions. During this whole period, too, the economic picture at home and abroad was complicated by the financial "shenanigans" of Ivar Kreuger, the Swedish match king, Samuel Insull and Serge Stavisky.

Through business conferences in October, 1931, the Chief Executive organized a program to combat the fast-mounting crisis brought on by the events in Europe and to strengthen confidence at home. He urged the formation of a bank credit pool to aid banks in need. He proposed measures to lend on frozen assets and to relieve mortgage foreclosings on homes and farms.

To ease the strain on agriculture, the Federal Farm Board was again directed to support farm prices and to lift them from the disastrous slumps which had occurred since April.

In this greatest peacetime danger the country had ever faced, the Chief Executive realized that some measure of wartime power was needed. He called a meeting at the White House of thirty-two leading senators and congressmen of both parties, for the evening of October 6. To this representative group he outlined the dangers in the world situation, including the menace to Germany and Central Europe of Communism and Fascism. He stated to the stunned audience that it was not a question of saving Germany and England—in the near panic, it was a question of saving the United States of America.

The President proposed a program to ease credit, including the creation if necessary of a corporation (the subsequent Reconstruction Finance Corporation) to make loans not available elsewhere to stiffen the whole economic system. At that meeting, which lasted until early the next morning, Hoover secured approval in principle from the members of Congress present for the proposals which required legislation. A joint statement was issued to the press, covering the measures agreed upon to check the continued depression caused by the succession of events in Europe. Within twenty-four hours, panic was dissipating.

In view of the impending deficit, at his press conference on November 6, the President announced proposed cuts in the next government budget. He stated that he would seek authority from Congress for further reductions. He was opposed to the many plans being offered for increased expenditure, since he thought additional appropriations should be confined to relief needs in meeting distress in agriculture and problems of unemployment through supplementary aid to the state, local and voluntary programs.

By mid-November, 1931, the third great crisis seemed to have been weathered, largely as a result of the President's leadership. Unemployment was once more decreasing, business activity was up, and the prices of commodities and securities had risen sharply. Hoarding ceased, with gold returning to the banks. Bank failures had almost stopped, and the outward flow of gold reversed. To avoid having to let any government workers go due to the proposed budget cuts, Hoover announced his plan for the sharing of work among federal employees concerned. The people were hopeful and the dollar still "rang true on every counter in the world." Again, the United States showed signs of recovery.

But the impact of the European economic hurricane on America continued and by December the country was under renewed severe strain. The 72nd Congress convened on the seventh of the month and for the remainder of his term as President, Hoover faced an opposition Congress. In his Annual Message to the Senate and House he expanded his program of economic defense and recovery measures. During the preceding month he had conferred with more than 160 members of Congress, both Republican and Democratic, in an effort to handle the emergency measures on a nonpartisan basis in the dangerous situation.

Democratic leaders attacked the President's proposals and continued to blame him openly for the depression. By the Christmas recess of Congress, only the German Moratorium had been approved, though with an amendment opposing any reduction or cancellation in the debt owed by foreign countries.

By January, 1932, unemployment had risen distressingly to an over-all total of about 10,000,000. There was one bright note in the report from the Surgeon General on the effectiveness of the relief operations which disclosed that public health was holding up well. Through interviews with individual members and another message to Congress, Hoover continued to press the urgent need for constructive action, stating, "We can and must replace the unjustifiable fear in the country by confidence."

The Reconstruction Finance Corporation Act was signed by the President on January 22, but he was disappointed by the failure of Congress to grant all of the powers he had requested. Also, the six weeks' delay on this emergency legislation, he felt, had resulted in needless bank closings and suffering. On the same day, a long-drawn-out wage dispute between the railways and their employees was successfully mediated by the

President, who intervened by telephone to Chicago where negotiations were being held. Talking to leaders on both sides,
he secured an agreement and a strike threat was averted.

The following day, Hoover signed the act providing additional capital for the Federal Land Banks. Other amendments
to the Farm Loan Act that he had proposed were delayed until
March, 1933.

By February, the economic situation had again deteriorated
and the whole world was shaken by the Japanese attack on
Shanghai. The President determined to fight the increased
domestic hoarding of coin and currency, which was restricting
credit and causing runs on sound banks, with some failures. He
felt that the currency-tinkering measures proposed in Congress
were adding to the public fears. An anti-hoarding campaign
was organized under Colonel Frank Knox, and the situation
was checked for the time being.

On February 7, the newly appointed Secretary of the Treasury, Ogden L. Mills, advised the President that the long-feared
gold situation had become critical and the United States was
in danger of being forced off the gold standard within two or
three weeks. Due to foreign drains, hoarding and the lack of
"eligible" paper to cover 60 per cent of the currency, there
was only about $300,000,000 of free gold available to cover
further foreign withdrawals and earmarking or conversion of
foreign-owned deposits into gold bullion, which were then
taking place at the rate of $100,000,000 a week. And foreign
deposits in the country subject to withdrawal on demand totaled
about $1,000,000,000!

After further consultation with Federal Reserve officials and
General Dawes, President of the RFC, on the dangers of the
gold crisis, the Chief Executive summoned the Republican and
Democratic Senate majority leaders, the ranking members of
the Senate Committee on Banking and Currency, and Administration officials to urge them to carry out the proposal of
the October agreement to widen Federal Reserve eligibility

provisions and to adopt additional credit expansion measures.

Senator Glass then reversed his stand and agreed to introduce the needed legislation. The House leaders went along with Senator Glass's decision. At Hoover's suggestion, Congressman Henry B. Steagall, chairman of the House Committee on Banking and Currency, joined in sponsoring the legislation known as the Glass-Steagall Bill. It was passed and became law on February 27, without any debate as to the gold situation. The danger of being forced to abandon the gold standard was averted, but again delay had hampered the alleviation of distress. In the prevailing jitters, it was some time before the President was able to talk about his successful navigation through this crisis.

During the whole session of Congress, from December 7 to mid-July, 1932, President Hoover declared he continually fought for his recovery program against "Democratic tactics" of obstruction and delay. He owns to having been badly battered and no doubt the constant parrot calls that he was the "sole creator of the world depression" did get under his skin.

The widespread repetition of the erroneous terms "Hoover depression" and "Hoover breadlines" must have had a bitter ring to the humanitarian who had received world-wide acclaim for his work in saving millions from starvation in the war and post-Armistice periods. These terms of misrepresentation, sent out in waves of manufactured political attack, were at opposite poles from the "Hoover relief," "Hoover luncheons," and the "Hooverizing" of World War I days. But the President had no time to reply to the "smears" and "such stuff." In response to the urging of friends that he fight back, he would answer, "If the American people wish to believe such things as this about me, it just cannot be helped."

In the late spring of 1932, there occurred one of the many incidents which, if publicized, would have softened the criticism unjustly heaped on Hoover for events beyond his control. Three children of an unemployed man who had been arrested for car stealing hitchhiked to Washington to ask the President to free their father. They believed that the man in the White House could do anything.

The first thing in the morning, the President asked the Attorney General for a report on the case. Then the children, two girls and a boy, were shown into the Presidential office. The Chief Executive greeted them with a smile and shook hands. He turned to the oldest, a girl of thirteen: "Now, tell me the whole story."

She began haltingly, but the President put her at ease and let her tell the story of a family's misfortune in her own way.

The expression on his face showing how deeply he was moved, the President told her that he was getting the records of her father's case. "I know there must be good in a man whose children are so well behaved and who show such loyalty and devotion to him," he continued. "I will use my good offices."

He gave each child a memento and promised that their father would be waiting for them when they reached home. After they had left, he buzzed for his secretary. As Joslin entered the room, the President was standing by a window, looking out. Without turning around, he asked the secretary in a choked voice to make arrangements immediately to have the father released on bail while awaiting trial.

But as to publicity about this humanitarian act, no—only the barest announcement.

The fifth major crisis began to develop in the United States about the middle of March, 1932, with an economic deterioration which has been largely attributed to the delays in Congress and the lack of co-operation in the President's recovery program, in addition to financial storms from Europe. There were sharp declines in commodity and security prices, large withdrawals of foreign gold and a resumption of domestic hoarding. The low point was reached in mid-July. Unemployment was at 12,400,000 persons.

All during this time, the President increased his struggle, persistently and patiently working with the various groups concerned and through public appeals. The expanded Federal Reserve activities, the RFC work and the firm resolution to balance the budget helped. Early in July, it became evident that the President would secure a large part of his important measures and that he would be able to defeat unsound proposals.

Confidence began to rise, coinciding with the adjournment of Congress on July 18. Other measures of Hoover's program passed were the Home Loan Banks, though delayed eight months and greatly restricted; increase in federal revenue of about $1,000,000,000, which was $400,000,000 less than asked; reduction in expenditures of about $300,000,000 out of the $700,000,000 proposed; restricted authority to reorganize government departments; appropriation of wheat and cotton to the Red Cross for relief and continued public works at the rate of $700,000,000 a year.

Added grants won for the RFC comprised $1,500,000,000 for reproductive public works and $300,000,000 to aid the states for direct relief, to be distributed through state and local committees. Two provisions of importance to small depositors were not passed. A loan publicity clause was included to which Hoover objected because of its adverse effect on business if carried out.

Congress did not pass the President's request for $120,000 to underwrite continuing the Unemployment Relief Organization, so Hoover raised the money from private sources, one of which was his own pocketbook.

Among the proposals which the President and his associates found unsound and aided in defeating were the Patman Bonus Bill, including the provisions for paper money unsecured by specie, "pork barrel," "universal loan," omnibus pension and other bills.

This was the distressing and difficult time of the Bonus

March demonstrations, when about 12,000 veterans and others had come to Washington in an effort to obtain immediate cash payment of a deferred bonus from Congress. When the Bonus Bill failed to pass the Senate on June 18, President Hoover asked the chairmen of the Congressional Committees to appropriate loan funds to buy tickets home for the real veterans. About 6,000 accepted this aid and departed. Among those remaining, the former President has disclosed, were many who had never served in the Army and a proportion of Communists, as well as ex-convicts. Some Communist participation in the Bonus March and the increased party direction in the later events has been revealed from first hand knowledge by John T. Pace, an acknowledged Communist who left the party in 1935.* Another account of this participation is given by Benjamin Gitlow in his book, *The Whole of Their Lives.*

On July 28, the explosive situation developed into a battle when the Washington police tried to evacuate marchers from some old government buildings slated to come down in a public works construction program. In the fight, two of the marchers were killed and many police were wounded. President Hoover was called on for federal troops by the District of Columbia authorities and General Douglas MacArthur was directed to take charge. He restored order without firing a shot and the unfortunate episode ended in the evacuation of the marchers and members of their families beyond the District line, although the President had only planned that the rioters be returned to camps outside the business area. In his statement on the military action, General MacArthur declared that the President could not safely have waited any longer before using force, in the vain hope of avoiding trouble and friction.

The whole world was ready for an upturn. Abroad, the Lausanne Conference, which reduced German reparations,

* Congressional Record, August 31, 1949 House Un-American Activities Committee, 82nd Congress, 1st Session 1951 Hearings, vol. 2 p. 1925, Communist Tactics Among Veterans' Groups

and the stiffening of the European economy by balanced budgets and stronger currencies began to have their effect. The calling of a World Economic Conference, at Hoover's instance, contributed to rebuilding confidence.

From late June to late September, 1932, the Federal Reserve Board index showed sharp rises in business and prices generally. Exports rose. The movement of gold reversed, showing international confidence in America. The net number of bank failures over openings changed to a net amount of bank openings and the American Federation of Labor reported an increase in employment of 800,000, a reversal of the usual seasonal trend.

In his *Economics of Recovery*, Leonard P. Ayres states that "the corner was turned even in this country in the summer of 1932 . . . probably the most important factor in preventing our incipient recovery in 1932 . . . was political in nature."

William Starr Myers, Professor of Politics at Princeton University, and Walter H. Newton, former Member of Congress and Secretary to President Hoover, wrote in *The Hoover Administration* that:

> History now records that the Great Depression reached its low point in June and July, 1932. Recovery began all over the world and has continued in greater or less measure in other countries until today. And President Hoover was the world leader who had contributed most to this victory over chaos. The battle against the depression had been won.

But in the United States 1932 happened to be a Presidential election year.

Never
Brook
Defeat

CHAPTER 16

Lhe encouraging economic upturn after the country passed through the bottom of the depression did not bring political gain to the Administration. The postponements and obstructions in Congress in effect contributed to this lag. In any event, recovery was delayed too long to influence the forthcoming Presidential election.

As the nationally elected President is the natural repository of the nation's ills, rather than the district and state elected members of Congress, Herbert Hoover was instinctively blamed for the hard times and resulting distress. In the public mind, he was inescapably associated with the early depression years.

The President was under no delusions about the criticism he incurred by right of office, in addition to that which stemmed from the function of the opposition under representative government. Besides the metropolitan newspapers that he read daily, pertinent articles and editorials from 500 papers across the country were supplied by a clipping bureau. Since Lincoln, no president had been so condemned for conditions.

In the background of the 1932 campaign, however, there was the continuous personal attack on the President, himself, which greatly influenced the political contest. He was charged with:

A "second Teapot Dome" in which oil shale lands worth billions were leased or about to be leased by the government— Investigation by the Department of the Interior proved that the acreage in question was a tiny fraction of the oil shale lands owned by the government and had no substantial commercial value. The newspaper in which the charge was published subsequently printed an apology.

Involvement in a "sugar scandal"— Investigation was made by a Senate Committee and the Democratic chairman, Senator Walsh, declared the charge erroneous.

The Arkansas "hunger riot"— Investigation by the President's Military Aide disclosed this to be a fake.

Misappropriating $100,000,000 from the United States foreign relief grants during the Armistice— As Secretary of the Treasury, Senator Glass had full responsibility for the funds and he exonerated Hoover.

Partisan favor in the RFC loan made to save the Dawes bank in Chicago— This was refuted by the fact that Democratic members of the RFC Board had recommended the loan. It was later repaid in full.

Probably the most effective personal attack resulted from the Bonus March riot of July 1932. Hoover was accused by implication of "murdering veterans" on the streets of Washington. As previously mentioned, the facts disclose that not a shot was fired and no one was killed after the federal government took charge of the critical situation through the Army under General Douglas MacArthur. John T. Pace has declared that he revealed the Communist role in the Bonus March and direction in the subsequent riots between marchers and the Washington police because it was his duty to set the record straight and expose the misrepresentations. And he has told, too, about his national speaking tour, under Communist auspices, to agitate against President Hoover and General MacArthur.

Another pre-election day feature was a rash of "smear Hoover" books. These and other charges continued to circulate very widely and were built up by whispers and rumors. President Hoover had neither the temperament nor the machinery with which to cope readily with such personal attacks or calumny. He tried to ignore misrepresentations, except those that specifically concerned his integrity and that of his Administration.

With the nomination for President of Governor Franklin Delano Roosevelt of New York by the Democratic Convention at Chicago on July 1, 1932, the official campaign was underway and it was soon stepped up into high gear. President Hoover accepted the Republican nomination on August 11. He had little hope of winning but felt it was obligatory for him to fight the campaign out to the end. The depression was a major enemy in the contest, particularly as the opposition strategy sought to fasten the responsibility for the world-wide economic disaster, which they contended was exclusively of domestic origin, as well as the resulting personal misfortunes of the American citizens, on Hoover alone.

His part in the campaign absorbed what little time the President could spare from normal administration duties and the depression struggle. He made only nine major speeches in swings around the country. Mrs. Hoover went with him on the campaign train, and he made a few informal talks at tank stops. The preparation of public addresses still rated among his hardest tasks, but he never gave a ghostwritten public statement of any importance. However, the Republican candidate could not match the effective delivery and the superb showmanship of the Democratic standard bearer.

Opposing him in speechwriting, besides the Democratic candidate himself, were the members of Governor Roosevelt's "brain trust."

In speeches up and down the land, the Democratic candidate presented his program of political and economic proposals for the country. In blaming Hoover for the world-wide depression, he asserted that the President "did absolutely nothing" about it and was "still doing nothing," and that the Smoot-Hawley Tariff Act of 1930 forced practically all the principal commercial countries off the gold standard. Hoover was accused of neglect of humane services including prison reform, child welfare and the abolition of child labor. He was also charged with reckless extravagance in federal expenditures, the stock market "boom and bust" of 1928–1929, the overbuilding of industry, losses in foreign loans and the drying up of credit abroad through curtailment of lending. All of which he answered with his record.

Hoover fought the "did nothing" charge by explaining all the countless methods and measures employed in combating the depression. When the President told of the successful fight to keep America on the gold standard, Senator Glass denied that such a crisis had ever existed but he was reminded by Senator Watson of the confidential conference the preceding February.

Hoover opposed, of course, the charge that he was responsible for the "boom and bust" in speculation, but he did not reveal the part played by the Federal Reserve credit policies of 1925–1928, as he felt he might impair confidence in the national economy and imply an attack on President Coolidge.

The theory advanced by the opposition that America's industrial plant was built to capacity, perhaps overbuilt, and the last frontier reached, was deplored by the President as denying the American dream of unlimited opportunity and progress. This was the counsel of despair!

Hurt by the continual charges that he was neglecting the people, as well as by the wide-spread personal misrepresentations, the President, speaking at Fort Wayne, Indiana, early in October, 1932, uttered his only harsh word on these scores in public:

> When you are told that the President of the United States . . . has sat in the White House for the last three years of your misfortune without troubling to know your burdens, without heartaches over your miseries and casualties, without summoning every avenue of skillful assistance irrespective of party or view, without using every ounce of his strength and straining his every nerve to protect and help, without using every possible agency of democracy that would bring aid, without putting aside personal ambition and humbling his pride of opinion, if that would serve—then I say to you that such statements are deliberate, intolerable falsehoods.

Democratic strategy did not include attacks on foreign policy, except in relation to the tariff and foreign loans. Another issue was left out of the general campaign—the question of direct relief which later was high on the list of Hoover "indictments" by the opposition. This neglect of a later "hot" issue can probably be attributed to the fact that the unemployed were being well cared for by the organization set up by the President on a volunteer co-operative basis and that to charge the opposite then would have antagonized the many devoted people who were carrying on this good work. They included as many Democrats as Republicans!

On the prohibition issue the majority opinion of the country had jelled in favor of repeal. The President had come out for an amendment allowing the states to deal with the prob-

lem individually, but the Democratic platform plank on repeal was more clear cut than the Republican stand.

Although some Democratic speeches were conservative in
their economic tone, the President was convinced that within
the party there was a minority group "intent, consciously or
unconsciously, on collectivism." On the opponents' future
political calendar, too, he charged, there were still some of
the very same currency-tinkering and greenback measures
which he and his associates had managed to defeat in the recent session of Congress.

The economic upsurge, strong though it was, came too late
to rechannel the country-wide tide that was running strongly
toward the Democratic party. After three unhappy years of
depression, the pent-up feelings of the majority wanted a
change, regardless of any hopeful signs. The Maine elections
disclosed the strength of the Democratic swing. Even the most
conservative advance poll predicted a national Democratic
sweep.

On November 8, 1932, Franklin Delano Roosevelt carried
forty-two states, with a popular vote of 22,821,857 against
15,761,841 for Herbert Hoover. The electoral vote was 472
to 59. That his defeat was expected hardly made it easier for
Hoover. Did he remember then having written years before
that it was the "bitter experience of all public men from
George Washington down that democracies are at least con-
temporarily fickle and heartless?" And, in the growing distress and unrest in the country, he faced four heartbreaking
months without real power to work for recovery. The opposition Congress and the majority of the people naturally
looked to the President-elect for the nation's future policies.

The economic upswing, in which unemployment decreased
by 1,000,000, was first checked by the Maine election. Recovery continued in the rest of the world but the risks inherent in
the change of administration and policies brought on an atti-

tude of stop, look and wait. After the Presidential election, a new decline set in.

The Hoovers had gone to Palo Alto to vote and, on the day following the election, the President initiated a policy of co-operation with the incoming administration. On November 22, the President-elect, accompanied by Raymond Moley, conferred with Hoover at the White House on the war debts, but he disavowed any responsibility on his part, on the grounds that this lay with those then vested with executive and legislative power. This disappointed the President, as he knew no action would be taken by the Democratic Congress without Roosevelt's approval. Although Hoover and Secretaries Stimson and Mills, who were present, thought that the President-elect had agreed to all their proposals, he accepted Hoover's four debt principles but in the end rejected reactivation of the War Debt Commission on bi-partisan lines and suggested that Hoover negotiate through diplomatic channels. To Hoover this was futile, as no foreign government would treat seriously with an outgoing, lameduck administration.

In the face of the weakening economic situation, the President tried once more in mid-December for co-operation with the incoming administration in getting the debt negotiations, as well as the machinery for the World Economic Conference, underway, to strengthen world-wide confidence. But Governor Roosevelt again declined to participate. This resulted in the postponement of the conference.

Hoover initiated further efforts to balance the budget by increased tax revenues and cuts in government expenditure at the short session of Congress. He was supported by the Democratic leaders, with Roosevelt going along. Some time later, the President-elect suddenly opposed the revenue measure and nothing further was done by Congress during that session to balance the budget. Hoover's was the last attempt in budget balancing until the postwar period.

President Hoover wanted to ask Congress for larger supplementary relief grants, to be distributed through the committee system, but it was impossible for the Administration to get a bill through Congress without the President-elect's approval. Roosevelt proposed to handle the problem through direct federal aid.

One development of those difficult times still persists in hurting Hoover. Some apple growers' association in the Northwest worked out a plan for marketing its abundant apple crop at high prices by hiring unemployed men to sell the fruit at street corners in many cities. For years afterward, the mere mention of President Hoover's name brought forth from many political opponents a scathing reminder of the depression, with some such barbed comment as, "Do you want to return to selling apples?"

By December 30, the country had slipped back sharply from recovery. Unemployment had risen over a million and a half from the election-time estimate by early January. Failure to act on the budget, directly contrary to campaign promises, increased uncertainty and fear in the country.

Republican campaign charges that there would be tinkering with the currency if Governor Roosevelt were elected were vigorously denied in speeches by Senator Glass and the Democratic candidate. But by January, the prevalent rumors that the gold standard would be abandoned for some sort of managed currency or evaluation came out into the open, striking a grave blow to public confidence. President Hoover's "visions of rubber dollars" unhappily were coming true.

Democratic insistence on publishing the RFC loans resulted in a further breakdown of confidence and many bank closings. Soon after coming into office, the new administration stopped the publication of the loans.

Although urged to do so by some prominent economists and the press, the President-elect refused to make any comment on his currency plans.

The rumors and statements on monetary changes and lack

of denials brought on an alarming flight from the dollar. Domestic hoarding of gold and currency was resumed and a general panic of depositors developed. As the crisis grew and bank closings increased, restrictions on withdrawals and bank holidays were declared in different states.

Hoover again urged passage of a Bankruptcy Bill, as the delay was causing continued suffering. He continued his attempts to secure Roosevelt's co-operation in the growing crisis.

The President wanted to use an unrepealed World War I law to control bank payments and foreign exchange, but was advised that legally it could not be used without the approval of the President-elect who controlled the incoming Congress. Through William H. Woodin, selected as Secretary of the Treasury, Roosevelt declined all Hoover's suggestions.

On March 3, in the acute panic, Hoover finally called Governor Roosevelt on the telephone, to secure his approval to enact the old war law, but the President-elect refused.

By the morning of Inauguration Day, banking was mostly restricted or suspended across the nation through continuing State Proclamations.

The President was up at six o'clock, finishing the formal business of his administration. He had had less than four hours' rest. For the past ten days he had not been able to have five hours sleep any night. "If I can keep awake through these ceremonies today and get to New York, I shall go to bed for forty-eight hours and don't any of you dare call me up!" he warned his staff.

Second only to his prayer that the United States would be completely past the depression during his term was Hoover's wish that he might turn the government over to the incoming administration in as sound a condition as possible. This sixth crisis, which he had had no real authority to meet, was a nightmare to him. He had worked unceasingly to obtain the co-operation of the new administration but this was denied him.

In a Lincoln Day address, he warned that the country would soon be at the fork of three roads:

The first is the highway of co-operation among nations. . . .

The second road is to rely upon our high degree of national self-containment. . . .

The third road is that we inflate our currency, consequently abandon the gold standard, and with our depreciated currency attempt to enter a world economic war, with the certainty that it leads to complete destruction, both at home and abroad.

Only as the clock chimed in the morning of March 4 did the President admit there was nothing more he could do.

At the Capitol he signed bills and resolutions passed by Congress in the concluding hours of the session. After saying good-by there to many who had worked with him during the four years, he took part in the inaugural ceremonies for the new president. Then, with Mrs. Hoover, he boarded the train for New York. From the observation platform of the last car, he looked into the tense faces of the thousands who had gathered to wish him well. Deeply touched by this evidence of friendship, he disappeared inside at the first movement of the wheels.

Some watching the train pull out felt this was a tragic situation. Those who were closely associated with Herbert Hoover behind the White House wall of silence, which he had imposed for the public good, knew how tragic it was to the man who had labored so hard to serve his country through unparalleled disaster and unequaled handicaps.

His colleagues had long noted with concern the lines, brought into bold relief by the light from the bronze lamp at his desk, which work and worry had etched on his face.

"What I have tried to do during these years," Herbert Hoover explained to his secretary during his last days as President, "has been to save the American people from disaster. They do not know what they have missed. Because they don't know what they have missed, they are dissatisfied with what has been done. In such circumstances they turn to other leaders.

"A former European official recently observed," Hoover continued, thumbing the curlicue on the arm of his chair, "that statesmen, in trying to prevent disaster, kill themselves off. He might say that my tactics have been wrong, that I should have waited until the American people were half-drowned and then have waded in and tried to save them. In such an event, they would, of course, have known what it was all about. But it would have meant catastrophe!"

Keeping
His
Word

CHAPTER 17

Immediately after the inauguration, to the former President's astonishment, President Roosevelt used the same unrepealed World War I power which Hoover in vain had urged him to approve—not to keep the banks open, but to close them! Hoover, who had fought off five greater crises, declared that the bank panic and collapse of March, 1933, was the "most political and most unnecessary bank panic in all our history," and that all that had been needed was to limit bank payments and foreign exchange to necessary business until the panic cooled. The banks were solvent and in time paid 99 per cent of their deposits. Declaring a national bank holiday, Hoover realized, was the dramatic way to create an emergency in solving the crisis. Soon after the end of an extended closing, over 5,000 banks were back in business, with the aid of Secretary Mills and other Hoover Treasury officials working with the new administration.

In his message to Congress of March 10, 1933, President Roosevelt asserted that the failure to balance the budget had had an undoubted effect on the growth of the banking crisis!

Hoover has pointed out that the fright of the bank depositors could not have been caused by fear of his outgoing administration which had only a few days to run, nor by fears of further blows from abroad, for the foreign countries were steadily recovering. Rather, he felt that, beyond the natural indecision between party changes, it was caused by fear of the monetary and other policies of the incoming administration, which departed from traditional American practice, and it was induced too by the President-elect's failure to affirm certain campaign promises on maintaining a sound currency based on gold and to co-operate.

The United States, alone of the nations with free economies, had slipped back from the world recovery, in motion since July, 1932.

After almost nineteen years in public service, Herbert and Lou Hoover retired to Palo Alto, California, to recuperate from their tasks. For the first time, they were able to live for more than a few days at a time in the dream house, which Mrs. Hoover had designed. Changing from the White House to a simple cottage might have proved a hard bump to some families, but the Hoovers had long alternated between great cities and primitive frontiers and so were acclimated to sudden changes in their scale of living. Their return to California was marked by a hearty welcome home from the Governor as well as by an enthusiastic reception staged by the Stanford students —and Hoover found awaiting him some 20,000 letters expressing loyalty and devotion.

For Herbert Hoover's family, the departure from the White House was in effect a release from worry, as they had feared the President's health might give way under the great strain and the terrific pace at which he worked.

Then, too, both of his sons were established in California at that time. Herbert, Jr. was living in Pasadena with his wife and their children. He was teaching Business Economics and Aeronautics at the California Institute of Technology there. Allan, still a bachelor, was working in a Los Angeles bank and living at the University Club in that city.

A former President carries away from the White House with him no privilege, pomp or even honorary title. He becomes just plain "Mister." However, an ex-President is recognized everywhere and still has value to autograph hunters. On one occasion, a boy insisted on three autographs from Hoover.

"Why three?" the former President asked.

"It takes two of yours to get one of Babe Ruth's, when I swap," came the ingenuous reply!

Hoover's activities in behalf of benevolent institutions, his crusades against parts of the New Deal and the promotion of national policies kept him busy and constantly traveling. As he found it important to spend considerable time in the East, the Hoovers took an apartment in New York City for part of the fall and winter months each year, beginning in 1934. Wherever he went, up and down the land, he received pleasant, even affectionate greetings and no derogatory word—to his face.

But the political attacks and misrepresentations were to be intensified, rather than diminished, as might have been expected, on Hoover's exit from the Presidency. The man who had not been considered good theater had now been turned into a "symbol of iniquity," at immense effort and expense, according to Eugene Lyons. This symbolic Hoover was too valuable a stage property to be permitted to retire in comparative peace. The "do-nothing" myth was enlarged and embroidered. The former President could not read the newspapers, listen to the radio or go to public places without risk of a senseless insult. Later on, Hoover asserted that it was suddenly discovered by the opposition that there had been much starvation in the United States before March 4, 1933, and this was widely broadcast. As told earlier, the work of Hoover's relief setup was not criticized in the campaign. Had there been any failure to meet distress, the ex-President commented, the chance to make an issue of it would not have been overlooked!

How a man with such sensitive qualities could stand up under this continuing attack is better understood from a conversation Hugh Gibson had with Mrs. Hoover during the President's term. Mr. Gibson remarked to her on the outward calm with which her husband was bearing up under a particularly strong attack. She answered, "You see, Bert can take it better than most people because he has deeply engrained in him the Quaker feeling that nothing matters if you are 'right with God.' That was dinned into him so thoroughly as a youngster that, even if unconsciously, it helps him at a time like this."

One affront, which must have hurt him very much and required all his strength to face it calmly, was the renaming of the Hoover Dam. In May, 1933, Secretary of the Interior Ickes ordered the name changed to Boulder Dam. It was customary to name a large dam for the President during whose term of office it was undertaken. In this case, moreover, the President concerned had been especially responsible for the enterprise. Through his chairmanship of the Colorado Commission, Hoover had been instrumental in preparing the way for the giant dam. He had personally guided the engineering, largely organized the required legislation and overseen the construction which was about two-thirds completed by the end of his term in 1933. The President had stopped at the dam site on his return to Washington after the November election and had hinted in an address that he would like to be present at the opening—as a bystander. When the dam was dedicated in September, 1933, however, he was not officially invited and did not attend—and the dedication speech given by President Roosevelt failed to mention Hoover's valuable contributions to the tremendous project.

Under the new regime, investigation of the previous administration was undertaken. Due to the caliber and integrity of the Hoover Administration officials, these attempts failed to prove any charge of wrongdoing.

Another effort by the New Deal to discredit Hoover's Administration was the attack on the airmail contracts negotiated by Walter Brown as Postmaster General in 1930. All airmail contracts were canceled in February, 1934, without hearings, and the Army was ordered to fly the mail. Colonel Lindbergh, among others, warned that the Army was not equipped for airmail service and, unfortunately, twelve officers were killed in the attempt. The Senate investigation could find no trace of any malfeasance in the contract negotiations and an attempt to involve the former President's older son, Herbert, Jr., in the inquiry backfired. Under public pressure the contracts were reinstated with slight modifications.

At another time, an effort to discredit Hoover through his younger son, Allan, also blew up, but caused his father anguish.

He was charged with receiving a big federal subsidy for curtailing crops as the largest owner of a southern California land company. The facts were that Allan owned only a few shares on which the subsidy was about two dollars which he refused —instead of the alleged thousands!

The Hoovers are a very closely knit and loyal family and the ex-President must have regretted these attacks on him through his sons as much as the boys regretted any thought that they might trade on his name. During Hoover's term as President, Herbert, Jr. took a summer job in Baltimore under an assumed name. At another time, he was offered an important West Coast position and he turned it down, realizing that it was much too big a job for him. "My father's name is not for sale," he declared to a friend of the family in explaining his refusal.

While following his diverse interests and traveling around the country, Herbert Hoover was able to observe the New Deal acts in practice, along with some of the principles that he had advocated, and he found many of the warnings that he had voiced during the campaign, amply confirmed.

The majority of the citizens had voted out Hoover's Administration—which they associated with hard times—and had adopted the New Deal with a customary willingness to try anything once. They accepted beneficial action without realizing that in such terms as Economic Planning, Production for Use and Planned Economy lay inherent dangers to their freedom.

In his campaign, Hoover had repeatedly warned against the "collectivist" ideology which he asserted was now to be imposed in part on America—"You cannot extend the mastery of government over the daily life of a people without somewhere making it master of people's thoughts and souls." And he had advised that the opposition's demand for a change and a new deal included an effort to "crossbreed some features of Fascism and Socialism with our American system."

To Herbert Hoover, there was no middle road between any type of regimented government and the American system. After a period of resting and watching on the sidelines, he set forth in March, 1935, to oppose many actions of the New Deal with no thought of how it might affect his standing in public favor. His addresses and the statements he had made on the New Deal and many other vital subjects through the years have been published in a series of seven volumes entitled *Addresses and Further Addresses Upon the American Road*. An account of these times is also to be found in *The Memoirs of Herbert Hoover*, Volume 3.

The former President opposed recognition of Soviet Russia as had Presidents Wilson, Harding and Coolidge before him. This was granted under President Roosevelt in November, 1933. He cited such examples of Soviet interference in the United States as the Bonus March of 1932 and the flooding of the world with Soviet-printed counterfeit American money during the next year. He pointed out as well their unfavorable international reputation. He declared that, contrary to the "scrap of paper" agreement, "Communist and Communist-front organizations bored into every vital organ in our country, including the government," and a few American labor unions.

Hoover deplored the ending of the World Economic Conference in July, 1933, by President Roosevelt's "bombshell" message postponing currency stabilization. The English economist, J. Maynard Keynes, proclaimed Roosevelt "magnificently right," to which Raymond Moley, the President's monetary representative, quipped, "Magnificently left, Keynes means." Secretary Hull, head of the American delegation, believed that two tragic results accrued from the ending of the conference—world recovery was retarded and, from then on, Germany, Italy and Japan felt they could rearm in comparative safety, due to lack of unity between Britain, France and the United States.

In addition, Herbert Hoover opposed the great centralization of power in the Executive under the strong, magnetic leadership of Roosevelt, the reduction of the legislative arm to a "rubber stamp" and the eventual "packing" of the Supreme Court with the President's appointees, although the Court Bill, to fill the vacancies caused by retirement or death, was defeated. The Senate Judiciary Committee declared the bill should be so emphatically defeated that its parallel would never again be presented.

Hoover had long warned on the dangers of a huge, self-perpetuating bureaucracy and political use of relief funds.

He opposed the Administration's rapid moves into a managed currency, fiat money and the abandonment of the gold standard as a moral issue in addition to the question of economic freedom. Senator Glass bitterly attacked the President on the Senate floor, charging there was no need for the United States to go off the gold standard with nearly 40 per cent of the world's gold. The suggested 50 per cent devaluation of the gold dollar meant to him national repudiation and dishonor.

With the Thomas amendment to the Agriculture Adjustment Act of May, 1933, Congress gave the Chief Executive authority over money as absolute as that of Tiberius Caesar, Hoover contended, asserting that the amendment fulfilled the dreams of every American currency tinkerer since the Republic was founded.

The Administration's gold operations were criticized by Keynes, upon whom two administration advisers leaned heavily for support. He described the "gyrations of the dollar" as more "like a gold standard on the booze" than a managed currency.

Hoover charged that devaluation of the dollar had a very adverse effect on foreign trade, causing it to decline, and he pointed out that devaluation resulted in increasing American tariffs 49 per cent on both dutiable goods and goods previously free of duty by raising the price of foreign currencies to the American buyer. Subsequent tariff reductions under the Reciprocal Trade agreements, he felt, restored approximately the Smoot-Hawley level!

The former President asserted that the unlimited silver purchases had the unfortunate result of draining China, India and Mexico of silver needed to maintain their silver standards.

He charged that the New Deal introduced the "spectacle of Fascist dictation" to business, labor and agriculture and inveighed against "planned scarcity," the resulting wide misuse of funds and government coercion in general. On May 15, 1935, he issued a blast against the National Industrial Recovery Act, known as the NRA. Title 1 of this Act was declared unconstitutional by the Supreme Court two weeks later. Long forward-looking in his views on the rights of labor, including collective bargaining, work hour decrease and wage increase, Hoover protested much of the New Deal labor policy and practices, with their resultant "stirring of class warfare in the most classless country in the world."

As the years passed, Hoover's speeches gained noticeably in sparkle and shed some austerity in comparison with his Presidential addresses. Many have brought out his sense of humor and a quiet satirical quality. Of planned scarcity he commented, "It is the more abundant life—without bacon."

The former President opposed the government policy of entering the power business, and he attacked this plan as the introduction of socialism through electrical power, citing the Tennessee Valley Authority.

Hoover charged that the planned economy of Roosevelt's regime had become planned extravagance, despite the campaign promises to reduce government expenditures by 25 per cent. Only in services to veterans and in defense appropriations did he find decreases shown—at a time when dictators were threatening world peace. He cited the increase in the national debt from about $20,000,000,000 at the end of his term to about $47,000,000,000 at the close of Roosevelt's second administration.

Hoover deplored the New Deal propaganda activities, citing the presence of "public relations" men on the staff of every New Deal bureau and the sharp rise in cost of free mailing by the executive departments—$23,000,000 more for 1936 than 1932. In May, 1939, a Democratic senator stated that about 30,000 government employees were taking part in propaganda activities.

Herbert Hoover—the symbol of a way of life, rather than the man himself—was the target of many of the propaganda attacks from all sources. In late December, 1935, while speaking at St. Louis, he made one of his few allusions to his personal ordeal. He warned of the disaster in the "dark alleys of inspired propaganda," where "ideals and men are assassinated with poisonous whisperings."

At this period, he was studying and reviewing his feelings and convictions about the American way of life. This resulted in the publication of his *Challenge to Liberty*.

Eugene Lyons in his book, *Our Unknown Ex-President,* told that, around 1935, American Communists and fellow travelers joined in the anti-Hoover line which they pushed in every corner of American life that could possibly be reached by infiltration. For a while, the Roosevelt Administration was also attacked, until Moscow adopted its "democratic," united-front line about the middle of 1935.

By the spring of 1936, there were a million more unemployed than on the day Roosevelt had been elected. Blame for this was heaped on economic royalists, Republicans, recalcitrant Democrats—and Herbert Hoover.

The campaigns of 1936, 1940 and 1944 were waged in turn against Republican candidates Landon, Willkie and Dewey. However, Hoover was in effect the candidate, as the Depression continued to be a major theme followed by the war, and the Democratic opposition was concentrated on him. Unhappily, the Republicans, for the most part, left their political past undefended. The Hoover record that was learned by millions of new voters was a Democratic version.

Hoover, of course, favored some of the actions taken under the New Deal Administration, though often regretting certain patterns and principles set up in the measures. For example, he approved the meritorious objective in Social Security, while he pointed out the "unsound" method of financing old-age pensions.

The former President was opposed to some of the New Deal accounting, including the "Twin Budgets." He attacked the intellectual honesty of certain features. He cited an act of February, 1938, passed by the House and Senate, in which debts to the RFC of ten New Deal agencies were canceled, bypassing Congress' power of the purse and the safeguards of examination and check by appropriations committees.

In a speech Hoover remarked on his sympathy for the humble decimal point, saying that, "His is a pathetic and hectic life, wandering around among the regimented ciphers trying to find some of the old places he used to know."

Hoover also questioned the New Deal operation in changes of statistics based on index numbers by altering the base.

The United States failed to regain pace with the world recovery which started in July, 1932, following the slump that had set in, Hoover asserted, due to fear and apprehension of the policies planned by the incoming Administration. He contended that his policies were in the main right, citing the fact that twelve nations retaining free economies and holding to these policies recovered their prosperity within two to three years and moved to levels above those of 1929.

But America, Hoover pointed out, continued to have huge unemployment, subnormal productivity and costly relief measures until the country's manpower and industries were completely taken up, eight years later, in 1941, by the demands of World War II. Despite beneficial changes incorporated into the government, the New Deal had failed to solve unemployment and in some quarters the condition was regarded as permanent, which Hoover deplored as denying hope to the idle of regaining jobs and making their own way.

After five discouraging years, Hoover recounted that some New Dealers turned to the theory, partly Keynes' in origin, that the government must tax or borrow away savings and spend them, and that there was no need to bother about the size of the government debt—it was not a debt at all! This in a country built on thrift and free enterprise.

The cause of the United States' failure to recover prosperity was presented by Hoover as primarily the Administration attempts to regiment the American system of life. As a consequence of these Planned Economy devices, including spending, recovery did not come to the country under President Roosevelt during peacetime. Hoover offered the verified figures of the numbers of unemployed, the number on relief and the subnormal productivity as infallible proof that the Great Depression extended until the advent of World War II.

Increase of employment above that of 1929 quickly took place in those nations with free economies, but the United States and France, "hobbled" by New Deals, continued under depression conditions until their economies responded to war needs, as did Canada whose economy was so closely allied to that of this country.

After January, 1940, war production and the large mobilization began to affect employment in America. At the time of Pearl Harbor, however, those unemployed still numbered more than 8,000,000. World War II then closed over the "debacle" of Planned Economy, Hoover asserted, pointing out that in addition to promoting economic failure, the New Deal had not succeeded in sustaining its movement toward regimentation. "The traditional American love of freedom and devotion to constitutional processes," he stated, "proved too deep for its schemes to work."

As a result of Planned Economy measures, topped by necessary war controls, Hoover declared that a reversal of feeling about parts of the New Deal and its methods grew stronger and stronger among the citizens of the United States. The first real swing back to free enterprise he felt was evidenced by the 1946 Congressional elections. According to an estimate made by a member of the body, Republicans and conservative Democrats in the new Congress repealed some 70,000 New Deal and war measures, regulations and orders. This helped to restore the balance of the American system. There have been setbacks since but that it has survived, Mr. Hoover has declared, is proof of its vitality.

In addition to his efforts in behalf of his country's well-being, the former President continued to maintain his interest in humanitarian, educational and scientific institutions, giving a great deal of his time, skill and personal energy and working through a host of organizations. He has served in many capacities, from trustee to fund raiser. In 1936, he became chairman of the Boys' Clubs of America, and he devoted enormous effort to this project which builds character and good citizenship among its young members in less privileged areas. Under his guidance, over twenty years later, this country-wide movement aided half a million boys through more than 500 clubs, with assets of over $100,000,000. The national headquarters in New York City is named the Herbert Hoover Building.

A trustee of Stanford University since 1912, Herbert Hoover, Class of '95, has aided in every part of its welfare, including the raising of large funds. He was instrumental in the establishment of the School of Business Administration, which had grown to an enrollment of over 400 in 1955.

The collection Hoover started of the contemporary, fugitive literature of World War I during the Belgian Relief days was continued, and his "Operation Packrat" has mushroomed through the years. Seven hundred and fifty thousand dollars was raised to build the Hoover Tower on the Stanford University Campus, to house the collection. This 285-foot tower was dedicated in June, 1941, by the founder of the project, which is now known as The Hoover Institution on War, Revolution and Peace. The collection was of immediate use in aiding research for World War II operations. German maps of the Japanese-held Pacific Islands, gathered by Hoover agents in Berlin, were studied or copied by members of the Armed Forces, and French maps from the Packrat collection were used in planning the invasion of North Africa. Records available there also enabled the federal government to map the locations of the Soviet Russian slave labor camps. Among the most unique items are a copy of the first edition of *Pravda*, the Goebbels diaries, German Anti-Comintern records and the diary of General Joseph Stilwell. Countless research treasures of World War II, the Korean War and the Communist Revolution in China have been accumulated. A Belgian woman whose life had been saved by the C.R.B., the commission through which Hoover had directed the feeding of enemy-held Belgium during World War I, collected Nazi papers to document the German occupation of her country during World War II and gave her cache to a Hoover agent after liberation.

In the beginning, Hoover supported the project all by himself. During the early years, he contributed $150,000 toward it. When it became necessary to provide proper storage and research quarters for the collection, former Belgian Relief men came to the rescue. Some of these are serving on the Advisory Board, including W. Hallam Tuck, Sidney A. Mitchell, Lewis L. Strauss and Perrin C. Galpin. Among members are Jeremiah Milbank, J. E. Wallace Sterling, president of Stanford University, and Allan Hoover. The institution is independently endowed.

The purposes of the operation are manifold. They include the salvaging and preservation of war research materials for use in the defense of the United States; the assembling of a complete record of peacemaking through pinpointed research and the publication of pertinent material; the protection of the American way of life from false ideologies; and the reaffirmation of the validity of the American Republic and the principles on which it was founded. "Sometimes," Herbert Hoover has said, "the voice of experience does call out to stop, look and listen. And sometimes people respond to that call."

Another enterprise which derived from Hoover's World War I activities, the Belgian American Educational Foundation, has exchanged Belgian and American college students for work on a graduate level and, in addition, has arranged for professors of both countries to give guest lectures. The Belgian exchange students, who constitute the greater part of the program, have been represented in large numbers on the teaching and research faculties of the Belgian universities. The roster has also included ten ministers in the Belgian government, among whom are numbered three prime ministers.

With the start of World War II on Germany's invasion of Poland in September, 1939, Herbert Hoover was appointed Chairman of the Commission for Polish Relief, serving from 1939 to 1942. He immediately went to work to bring food and other relief supplies to non-combatants—children in particular. Following the Soviet invasion of Finland, in December, 1939, he also took on the chairmanship of the Finnish Relief Fund. He continued this fine work for three years, helping to raise huge funds.

Touched by the many imploring petitions he received from native relief committees inside the occupied countries, Hoover organized the Committee on Food for the Small Democracies in 1940. Hundreds of Americans rallied to this cause with aid, and General Pershing made a public statement in support of the project. The former C.R.B. head also became chairman of the Belgian Relief Fund. But this time he was only able to arrange for the captive populations to receive minor supplies through private organizations such as the Red Cross and the Friends' Services.

As a result of the depression, his encounters with the New Deal, the well-organized anti-Hoover propaganda, and his opposition to World War II and American intervention in the conflict, Herbert Hoover became the object of "fairly deep unpopularity," as he himself owned. In late 1941, shortly before Pearl Harbor, his unpopularity struck a low point, due to his continued criticism of the totalitarian Kremlin regime and his unceasing demands that America help feed the starving children of France, Greece and other Hitler-held countries.

He, however, never deviated from his selfless struggle to aid the hopeless victims of war and, once again, Herbert Hoover, this outstanding humanitarian, would aid famine sufferers throughout the world when the war was won.

With the Japanese sneak attack on Pearl Harbor, all debate concerning military intervention in World War II was over, and the United States plunged into the conflict for survival. Although other prominent Republicans were forgiven their political views and taken by the Administration into the war effort, no job was offered Hoover—the brilliantly successful Food Administrator of World War I. This neglect was not due entirely to caprice, according to the author, Raymond Moley.

He believes it was the "result of political prudence, for Roosevelt entertained a view that only Hoover among the notables of the Republican Party possessed the massive convictions and intelligence to provide an alternative to the New Deal. Roosevelt actually believed that Hoover might well emerge once more as the leader and candidate of his party. . . ."

Through speeches, articles, statements and testimony to a Congressional Committee, Hoover warned the country of the growing dangerous food crisis at home and abroad and offered constructive suggestions based on his unparalleled experience in this field. Through his leadership, public opinion was aroused and his proposals were mostly adopted by the Administration.

In 1944, Herbert Hoover suffered his greatest personal loss when Mrs. Hoover died suddenly in New York City. In accordance with her wish, Mr. Hoover presented their house on the Stanford Campus to the university, to be used as the residence of the president. The transfer included an annual gift to the Hoover Institution from the university of $10,000 for six years, to be used in research and the publication of documents advancing peace in the world—Lou Henry Hoover's greatest hope.

At the end of World War II, President Harry S. Truman called Hoover into service, to help with the gigantic famine which inevitably followed in Europe and other parts of the world. This was the first request for aid of any kind received by the former President from the White House in twelve years. His wise recommendations for the relief of France, Italy and Belgium were accepted. During 1946–1947, Hoover served as Co-ordinator of Food Supply for World Famine for many nations. With volunteers drawn from among his former experienced colleagues in starvation relief, he visited thirty-nine countries on a 57-day trip by plane. Hard work and travel consumed many hours of his nights as well as his days. Perrin

Galpin estimates that Hoover alone wore out 127 pencils during this humanitarian journey. He then made another flying trip to Latin America to visit food exporting countries there in the search for available foodstuffs. Mass starvation was prevented but there was still great suffering, until the good harvest of 1946 brought local relief. Nevertheless, grave problems continued in certain countries and, at President Truman's request, Hoover again took a hand. Besides food and reconstruction, economic policies were also involved. Hoover aided in restoring free enterprise to West Germany and Japan. During his special mission to Germany and Austria, Hoover reestablished a canteen system for feeding the children and special groups numbering over 6,000,000.

As a result of his world-wide personal survey, Hoover estimated that there were about 30,000,000 children in critical need. Jointly with others, he established the United Nations International Children's Emergency Fund. He was instrumental, too, in organizing CARE, which has transmitted many millions of food packages to people, particularly the destitute, in foreign countries. Other supplies, such as farming tools, can also be sent.

Herbert Hoover's return to humanitarian work on a large scale, and his courage in undertaking such arduous tasks, set off a new appreciation of this First Citizen throughout the country. After a long term of unpopularity, roughly coinciding with the New Deal era, he came into his own again in the role of Elder Statesman. The critical tone in the press and radio suddenly turned deferential. The uneasy conscience of many citizens was expressing itself in belated recognition. Even those who refused to accept his ideas seemed awed by his moral stature. Only in the extreme left camp did slander continue unabated. As a symbol of the new feeling, the Republican Congress passed a bill in 1947 restoring the original name of Hoover Dam to Boulder Dam. This was signed by President Truman. Hoover's birthday that year was front page news and marked by editorial tribute. Again a leading figure in his own Republican Party, he was consulted continually by members of both parties in the House and Senate and by Congressional Committees.

In 1947, another task came to Hoover for which he had unparalleled qualifications. He was then appointed to the Commission on Organization of the Executive Branch of the Government, of which he was elected chairman. He had long worked, in the Harding and Coolidge Administrations and during his own term for authority, to reduce waste and increase efficiency in the executive branch. This assignment not only made justice—but drama.

The bipartisan Commission of twelve men immediately went to work to obtain the necessary information. Twenty-four task forces undertook research on different subjects such as the Office of the President, Records Management and Foreign Affairs.

After analyzing the vast data, the Commission proposed about 273 recommendations. Many of these were adopted under the Truman Administration and still others under President Eisenhower—comprising about three-quarters of the program in whole or in part. In urging the acceptance of the proposals before the Citizens' Committee on the Hoover Reports, the chairman declared, "We have need to re-establish faith that the whole of the preamble to the Declaration of Independence and the Gettysburg Address are still related to government. If the republic is not to be overwhelmed, the people must have such methods and systems as will enable good officials to give them good government." And he warned that the crusade "to reduce cost of government is a necessary condition to winning the cold war."

At the approach of Herbert Hoover's seventy-fifth birthday, August, 1949, great honors were in store for the thirty-first President. On August 2, Congress passed *A Unanimous Resolution of Appreciation:*

Resolved by the Senate (the House concurring) that the Congress hereby extends to the Honorable Herbert Hoover . . . its cordial birthday greetings. . . . and expresses admiration and gratitude for his devoted service to his country and to the world; and that the Congress expresses its hope that he be spared for many years of useful and honorable service.

The acclaim for Herbert Hoover was nation-wide—and world-wide—with hundreds of laudatory radio comments, over 2,000 syndicated and original newspaper editorials, proclamations or statements from state governors, greetings from more than a hundred foreign governments or organizations and over 25,000 letters. One newspaper writer continued to dislike Hoover's high collars and a very few, perhaps about twenty-five, still clung to their earlier negative beliefs.

The *New York Herald Tribune* wrote of Herbert Hoover: "like only one or two other statesmen in our history he has been able to go from service to service, making the Presidency only one step in a career which reaches its climax in the total and cumulative record of work done, good causes unselfishly pursued and arduous responsibilities carried through to the end. If ever a man were entitled to feel the deepest kind of satisfaction and content, it is Mr. Hoover—"

A new step came in 1953 with Hoover's appointment to a new Commission on Organization of the Executive Branch of the Government, with wider powers including policy study, created by Congress. He became chairman of this one, too. This was during President Eisenhower's first Administration. The Commission brought in 314 recommendations, about 64 per cent of which have been adopted in whole or in part. The work of the two commissions under the brilliant guidance of Herbert Hoover resulted not only in greatly improved administrative efficiency but also in an enormous saving of the taxpayers' money. It has been estimated that economies totaling $7,000,000,000 can be traced to the first Hoover Commission's Reports and that savings of upwards of $3,000,-000,000 a year will result from the recommendations of the second commission. As blueprints for good government, the Hoover Reports have gone a long way toward revitalizing the federal structure and rendering it more responsive to the needs of the people. From a level of about $4,623,000,000 budget expenditure in 1933, the biggest business in the world operated at a budget rate of $71,936,171,353 in 1958.

Task force reports made include those on Federal Transport functions, Civil Service, Surplus Property, Foreign Aid and Water Resources and Power. A sharp cut in government money lending service and the termination of many government activities competing with private business were urged. In line with Hoover's own feeling, it was held that government should only undertake functions not feasible for private business and financial institutions and then only for "justifiable" Federal purposes.

It is hoped that more of the proposals made by the second Hoover Commission will still be enacted, including those recommendations which would result in immense governmental saving.

And so the circle had come full turn from the Hoover luncheons, Hoover relief and Hooverizing of World War I . . . through the misnamed Hoovervilles and Hoover depression . . . and on to the indelible achievements of the Hoover Commissions.

As Elder Statesman, Hoover's advice was sought at each new turn and crisis, be it the Communist Chinese threat to Formosa or the Iron Curtain situation. He continued his speeches and writing along the American Road, keeping his word pledged to public service for the American people—and to those abroad whom he could help. His *America's First Crusade, The Problems of Lasting Peace,* * *The Basis of Lasting Peace* * and *The*

* with Hugh Gibson

Ordeal of Woodrow Wilson are to be considered permanent contributions to an understanding of the growth and aspirations of the United States.

The public positions Herbert Hoover had held and the distinctions conferred upon him filled a 57-page 1957 booklet. His honorary degrees from American and foreign universities number eighty-nine. He had received very many medals, 177 testimonials and awards from all parts of the world, too, as well as numerous honorary memberships in scientific, civic and charitable organizations. Streets, plazas, a planet and a rose have been named in his honor. He was especially touched by the knowledge that thirty-three schools in the United States are named for him and one in West Germany. A second round of honors from previous grantors started some time ago, including a second joint resolution of Congress in 1954.

At the request of President Eisenhower and Chancellor Adenauer of West Germany, Hoover undertook a mission to Germany in 1954, and in 1956 he served as honorary chairman of First Aid for Hungary. At the Brussels Fair, held in 1958, he represented the President on United States Days—July 2–4. This gave the Belgians a further chance to express their appreciation to him for all that he had done for their country.

As engineer, humanitarian and statesman, Herbert Hoover had reached the summits of three careers.

Politically his Administration was shattered by the Great Depression, arising from the effects and dislocations of World War I and the "imponderable of the (American) people's political habits," doubly strong in the depression. As President, he was hampered by his innate reserve and lack of histrionic ability, which prevented his selling himself and his policies to the crowds, and by a lack of political mastery and dexterity.

Economically, he contended that his Administration finally won the Battle of the Depression, after three and a half years of struggle, with the United States economic upturn from July, 1932. The recovery continued among the other nations of the world with free economies, but the United States, which should have led the way, Hoover asserted, slumped back into further depression, due to people's fear of the monetary and other policies of the new administration.

Herbert Hoover had unlimited faith that America will always be strong if we continue to live up to the God-given principles on which the Republic was founded. He believed unquenchably in the "resistless, dynamic power of American enterprise." As he stated in October, 1930, "We have known a thousand temporary setbacks, but the spirit of this people will never brook defeat."

Historical perspective is still somewhat clouded by myth and misrepresentation. In the view of Ray Lyman Wilbur and Arthur M. Hyde, as told in their book, *The Hoover Policies:*

> History will record that despite many handicaps President Hoover guided the Nation safely through perilous times and placed it on the road to recovery in 1932. It will also record the effective care of distress, the unparalleled industrial peace of the times, and the fidelity to national obligations.
>
> It will record that Hoover originated and developed more new government policies for the correction of business abuse and the advancement of economic life than any President up to his time. It will record that it was Hoover who laid the foundations for an era of social progress in this country. It will record that with these great accomplishments he held to Constitutional Government and to the fundamental ideas of free men.

In a moving tribute to his longtime friend, Senator Robert A. Taft, Herbert Hoover told of his associate's magnificent courage and unwavering devotion in the service of his country:

> Bob's other outstanding quality of character was his intellectual and moral integrity.

His sense of duty, his acknowledgment of obligation, his essential loyalty and patriotism were unusual in a day when men compromised their souls for the crumbs of popularity.

This tribute can be read for Herbert Hoover, too.

Many people have sought to describe this Elder Statesman who rose from a poor orphan to world-wide acclaim. One biographer asserts that the crowning quality of Hoover's personality is shyness. Herewith it is submitted to be—patriotism.

All
Along
the Way

CHAPTER 18

Herbert Hoover lived longer, after leaving the White House, than has any other American president. John Adams, the leader in the Continental Congress in the struggle to declare independence, had survived for exactly twenty-five years and four months since the end of his term as the nation's second president when he died on the Fourth of July, 1826, fifty years to the day after the Declaration had been approved by the colonial delegates. Hoover had passed Adams' mark on July 3, 1958. He lived six years, three months and sixteen days longer. Adams, however, outdistanced Hoover in age by almost six months.

On the date when Mr. Hoover overtook Adams' record, he was in Belgium, serving as President Eisenhower's personal representative at the Brussels World's Fair, July 2–4, 1958.

July 5th was designated Herbert Hoover Day in Belgium. On his Honor Day he gave a speech at the Reunion of the Belgian

Relief Commission that he headed in World War I and the Belgian Comité National. These honors marked the first of his many great humanitarian works—the organization of the feeding of enemy-occupied Belgium during World War I and in the postwar period after liberation. This was also the first large-scale international relief operation in recorded history.

There was further recognition of Hoover's services as Chairman of the Commission for Relief in Belgium and of his work for Belgian Relief (1939–1942) and his aid after the second World War. When King Baudouin made a three-weeks' tour of the United States, in May, 1959, the Belgian monarch was honored in New York City on the 29th, at a dinner sponsored by the Belgian-American (originally C.R.B.) Educational Foundation. On this occasion, Herbert Hoover gave the main address.

As part of his other humanitarian work, previously described in this book, Hoover supervised aid to liberated Finland following World War I and he was chairman of the Finnish Relief Fund (1939–1942). He went to Finland in 1946 and again aided that country in the post-World War II famine. In 1949, he received a Legislative Citation of Appreciation from the People of Finland.

Herbert Hoover served as honorary chairman of the American-Baltic Commemorative Committee in 1960, which marked the 20th anniversary of the Soviet invasion of Estonia, Latvia and Lithuania.

In October, 1961, President Urho K. Kekkonen of Finland arrived in New York City for a four-day visit at the start of a national tour. That afternoon, President Kekkonen, who was staying at the Waldorf-Astoria Hotel, paid a call on Mr. Hoover, then eighty-seven years old, at his apartment there. The two conversed informally.

During these years, Mr. Hoover was working on a detailed and documented account of the vast extent of the relief and rehabilitation in wars, postwars and famines in Europe and elsewhere which the generosity of the American people had made possible in very great measure; of the operations that carried out the work which he had headed in governmental and other posts, and of the participation of other organizations.

An American Epic was the title chosen for this work. Originally planned to be published in three volumes, it was eventually expanded to four. In the Introduction to this epic (in the first volume), Herbert Hoover stated:

"Never before has a nation undertaken such burdens, consciously and collectively, that human life, and even civilization might be preserved.

"Our people accomplished this task of compassion by self-denial, by longer hours of labor and greater tax burdens—and with no return other than to their own consciences. . . .

"These American labors not only saved human lives, they saved civilization for the Western world. They erected dams against the spread of Communism."

Herbert Hoover undertook to write the "whole magnificent story" of this American relief epic, as he had participated in "many of these efforts," had the assistance of many of his colleagues in the operations and had access to documentation not previously available to others.

For twenty years he had worked part-time on the Epic. In the research for the project, 3,500,000 items were inspected. Mr. Hoover personally studied 400,000 of these.

Hoover declared that, while other nations contributed within their means, 95 per cent of the enormous cost involved in these life-saving enterprises during both World Wars and their aftermaths was borne by the citizens of the United States. He cited the vast organizational, supply and transportation requirements for this relief and reconstruction. To carry out the work, the services of "hundreds of thousands of self-sacrificing people" in each nation aided had been needed, too.

An American Epic consists of:

VOLUME I: Introduction
    The Relief of Belgium and Northern France,
    1914–1930 (1959)
The exciting story of feeding enemy-occupied Belgium
and Northern France in World War I and postwar, undertaken by the Commission for Relief in Belgium, organized
and headed by Hoover.

VOLUME II: Famine in Forty-five Nations
    Organization Behind the Front, 1914–1923
    (1960)
Provision of food for the Allies and Neutrals during the
war and preparation to meet the postwar famine in forty-
five nations. Hoover's role as United States Food Administrator and, later, as Director-General, American
Relief Association; Director-General, Relief and Reconstruction (thirty countries in Europe), and in numerous
other posts.

VOLUME III: Famine in Forty-five Nations
    The Battle on the Front Line, 1914–1923
    (1961)
Concludes account of the battle against the great famine
in Europe and a part of Asia during World War I and its
aftermath.

VOLUME IV: The Guns Cease Killing and the Saving of Life
    from Famine Begins, 1939–1963 (1964)
Narrative of American actions to relieve starvation over-
seas during and after World War II. Mr. Hoover's part as
Coordinator, Food Supply for thirty-eight Nations in the
Worldwide Famine of 1946–1947.

"During these famines of both world wars," Mr. Hoover
stated in Volume IV, "the American people furnished the margins of food and medicine which saved the lives of more than
1,800,000,000 human beings, largely women and children,

most of whom otherwise would have perished."

Among the numerous honors and recognition for his aid accomplishments at home, a debt of gratitude was paid to Mr. Hoover in January, 1961, by the State of Florida for his leading role in the Lake Okeechobee flood control.

The hurricane-driven flood waters of the large central Florida lake caused terrible loss of life in 1926 and 1928. After both hurricanes, Hoover visited and appraised the disaster areas. At the time of his visit in February, 1929, he was President-elect.

Hoover, an experienced engineer, recommended that large levees or dikes be built along the shores of the 730-square-mile lake for many miles. He felt that these would prevent another such catastrophe, as well as annual flooding during the rainy season. His appeal to Congress for funds to build the dikes was approved and construction started in 1932.

In subsequent hurricanes, the dike system at Lake Okeechobee has held and no human lives have been lost.

In November, 1959, the Florida State Chamber of Commerce passed a resolution to name the dikes in Mr. Hoover's honor. On July 14, 1960, by Act of Congress, the Lake Okeechobee levees were designated the Herbert Hoover Dike, in commemoration of his "humanitarian efforts and interest in public safety."

Other organizations joined the Florida Chamber of Commerce in plans for a ceremony that was held at Clewiston, about sixty miles west of West Palm Beach, on January 12, 1961. A plaque, prepared by the U.S. Army Corps of Engineers, was dedicated in Hoover's honor. In his remarks, the former President said that the American people had contributed huge sums to such projects. "And I know," he continued, "there has never been a substantial complaint over the tax burden to build this and other great public works which add to the safety of our citizens and the increase in national productivity."

Mr. Hoover continued to be very active in many organizations devoted to benefiting children and young people at home and abroad. Among these were the United Nations International Children's Emergency Fund (UNICEF) and the Boy Scouts of America. But the Boys' Clubs of America to which he had devoted his organizing ability and which he headed personally was closest to the former President's heart.

When Herbert Hoover was elected chairman of the Boys' Clubs of America in October, 1936, there were 140 clubs with a total membership of 140,000 boys. Through the years that followed he worked tirelessly, enlisting supporters for the movement.

In October, 1960, the Herbert Hoover National Headquarters Building in New York City was dedicated. In his remarks, Mr. Hoover said that "never before has our country needed" great character-building organizations such as the Boys' Clubs "more than now."

He paid tribute to the many individuals and to the foundations whose contributions had made the headquarters possible. Not the least of these and, to him, the most touching were the gifts of pennies, nickels, dimes, bricks and handwork by the boys themselves for the building and its equipment. Two boys, unable to contribute money, had given a pair of "more than slightly used" bricks. The board chairman had made sure that these bricks were used in the foundation of the headquarters.

In his address to the Annual Convention of the Boys' Clubs, earlier that year, Mr. Hoover said:

"The purpose of these clubs is to give them (the boys) an alternative to the life on the cobblestones and the pavements. Under skilled guidance the boys receive two great services: They are organized into sports teams. And the rules of sports are second only to religion as moral training. The second great service is in our shops and reading rooms where the boys are given opportunity to determine their bent in life. . . . The Boys' Clubs are not a cure; they are a preventive of youthful delinquency.

"These days we hear much about National Goals. The greatest national goals of all human history were established in the Declaration of Independence and the Constitution of the United States." The Boys' Clubs and similar organizations supported these goals, he declared. In conclusion, he asked if support of these character-building institutions was not also a national goal.

To the boys, personally, Mr. Hoover was a beloved friend, interested in helping them and giving each one a chance. On his birthdays, thousands of messages came from boys in the clubs. At his insistence, each boy received an acknowledgment, many of them personally written and signed by the former President, showing that his greeting had been read and appreciated.

At the time of the devoted chairman's death, there were approximately 635 clubs, with a total membership of 600,000 boys in 450 communities, which represented cities, towns, suburban and rural areas.

On the future of America's youth Mr. Hoover wrote in an article published in *Seventeen* in 1962: "I think the opportunities for our youth today are greater than ever before by virtue of all the scientific invention and technological improvements that have gone on.

"We have expanded the number of jobs enormously, the number of new areas for adventure, for individual initiative. You have plenty of promise ahead of you."

On May 2, 1960, at its annual meeting in Washington, the Chamber of Commerce of the United States of America presented its Great Living American Award to five men—Herbert Hoover in absentia, Bernard Baruch and three others. The award is given to the individual "who, under our system of free enterprise, has made a lasting and significant contribution to society."

As Mr. Hoover was unable to go to Washington to attend, the award and citation were presented to him in New York, a few days later. The citation honored him for statesmanship, devotion to the concept of government as the servant, not the master, of the people, reorganization of the Executive Branch of the Government and "vast" selflessness in relieving suffering in the world, among other qualifications.

The 1960 Republican National Convention, held in Chicago, opened on July 25th. At the evening session, the delegates and alternates "erupted in a demonstration of affection" for their former standard bearer as Herbert Hoover arrived to address the convention.

"Today," he warned, "America is in the midst of a frightening moral slump." He cited the increase in crime and corruption.

"This nation needs a rebirth of a great spiritual force, which has been impaired by cynicism and weakened by foreign infection."

He reminded his fellow Republicans that they were there to declare guidelines as well as to nominate candidates for president and vice president. "Yours is the task to stop this moral retreat, to lead the attack and recapture the meaning of the word America. Thus can opportunity and the spiritual future of your children be assured."

The former President was given a second ovation at the conclusion of his speech, and another on receiving the Young Republicans award.

On the day before the Hoover Dike Ceremony, in January, 1961, the former President and the President-elect, John F. Kennedy, met in Florida. The President-elect asked Mr. Hoover if he had any advice for him on his assuming the Presidency. Hoover replied that all ex-Presidents are always ready to give advice to a new one. "You'll hear from them all," he declared, adding that the problem was "deciding which advice was right."

President Kennedy was the first Democratic Presidential candidate in twenty-eight years not to make Mr. Hoover a campaign target. This was due in part to the fact that the former President was an old friend of the Democratic standard bearer's father, Joseph P. Kennedy, and had had Senator John F. Kennedy's co-operation in getting the necessary enabling legislation for Hoover's government reorganization on recommendations.

In March, Mr. Hoover declined President Kennedy's offer of Honorary Chairmanship of the Peace Corps with regret. Due to his commitments to nine educational, scientific and charitable institutions or movements whose annual expenditures amounted to nearly $100 million and his age—twice that of the President's —he did not feel he could undertake the assignment, but said that he would be available for information and advice.

Following the Cuban invasion débâcle in April, 1961, President Kennedy conferred with many Republican leaders on this international problem, as well as on Laos, and other growing crises, seeking both advice and to ward off partisan attack. On April 28th, in New York City, he paid a call on former President Hoover, a Republican who had known both the heights of success and the depths of adversity.

On June 27, 1961, Herbert Hoover made the keynote speech of Philadelphia's Freedom Week, marking the 185th Anniversary of American Independence.

During the midday ceremony at Independence Hall, Hoover was presented with the first "City of Philadelphia President's Freedom Award," in honor of his long efforts in behalf of world freedom. His talk, directed primarily to the young men and women of the nation, was carried on a national radio network.

"The validity of our beliefs in freedom," he warned, "is at stake on a global battleground."

Citing the "costly burden of our defense against the implacable foe who lurks in the Kremlin," which the young people "will inherit," and the hope for the co-operation of other nations in this defense of mankind, he stated that in the end, "the safety of America must rest upon our own well-armed right arm, whatever the sacrifice this entails. I am confident of your courage."

It can safely be estimated that Mr. Hoover worked harder as an ex-President than any other chief executive has to date. On the eve of his eighty-seventh birthday, in 1961, at his annual anniversary press conference, he explained that he still worked nine hours a day.

A staff of six secretaries was kept busy handling his various affairs. He was then writing three books and, during the preceding year, had delivered seven major addresses—which he had written himself. This totaled two more speeches than the year before. His correspondence entailed answering 34,805 letters.

In addition, during that year he had traveled to Florida, Washington, Philadelphia and California.

Topics touched upon by the former President at this 1961 birthday press conference included Berlin, Khrushchev, summit sessions, the moon, crime, fishing and baseball. Queried on the threat to Babe Ruth's home run record, the avid baseball fan replied, "I'm for anybody who can bat a home run, in baseball or anything else."

In regard to growing old, he told the press, "The only way to live a satisfactory life when you get old is to keep working at something."

The former President's interest in many of his lifetime activities, such as those concerned with education and engineering, and in national and world affairs, continued unabated. The welfare of his Alma Mater, Stanford University, was always a favorite objective.

A trustee of Stanford for forty-nine years, Herbert Hoover became an Emeritus Trustee in 1961. That same year, he undertook the Honorary Chairmanship of the Stanford PACE Program. This fund drive raised $109.2 million ahead of schedule, including a Ford Foundation incentive grant of $25 million.

In 1963, Hoover was given the first Herbert Hoover Gold Medal by the Stanford Alumni Association.

"Once an engineer," the ex-President said, "you are always an engineer at heart."

In March, 1959, Hoover received Tufts University's highest award, the Hosea Ballou Medal, for distinguished service in engineering.

When a new engineering center was needed, because of outgrown quarters, Mr. Hoover's views in favor of continuing to have the headquarters located in New York City carried great weight.

He was one of the speakers in October, 1959, at the ground breaking ceremonies for the United Engineering Center, on 47th Street and First Avenue, opposite United Nations Plaza. The twenty-story building was to be financed by engineering and engineering-related companies, as well as by thousands of individual engineers.

On that occasion, the former President cited engineers as "the foundation of security in our defense and the increase of our standards of living and comfort."

The following June, while helping to set the cornerstone for the United Engineering Center, Hoover read a message to posterity which was then sealed in the cornerstone.

In the message, Mr. Hoover gave a prophetic appraisal of the world to come—to be read in 2060 A.D., by those citizens of the future who would open the receptacle.

"But civilization," he warned, "is faced with a major danger. At least 600,000,000 people have adopted Communism, which denies religious faith, which finds its inspiration in rank materialism and whose primary tenet is that, by conspiracy or military action, freedom will be extinguished in the world.

"Within all the problems of the free governments and of international life there are stabilizing forces. Religious faith, its inspiration to moral values, and the unextinguishable spark in man to be free may well be the salvation of progress and civilization. We can," he concluded, "at least bid our successors to make sure these forces live."

The final honor paid Hoover as an engineer during his lifetime was announced by Columbia University on the day of his death. Unfortunately, he did not know of it. As part of a survey conducted among the 7,000 graduates of Columbia University's School of Engineering and Applied Science in connection with the School's Centennial, the alumni were asked to name the greatest engineer America has produced over the past century. Thomas Alva Edison received the largest number of votes and Herbert Hoover was chosen next, in second place.

In March, 1962, all three ex-Presidents supported John F. Kennedy in his stand regarding A-Tests in the air. The President, Hoover said, "is right in resuming nuclear testing." He declared in a public statement, "We can do no other if we are to survive."

August of that same year brought an occasion of great importance to the former President. On his eighty-eighth birthday, at the site of his birthplace in West Branch, Iowa, the Herbert Hoover Presidential Library was dedicated. Privately financed, the library building was built by the Herbert Hoover Birthplace Foundation, Inc. The dedication ceremony was held in the twenty-eight-acre Hoover Birthplace Park, near the tiny cottage where the former President was born and also close by his father's blacksmith shop.

The Hoover Presidential Library-Museum was the fourth library to be established under Congress to make the records of White House Administrations available to the public as a lasting contribution to American and world history.

Among those attending the dedication were former President Truman, Governor Norman A. Erbe of Iowa, the two Iowa senators, Bourke B. Hickenlooper and Jack Miller, two Iowan Congressmen, James Bromwell and Fred Schwengel, Mr. Hoover's sons, Herbert, Jr., and Allan Hoover, and their families. Admiral Lewis L. Strauss, chairman of the Birthplace Foundation, presided.

In his speech, Mr. Hoover proposed a Council of Free Nations to meet the world-wide "menace of Communism." He declared that, if the free nations were to survive, "they must have a new and stronger world-wide organization to meet this menace. . . . It should include only those nations who are willing to stand up and fight for their freedom and their independence."

He did not propose that the Council of Free Nations "should

replace the United Nations." But he did suggest: "When the United Nations is prevented from taking action, or if it fails to act to preserve peace, then the Council . . . should step in."

A crowd of about 45,000 persons attended the dedication.

In 1964, the Friends Meeting House that young Herbert had attended in West Branch was moved to a site just across the street from the Presidential Library, where the restoration of the building was carried out. At the Library dedication Mr. Hoover said, "I had a stern grounding of religious faith." All his life, this dedicated Quaker held firmly to the strong religious convictions imparted by his training in the over 100-year-old meeting house and by his parents.

Less than three weeks after the high point of the Library ceremony, the former President had an operation which resulted in a long convalescence. Mr. Hoover continued to work hard, to make statements for the press on public affairs and on the passing of notables from time to time—and to receive awards and honors.

In the Cuban crisis, in October, he supported President Kennedy in his stand for removal of the Soviet missiles that had been planted on the island.

In addition to articles and *An American Epic,* three more books were added to Herbert Hoover's long list of publications. These were the eighth volume of *Addresses Upon the American Road, 1955–1960* (1961); *On Growing Up* (1962), and *Fishing for Fun* (1963).

On May 22, 1963, New York City gave its warm welcome to Astronaut Major L. Gordon Cooper, Jr., with a parade, a ceremony at City Hall and an official luncheon. A week previously, the space hero had circled the earth twenty-two times in slightly over thirty-four hours—the fourth American to orbit our world.

The luncheon, held at the Waldorf-Astoria Hotel, was attended by 1,900 persons, including the host, Mayor Robert Wagner, then Vice President Lyndon B. Johnson, James E.

Webb, Director of the National Aeronautics and Space Administration, and five of Cooper's six fellow Astronauts.

Against the advice of his doctors, Herbert Hoover insisted on coming down to the luncheon from his Waldorf Towers apartment to honor the thirty-six-year-old Astronaut.

In a brief address, Hoover linked the names of Major Cooper and his fellow Astronauts with those of four other great American explorers—"Lewis and Clark, Lindbergh, and Byrd."

"Each of these men has added spirit and character to our country," he said. "There could be no greater tribute than this to any man and no greater service to our people."

In June, Mr. Hoover became ill and he was not able to hold the customary press conference on his eighty-ninth birthday.

At the tragic news of President Kennedy's assassination, on November 22, 1963, the former President made public a statement of heartfelt sympathy to Mrs. Kennedy and the Kennedy children.

The first time President Lyndon B. Johnson left Washington after becoming President was his trip to New York City, to attend the funeral of former Senator Herbert H. Lehman, on December 9th of the same year. Unprecedented precautions were taken to guard the President during his two-hour stay in the City.

As he entered the Temple Emanu-El for the Lehman services, he announced his decision to visit former President Hoover before returning to the airport. Security was immediately set up for his visit to the Waldorf Towers apartment of Mr. Hoover and he proceeded there after the funeral.

At a press conference at the LBJ Ranch in Texas, on December 27th, in reply to a reporter's question, the President stated that he was going to keep "the ex-Presidents of the United States fully informed and seek their counsel and advice from time to time.

"I have had extended conversations with Mr. Hoover, first with his son, who talked for him over the phone right after I took the oath as President, and later with President Hoover personally. On Christmas Day I had another conversation with him. He has given me some very constructive suggestions on the operations of the Federal Government that grew out of his retirement. We are studying these suggestions. We are applying them where they are appropriate. The Hoover Commission reports have been very carefully evaluated since I became President."

At the opening ceremony of the New York World's Fair, on April 22, 1964, a message was read from ex-President Hoover, who was Honorary Chairman of the Fair.

Mr. Hoover was unable to attend the 1964 Republican Convention, held in San Francisco—the first he had missed since his own nomination as the Republican standard bearer in 1928. His message to the Convention was read by Senator Everett McKinley Dirksen. When the Senator announced that "the grand old man of the Grand Old Party was listening," the Convention gave the former President a tremendous, long-lasting ovation.

A Resolution calling for official recognition of former President Hoover's ninetieth birthday on August 10, 1964, was passed unanimously by the U.S. Senate on July 23rd. A Proclamation by the President was authorized.

On the eve of his birthday, Hoover watched the Yankees play the Baltimore Orioles at Yankee Stadium on television—a baseball game dedicated in his honor. Special ceremonies marking the day were also held at other ball games throughout the country. While serving as Secretary of Commerce in April, 1927, Mr. Hoover had taken part in the first public demonstration of television.

Thousands of birthday messages were received from well-wishers, including President Johnson, ex-Presidents Eisenhower and Truman, King Baudouin of Belgium, Pope Paul VI and other heads of state, and hundreds of school children and Boys' Clubs members.

To mark both the former President's ninetieth birthday and his fifty years in full-time public service, a booklet was published by the Hoover Institution on War, Revolution, and Peace, in July, 1964. It contains a list of his public positions, tributes and awards given him and his publications.

"There is no greater honor that can come to a man than to have a school named for him," Hoover declared. Forty-nine schools bear his name.

Herbert Hoover received over a hundred medals and over two hundred testimonials and awards from all over the world. He was granted almost one hundred honorary degrees from United States and foreign universities. Overwhelmingly defeated in his bid for re-election to the Presidency in 1932, he was twice voted Joint Resolutions of Appreciation by Congress for his later work as head of the two Hoover Commissions.

The Hoover Institution on War, Revolution, and Peace continues to grow. According to the official estimate of April, 1965, its collections include approximately 670,000 books and pamphlets, 132,000 volumes of government documents from over 90 countries, 25,600 journal, periodical and newspaper titles and thousands of photographs and posters. A new building, to provide greatly needed expansion, is being added.

The Herbert Hoover Presidential Library at West Branch, Iowa, is rapidly developing into a major research institution to be used by historians and students.

Former President Hoover died on October 20, 1964.

A thirty-day mourning period was proclaimed by President Johnson. Flags were lowered to half-mast at the White House and on all federal buildings and grounds in this country, at embassies and military installations abroad, and on Navy ships at sea. Official New York City flags were also lowered, on the order of Mayor Wagner, for the thirty days.

The Supreme Court recessed out of respect to the late ex-President.

Tributes to his memory poured in from national and world leaders and from thousands of persons in this country and abroad. They came from President Johnson, ex-presidents Eisenhower and Truman, Queen Elizabeth of England, King Baudouin of Belgium, Prime Minister Lester Pearson of Canada, President Kekkonen of Finland and other world leaders.

Thousands of people filed past his flag-draped coffin in St. Bartholomew's Protestant Episcopal Church, in New York City, during the next two days. An honor guard at the bier represented the five armed forces of the nation.

In the midst of the intensive 1964 campaign for the Presidency, all four major candidates canceled campaign commitments to pay respects to Herbert Hoover. In tribute to the late former President, the political life of the country halted as President and Mrs. Johnson, his running mate, Senator Hubert Humphrey, and the Republican Presidential and Vice Presidential candidates, Barry Goldwater and William Miller, attended funeral services held at St. Bartholomew's Church on the afternoon of the 22nd. Many other prominent people in the life of the nation were also present.

Taken to Washington by train, the late former President's body lay in state in the Rotunda of the United States Capitol, on the catafalque used for President Lincoln's coffin and that of President Kennedy. Official state funeral services, held under the dome of the Capitol, were attended by President and Mrs. Johnson, members of Congress, of the Cabinet and of the Diplomatic Corps, and by government officials.

On Sunday, the Hoover coffin was flown to Iowa for his burial at West Branch, at the Hoover birthplace site. His late beloved wife has been re-buried there beside Herbert Hoover.

In addition to the countless contributions of incalculable value Herbert Hoover made to the American way of life—to become a part of the very fabric of his country—he has left another legacy which is of tremendous import to its future. This great American "fed more people and saved more lives than any man in history." To his nation he has bequeathed the grateful remembrance of many millions abroad who, themselves, or members of their families, were aided in desperate hunger and saved from starvation by the relief activities which Hoover organized and directed. He frequently pointed out that this was made possible in greatest part by the American people.

Herbert Hoover was always proud that he was a citizen of the United States. He expressed his pride and appreciation in loyal service. He had an enduring faith in the people of America and in his country's future.

Bibliography

Bane, S. L. and Lutz, R. H. *Organization of American Relief in Europe 1918–1919*. Stanford: Stanford University Press, 1943. (Hoover Library Publication No. 20)

Comité d'Accueil. *Manifestation Herbert Hoover 5 Juillet 1958*. Brussels: Fondation Universitaire.

Corey, Herbert. *The Truth about Hoover*. Boston: Houghton Mifflin Co., 1932.

Darling, Jay N. *As Ding Saw Hoover*. Ames: The Iowa State College Press, 1954.

Elliott, Orrin L. *Stanford University, The First Twenty-five Years*. Stanford: Stanford University Press, 1957.

Emerson, Edwin. *Hoover and His Times*. Garden City: Garden City Publishing Co., Inc., 1932.

Fisher, H. H. *The Famine in Soviet Russia 1919–1923*. New York: The Macmillan Co., 1927. (Hoover Library No. 9)

Gann, Dolly. *Dolly Gann's Book*. Garden City: Doubleday, Doran & Co., Inc., 1933.

Galbraith, John Kenneth. *The Great Crash, 1929*. Boston: Houghton Mifflin Co., 1954.

Galpin, Perrin C. (ed.) *Hugh Gibson, 1883–1954*. New York: Belgian American Educational Foundation, Inc., 1956.

Gay, George I. *The Commission for Relief in Belgium. Statistical Review of Relief Operations*. Stanford: Stanford University Press, 1925.

Gay, George I. with Fisher, H. H. *Public Relations of the Commission for Relief in Belgium*. 2 vols. Stanford: Stanford University Press, 1929. (Hoover Library Nos. 7, 8)

Gibson, Hugh. *A Journal from Our Legation*. Garden City: Doubleday, Page & Co., 1917.

Hard, William. *Who's Hoover?* New York: Dodd, Mead & Co., Inc., 1928.

Hinshaw, David. *Herbert Hoover: American Quaker*. New York: Farrar, Straus & Co., 1950.

The Hoover Commission Report on Organization of the Executive Branch of the Government. New York: McGraw-Hill Book Co., Inc., 1949.

Hoover Institution on War, Revolution, and Peace. Stanford University, 1963.

Hoover Medal Board of Award. *Herbert Hoover, Medalist.* New York, 1931.

Irwin, Will. *Herbert Hoover, A Reminiscent Biography.* New York: The Century Co., 1928.

————. *The Making of a Reporter.* New York: G. P. Putnam's Sons, 1942.

John Fritz Medal, Board of Award. *Presentation of the John Fritz Gold Medal Award to Herbert Hoover.* New York: American Institute of Mining and Metallurgical Engineers, 1929.

Joslin, Theodore G. *Hoover Off The Record.* Garden City: Doubleday, Doran & Co., Inc., 1934.

Kellogg, Vernon. *Fighting Starvation in Belgium.* Garden City: Doubleday, Page & Co., 1918.

————. *Herbert Hoover, the Man and his Work.* New York: D. Appleton & Co., 1920.

Leach, Henry Goddard. *My Last Seventy Years.* New York: Bookman Associates, 1956.

Lindley, Ernest K. *The Roosevelt Revolution.* New York: The Viking Press, 1933.

Lyons, Eugene. *Herbert Hoover: A Biography.* Garden City: Doubleday & Co., Inc., 1964.

————. *Our Unknown Ex-President.* Garden City: Doubleday & Co., Inc., 1948.

Michelson, Charles. *The Ghost Talks.* New York: G. P. Putman's Sons, 1944.

Moley, Raymond. *After Seven Years.* New York: Harper & Bros., 1939.

————. *27 Masters of Politics.* New York: Published for *Newsweek* by Funk & Wagnalls Co., 1949.

Moulton, Harold G. *Controlling Factors in Economic Development.* Washington: Brookings Institute, 1949.

Myers, William Starr. *The Foreign Policies of Herbert Hoover.* New York: Charles Scribner's Sons, 1940.

————. (ed.) *The State Papers and Other Public Writings of Herbert Hoover.* 2 vols. Garden City: Doubleday, Doran & Co., Inc., 1934.

Myers, W. S. and Newton, W. H. *The Hoover Administration.* New York: Charles Scribner's Sons, 1936.

Reeves, Earl. *This Man Hoover*. New York: A. L. Burt Co., 1928.

Smith, R. and Beasley, N. *Carter Glass*. New York: Longmans, Green & Co., 1939.

Sullivan, Lawrence. *Prelude to Panic*. Washington: Statesman Press, 1936.

Wilbur, R. L. and Hyde, A. M. *The Hoover Policies*. New York: Charles Scribner's Sons, 1937.

Wolfe, Harold. *Herbert Hoover*. New York: Exposition Press, 1956.

Index

Abyssinia, 86
Adams, Charles Francis, 222
Adams, John, 227, 228
Addresses and Further Addresses Upon the American Road, 282
Adenauer, Konrad, 297
Agnew, John A., 42, 45, 54, 60, 65, 74, 89
Alabama, 231
Alaska, 94
Albert, King of Belgium, 129, 133, 176, 186-187
Allies, 119, 132, 134, 136, 138, 141-143, 146, 147-149, 151-154, 156-159, 163-165, 167, 170, 173-175, 178-179, 182
American Bankers Association, 188
American Child Health Association, 194, 201-202
American Committee for Repatriation of American Citizens from Europe, 103-107
American Engineering Council, 193
American Expeditionary Forces, 146, 154, 160
American Federation of Labor, 199, 203, 240, 265
American Individualism, 192
American Institute of Mining and Metallurgical Engineers, 184, 193
American Legion, 256
American Red Cross, 204, 205, 240, 241, 263, 291
American Relief Administration (ARA), 154, 162-163, 189-190, 191-192
Argentina, 220
Arkansas, 17-19, 32, 267
Armenia, 165, 169, 190
Australia, 35, 36, 37, 39, 41, 45, 74, 75, 76, 79, 80, 102, 111, 114; Western A., 35-37, 43, 74
Austria, 165, 169, 242, 243, 246, 293
Austria-Hungary, 98, 100

Aviation, 205-206, 221, 234
Azerbaijan, 159, 165, 169

Bankruptcy Bill, 274
Baruch, Bernard, 251
Belgian American Educational Foundation, Inc., 176, 290
Belgium, 42, 101, 108, 109, 110, 111, 115, 118, 122, 124, 127, 130, 131, 132, 162, 165, 175, 176, 182, 289, 297
Benson, William S., 153, 157, 164
Berlin, 117, 127-128
Bewick, Moreing and Company, 35, 36, 37, 39, 40, 41, 71, 73-87, 90
Bible, 9
"Big Four," 156, 160, 161, 163, 164, 167, 169, 170, 173
Bolivian government, 219
Bolshevism, 94, 171
Bonus legislation, 241-242, 243, 256, 263, 264
Bonus March demonstrations, 263-264, 267-268
Boxer Rebellion, 53, 55-63, 64, 65, 67, 72, 227
Boys' Clubs of America, 288-289
Branner, John, 15, 16, 17, 26, 27, 95
Brazil, 219, 221
Brown, Walter F., 222, 234, 239, 281
Brussels, 108, 121, 126, 130, 133, 165, 175, 176, 297
Bryan, William Jennings, 25, 34, 108, 109, 117
Buenos Aires, 220
Bulgaria, 165
Bureau of Mines, 43, 45, 46, 48, 63
Burma Mine, 82-85, 87, 89-91, 125

California, 3, 13, 15, 26, 29, 32, 37, 43, 51, 64, 79, 90, 94, 109,

124, 125, 184, 186, 194, 218, 231, 278, 281

Canada, 3, 10, 110, 136, 142, 288

Carran, Mollie, 223

Castle, William R., Jr., 246

Cavell, Edith, 127

Challenge to Liberty, 285

Chang Yen-mao, 43, 45, 46, 47, 48, 49, 51, 52, 53, 55, 56, 58, 60, 63, 64, 70, 82, 213, 217

Chicago, 195, 260, 267, 268

Chile, 111, 218, 219, 220

China, 42, 43, 44, 46, 47, 52, 53, 54, 55, 63, 64, 65, 67, 68, 72, 109, 111, 284

Chinese Engineering and Mining Company, 42, 43, 45, 47, 48, 58, 63, 64, 65, 66, 67, 69, 70, 71, 72, 82, 109, 217

Chinwangtao, 43, 46, 63, 64, 71

Civil Service Commission, 196

Clemenceau, Georges, 147, 156, 169, 182

Colorado, 33

Commission for Relief in Belgium (C.R.B.), 111, 113-129, 131-133, 134, 147, 153, 164, 174, 175-177, 188, 289, 290

Commissions on Organization of the Executive Branch of the Government; *see* Hoover Commissions

Communism, 152, 156, 165, 169, 174, 182, 258

Communist Revolution in China, 289, 296

Congressional Campaign 1930, 241

Congressional Record, 213, 264n

Coolgardie, 37, 38

Coolidge, Calvin, 198, 200, 203, 204, 205, 206, 208, 209, 212-213, 214, 219, 221, 229, 282

Costa Rica, 219

Curtis, Charles, 223

Czechoslovakia, 165, 168

Dawes, Charles G., 246, 247, 260, 267

Delcassé, Théophile, 120-121

Democratic National Committee, 230, 254

Depression, 236-246, 256-264, 272-274, 278, 286-288, 297

De Re Metallica, 96-97

Detroit, 256

de Wouters, Edmond, 64, 65, 67, 70, 71, 72, 82

Dies Committee, 192

Egypt, 37, 85, 86

Eighteenth Amendment, 216, 235, 236

Eisenhower, Dwight D., 294, 295, 297

Emancipation Proclamation, 227

Empress Dowager of China, 46, 55, 63

England, 42, 46, 79, 83, 87, 96, 100, 101, 103, 104, 106, 115, 127, 128, 130; *see also* Great Britain

Estonia, 165, 167

Europe, 95, 98, 99, 100, 102, 103, 104, 105, 106, 107, 114, 131, 132, 137, 142, 143, 144, 145, 146, 147, 148, 149, 150-154, 156-165, 167, 171, 174-175, 177, 178, 179, 181-182, 187, 188, 189, 190, 192, 225, 236-237, 238, 240, 242, 243, 244, 247, 256, 258, 259, 262, 265, 292

Farm Loan Act, 260

Fascism, 258, 282

Federal Farm Board, 235, 239, 257

Federal Reserve System, 236-237, 239, 260-261, 263, 265

Finland, 165, 167, 175, 291

Foch, Marshal, 180

France, 37, 42, 55, 101, 114, 120, 121, 151, 152, 158, 165, 175, 176, 181, 182, 243, 245, 256, 283, 287, 291, 292

France, Northern (occupied), 109, 120-121, 162, 175, 176

Francis Ferdinand, Archduke, 98, 100

Franqui, Emile, 71, 109-110, 111, 121, 165

Free Enterprise, 203, 208, 230, 234, 278, 288, 296

Friends, Society of, *see* Quakers

Galpin, Perrin C., 115, 290, 292-293

Garfield, Harry A., 137, 142, 146

Garfield, James A., 9

Garner, John N., 244

Georgia, 165, 169
German-Austrian Credit Union, 242
German Moratorium, 244-245, 259
Germany, 42, 55, 68, 101, 116, 117-118, 123, 124, 143, 146, 148, 150, 159, 162, 163, 164-165, 167, 175, 180, 242-243, 245-246, 256, 283, 290, 293, 297
Germany, West, 293, 297
Gibson, Hugh, 108, 109, 110, 126, 132, 154, 280, 296n
Gifford, Walter S., 256
Gitlow, Benjamin, 264
Glass, Carter, 153, 244, 261, 267, 269, 273, 283
Glass-Steagall Bill, 261
God, 16, 125, 280
Govette, Francis, 75, 77, 81, 98
Grant, Ulysses S., 1
Great Britain, 55, 68, 101, 104, 107, 114, 116, 152, 165, 180, 246, 256, 283
Grey, Sir Edward, 108, 117
Guggenheim, Daniel, 195

Harding, Warren G., 193, 195, 196, 198, 199-200, 202, 282, 294
Harrison, Benjamin, 23
Haskell, William N., 170-171, 191
Henry, Lou; see Mrs. Herbert C. Hoover
Honduras, 219
Hoover, Allan, 5, 6, 7
Hoover, Mrs. Allan (Millie), 5, 8
Hoover, Allan Henry, 87, 96, 101, 107, 124, 125, 144, 181, 184-186, 209, 279, 281, 290
Hoover Commissions, 294, 296
Hoover Dam, 204, 230-231, 280, 293
Hoover, Herbert C. For biographical material and career see Table of Contents
Hoover, Mrs. Herbert C. (Lou Henry), 26-27, 28, 32, 36, 42, 43-45, 47-48, 52, 54, 55-56, 59-60, 61, 62, 64, 70, 72, 73, 75, 78-79, 85-87, 95-97, 101, 104, 105, 106, 107, 124, 125, 144-145, 181, 184-185, 186, 209-210, 218, 220, 221, 223, 227-228, 229, 252, 254, 268, 275, 278, 280, 292

Hoover, Herbert, Jr., 79, 85, 87, 96, 101, 107, 124-126, 144, 184, 185, 209, 279, 281
Hoover, Huldah Minthorn, 3-5
Hoover Institution on War, Revolution and Peace, 129, 177-178, 289-290
Hoover, J. Edgar, 211
Hoover, Jesse, 1-3
Hoover, May, 5, 32, 34, 35
Hoover, Theodore, 4-5, 32, 34, 35, 89
Hoover, Walter, 5, 7-8
House, Edward M., 131, 153
Hughes, Charles E., 187, 196, 199
Hungary, 156, 161, 165, 169-170, 245-246, 297

Indiana, 270
Iowa, 1, 3, 6, 9, 10, 27
Irwin, Will, 25-26, 92, 97, 99-100, 105, 110-111, 116, 136, 171, 205, 212, 218
Italy, 86, 152, 165, 182, 283, 292

Janin, Louis, 32-36
Japan, 55, 64, 68, 114, 257, 260, 283, 293
Jordan, David Starr, 14, 16, 95
Joslin, Theodore, 244, 245, 250, 253, 254, 262, 276

Kalgoorlie, 37-39, 74-75, 89
Kellogg, Vernon, 126, 127, 128, 132, 165, 171, 191
Kent, Frank R., 254
Kentucky, 232
Keynes, John Maynard, 182, 283, 284, 287
Korea, 89
Korean War, 289
Kreditanstalt, 242
Kwang Hsu, 43, 46
Kyshtim, 91-93, 94

Lansing, Robert, 180
Latin America, 114, 218-222, 293
Latvia, 165, 167
League of Nations, 181, 185, 187
Leatherstocking Tales, 4
Lewald, Theodor, 117, 127, 128
Lincoln, Abraham, 1, 267

Lindgren, Waldemar, 20, 22, 29, 32, 34, 79-80
Lithuania, 165, 167
Lloyd George, 119-120, 147, 156
London, 36, 43, 63, 64, 71, 72, 73, 76, 77, 78, 81, 85, 86, 88, 97, 98, 101, 105, 106, 109, 119, 120, 124, 125, 126, 147, 151, 152, 154, 246
Lowden, Frank, 213
Lyons, Eugene, 279, 285-286

MacArthur, Douglas, 264, 268
Maine, 271
Manchuria, 52, 69, 76, 257
Mayflower Mine, 31-32, 41
McKinley, William, 34, 227
Mellon, Andrew, 199, 222, 243, 244, 246
Memoirs of Herbert Hoover, 282
Mercier, Cardinal, 124, 182
Michelson, Charles, 213, 254-255
Miles, Laban, 4, 32
Miller, Nathan, 195
Mills, Ogden L., 244, 246, 260, 272, 277
Mining in Altai Mountains, 93-94
Minthorn, Henry J., 9-11, 14, 131
Mississippi River, 1, 19, 36, 204-205, 212, 232, 237
Moley, Raymond, 272, 283, 291
Monroe Doctrine, 218
Monroe, James, 228
Monterey, 26, 27, 42, 43-44, 79
Moreing, Charles A., 36, 40, 42, 43, 63, 64, 71, 76, 77, 78
Morrow, Dwight, 246

Nansen, Fridtjof, 144, 174
National Conference on Street and Highway Safety, 198
Newberg (Oregon), 9-11
Newberg Academy, 10-11
New Deal, 201, 233, 281, 282, 284, 285, 286, 287, 288, 292, 293
New England, 3
New Mexico, 33, 34
New York City, 88, 107, 114, 115, 124, 131, 176, 184, 186, 187, 190, 215, 216, 237, 275, 279, 289, 292
Nicaragua, 219
Norris, George W., 215, 231
North Sea, 123, 124, 128, 129

Ohio, 3
Oregon, 2, 9, 10, 12
Osage (Indian) Nation, 4

Pace, John T., 264, 268
Paderewski, Ignace Jan, 26, 144, 166
Page, Walter Hines, 103-104, 108, 109, 110, 111, 114
Palo Alto, 3, 14, 32, 107, 124, 187, 209, 272, 278
Paris, 88, 120, 147, 153, 155, 157, 158, 168, 173, 178, 181, 182, 183, 244
Pawhuska, 4, 107
Peace Conference, 151, 170, 173, 174, 178, 183
Peking, 42, 45, 54, 55-56, 62, 63, 67
Pershing, John J., 142, 143, 146, 148, 149, 154, 158, 159, 161, 163, 177, 190, 291
Peru, 219, 220
Petrograd, 88, 174
Poland, 25, 106, 165-166, 171, 290
Polk, Frank L., 170
Portland, 10
President's Committee for Unemployment Relief, 240, 241, 256-257, 263
Principles of Mining, 95

Quakers, 3, 4, 8-9, 10, 11, 12, 44, 87, 112, 131, 195

Radio, 206-207
Railway Labor Board, 202
Rapidan Camp, 229-230, 250, 253, 254
Reconstruction Finance Corporation (RFC), 258, 259, 263, 273, 286
Reward Mine, 30-31
Rickard, Edgar, 101, 103, 107-108, 151
Rio de Janeiro, 221
Robinson, Henry M., 159
Roosevelt, Franklin D., 233, 268-269, 271, 272-275, 277-278, 280, 282-283, 285, 286, 287, 292
Roosevelt, Theodore, 126, 194, 227
Rumania, 165, 170-171
Russia, 55, 68-69, 91-94, 111, 169, 174; *see also* U.S.S.R.

St. Lawrence Waterway, 233
Salem, 2, 11
San Francisco, 20, 24, 32, 34, 88, 95, 186-187, 234
Sims, William S., 134, 143
Smith, Alfred E., 216, 217, 228
Smoot-Hawley Tariff Act, 236, 269, 284
Smuts, Jan Christiaan, 179-180
Socialism, 203, 216, 232, 282
Solid South, 218
Sons of Gwalia, 40-42, 46, 74, 75
South Africa, 81, 102, 114
Standstill Agreement, 246
Stanford, Leland, 2-3, 15-16
Stanford University, 2-3, 12-16, 19, 22, 24, 25, 28, 29, 32, 35, 36, 46, 73, 79, 95-96, 124, 129, 177, 185, 199, 289, 292
Stimson, Henry L., 222, 243, 244, 246, 272
Strauss, Lewis, 145, 152, 189
Supreme Economic Council, 156
Swain, Joseph, 12-13, 14, 15

Tacna-Arica, 221-222
Taft, Robert A., 152, 189, 298-299
Taft, William Howard, 187
Tatum, Laurie, 13, 15
Teapot Dome, 200
Tennessee, 204, 231
Tennessee Valley Authority, 285
Tientsin, 45, 48, 56, 59, 61, 62, 63, 65, 66, 68, 72, 227
Tong Shao-yi, 48-49, 58, 60-61, 72, 217
Truman, Harry S., 292, 293
Turkey, 165

Ukraine, 191
U.S.S.R., 169, 174, 191-192, 240, 282
United States, 1, 16, 36, 46, 68, 71, 74, 79, 87, 91, 95, 102, 103, 104, 105, 109, 110, 117, 119, 123, 126, 127, 131, 132, 136, 138, 139, 142, 145, 148, 149, 151, 152-153, 155-157, 159, 164, 174, 179, 181-182, 189, 191, 200, 218, 219, 221, 222, 225, 233, 237, 238, 240, 242-243, 245, 247, 256, 257-259, 260, 262, 265, 274, 278, 279, 282, 283, 287, 290, 291, 297, 298

U.S. Chamber of Commerce, 199, 205, 239
U.S. Congress, 105, 138, 140, 147, 154, 188, 191, 194, 196, 198, 201, 202, 204, 206, 218, 224, 225, 231, 232, 233, 235, 239, 240, 241, 242, 244, 249, 252, 256, 258, 259, 260, 261, 262, 263, 264, 265, 266, 271, 272-273, 274, 275, 278, 284, 286, 288, 294, 297
U.S. Food Administration, 135-150, 151, 153, 156, 164, 168, 188-189, 191
U.S. Supreme Court, 283, 284
Uruguay, 219, 220

Versailles, Treaty of, 166, 179, 180, 181, 185, 187, 242
Vienna, 157, 160, 169
Volga River Valley, 191

Wallace, Henry C., 203
War Council, 145-146, 178
Washington, D.C., 22, 117, 131, 132, 134, 135, 136, 144, 154, 194, 196, 198, 202, 208, 209, 210, 219, 229, 244, 252, 254, 262, 264
Waterways, interior system of, 232
Weimar Republic, 244
West Branch Free School, 7
West Branch (Iowa), 1, 3, 5
White House, 222, 223, 227-229, 237, 238, 244, 249, 252, 257, 272, 275, 278, 292
Wilbur, Ray Lyman, 19, 95, 129, 222, 235, 251
Wilson, Woodrow, 109, 126, 131, 132, 134-135, 137, 138, 139, 141-143, 146-147, 150-153, 155-156, 159, 162, 163, 165-166, 170, 173, 174, 178-181, 186, 193, 282
Work, Hubert, 200, 204
World Economic Conference, 265, 272, 283
World War I, 94, 100, 101, 123, 132, 148, 177, 237, 242, 243, 261, 274, 277, 289, 290, 291, 296
World War II, 132, 141, 287, 288, 289, 290, 291, 292

Yugoslavia, 165, 168

Dorothy Horton McGee

was born at West Point, New York, where her father, a graduate of the United States Military Academy, was an instructor in law at the Military Academy. She has lived mostly on the north shore of Long Island and attended the Green Vale School, Glen Head; the Brearley School, New York City; and the Fermata School, Aiken, South Carolina.

Dorothy McGee's favorite hobby is sailing. She began sailing at the age of eight, at Quisset on Cape Cod, where her family had a cottage for the summer. She has enjoyed many seasons of racing and sailing at the Seawanhaka-Corinthian Yacht Club at Oyster Bay, of which she is a member. She has sailed on many kinds of boats, from a dinghy to a cup-defender, and in many waters, from Long Island Sound to the New England Atlantic Coast and Nantucket, as well as at Nassau, Bermuda and the inland lakes of Minnesota and the Adirondacks. A racing skipper in her own right, she has raced sailboats of several classes, including Star, Herreshoff Fish, Atlantic, Herreshoff "S" and Six Metre, the latter with a crew of four, and has won the "S" class at Larchmont Race Week and the Season Championship in the "S" class at the Seawanhaka-Corinthian Yacht Club.

Dorothy McGee is also greatly interested in American history. A member of several historical societies, she is a Fellow of the Society of American Historians and former Assistant Historian of Roslyn.

Her fiction books, *Skipper Sandra* and *The Boarding School Mystery,* are based on her sailing and school background. Historical books she has written include *Sally Townsend, Patriot; Famous Signers of the Declaration; Alexander Hamilton: New Yorker;* and *Herbert Hoover: Engineer, Humanitarian, Statesman.*